Lectionary for Masses with Children

Weekdays

APPROVED FOR USE IN THE
DIOCESES OF THE UNITED STATES OF AMERICA
BY THE NATIONAL CONFERENCE OF CATHOLIC BISHOPS
AND CONFIRMED BY THE APOSTOLIC SEE

PREPARED BY THE COMMITTEE ON THE LITURGY
NATIONAL CONFERENCE OF CATHOLIC BISHOPS

LTP

LITURGY TRAINING PUBLICATIONS

Concordat cum originali:

Ronald F. Krisman, Executive Director
Secretariat for the Liturgy
National Conference of Catholic Bishops

Published by authority of the Committee on the Liturgy, National Conference of Catholic Bishops.

ACKNOWLEDGMENTS

Editor: Elizabeth Hoffman
Copy Editor: Theresa Pincich
Designer: Kerry Perlmutter
Typesetter: Mark Hollopeter
Artist: Steve Erspamer, SM

NATIONAL CONFERENCE OF CATHOLIC BISHOPS
UNITED STATES OF AMERICA

DECREE

The *Lectionary for Masses with Children* for use in the dioceses of the United States of America was canonically approved by the members of the National Conference of Catholic Bishops on 13 November 1991 and was subsequently confirmed by the Apostolic See by decree of the Congregation for Divine Worship and the Discipline of the Sacraments on 27 May 1992 (Prot. N. 1259/91).

As of 1 September 1993 the *Lectionary for Masses with Children* may be published and used in the liturgy. The First Sunday of Advent, 28 November 1993, is hereby established as the effective date for use of the *Lectionary for Masses with Children* in the dioceses of the United States of America. From that day forward no other English lectionary for Masses with children may be used.

Given at the General Secretariat of the National Conference of Catholic Bishops, Washington DC, on 28 December 1992, the feast of the Holy Innocents.

\+ William H. Keeler
Archbishop of Baltimore
President
National Conference of Catholic Bishops

Robert N. Lynch
General Secretary

CONGREGATION FOR DIVINE WORSHIP AND THE DISCIPLINE OF THE SACRAMENTS

Prot. N. 1259/91

This Congregation has examined the request of the National Conference of Catholic Bishops of the United States of America for the confirmation of the approval for the *Lectionary for Masses with Children*.

We grant permission for the experimental use of the cursus of the lectionary for children. After a three-year period a full report of the experiment must be given and a renewal or definitive confirmation will be given.

The terms of the permission are as follows:

1. We ask that it be established as a first principle what is stated in paragraph 13 of the Introduction to the *Lectionary for Masses with Children:*

   "Proper balance and consideration for the entire assembly should be observed. Therefore, priest celebrants should not use this *Lectionary for Masses with Children* exclusively or even preferentially at Sunday Masses, even though large numbers of children are present."

2. a. In granting permission for the cursus to be used, independently of any approved version of the Scripture, no approved version is *a priori* excluded from use. However, there is one small modification regarding the cursus.

   b. Before the readings for the following celebrations, Christmas Day, Epiphany, Sundays of Lent, Easter Sunday, Ascension, and Pentecost, it is asked that a rubric be added stating that, "these readings may be used only when the celebration of the liturgy of the word for the children is held in a place apart from the main assembly." This is to ensure that on these days in the assembly the universal lectionary will take precedence over the children's lectionary.

3. On the basis of the assurance given that the *Contemporary English Version* of the Bible does not present any doctrinal problems in the sphere of the issue of the inclusive language question at present under study we grant permission for its experimental use but without granting a formal confirmation.

From the Congregation for Divine Worship and the Discipline of the Sacraments, 27 May 1992.

\+ Antonio María Cardinal Javierre Ortas
Prefect

\+ Geraldo M. Agnelo
Archbishop Secretary

CONTENTS

Decree of the National Conference of Catholic Bishops *iii*

Decree of the Congregation for Divine Worship and the Discipline of the Sacraments *iv*

Foreword *vi*

Introduction *viii*

Weekday Readings
- Season of Advent **3**
- Season of Lent **19**
- Season of Easter **57**
- Ordinary Time **91**

Gospel Acclamations for Weekdays in Ordinary Time **201**

Proper of Saints
- January **206**
- February **214**
- March **224**
- April **234**
- May **240**
- June **256**
- July **268**
- August **276**
- September **290**
- October **304**
- November **312**
- December **326**

Commons
- Common of the Dedication of a Church **340**
- Common of the Blessed Virgin Mary **346**
- Common of Apostles **354**
- Common of Martyrs **358**
- Common of Pastors **364**
- Common of Doctors of the Church **370**
- Common of Saints **376**

Sacraments
- Baptism **390**
- Confirmation (Holy Spirit) **398**
- Holy Eucharist **408**
- Reconciliation **416**

Masses for Various Needs and Occasions
- Beginning of the School Year **428**
- End of the School Year **434**
- In Thanksgiving **440**
- For Vocations **444**
- For the Unity of Christians **452**
- For Peace and Justice **458**
- For Productive Land and After the Harvest **464**
- For Refugees and Exiles **468**
- For the Sick **472**
- For the Dead **476**

Calendar **486**

Index of Readings **496**

FOREWORD

Throughout his ministry, our Lord Jesus Christ had a special concern for children. When his disciples tried to prevent parents from bringing their children to Jesus to bless them, the Lord became angry and reminded the disciples: "Let the children come to me! Don't try to stop them. People who are like these little children belong to the kingdom of God" (Mk 10:14). The Gospels record other incidences when Jesus healed sick children and even raised them to life (e.g., Lk 8:40–56, Lk 9:37–43, Mt 17:14–18, Mk 9:14–27).

The Church too has manifested a special care and concern for children through the ages. From the time an infant is baptized the Church seeks to enfold it in its loving embrace so that the child may grow in the love of God. Parents are reminded: "It will be your duty to bring [your child] up to keep God's commandments as Christ taught us, by loving God and our neighbor." And in response to their affirmative answer, the minister addresses the child and says: "N., the Christian community welcomes you with great joy. In its name I claim you for Christ our Savior by the sign of his cross." The welcome of children by the Church must not be a one-time event; rather, the Church, in following the example of Christ, continues to welcome all children, but especially the young, into its midst and into its liturgical assemblies.

A concrete expression of the Church's concern for the pastoral care of children is found in the *Directory for Masses with Children*, published by the Congregation for Divine Worship in 1973 as a supplement to the *General Instruction of the Roman Missal.* This document provides for adaptations that can be made when the eucharist is celebrated with young children so that the words and actions of the Mass will be more suitable to the comprehension of the children. The Directory, in particular, provides for the adaptation of the liturgy of the word and recommends that individual conferences of bishops see to the composition of lectionaries for Masses with children.

At the recommendation of the Federation of Diocesan Liturgical Commissions and with its assistance, the Committee on the Liturgy of the National Conference of Catholic Bishops undertook the project of preparing a children's lectionary for Mass. The task group responsible for this work compared the existing lectionaries for children in other languages and, always keeping an eye on the Roman *Lectionary for Mass*, elaborated the *cursus* of readings that is found in this *Lectionary for Masses with Children* and prepared the introduction to the Lectionary. The work of the task group, which consisted of experts in liturgy, scripture, and catechetics, was ultimately approved by the NCCB Liturgy Committee and by the entire National Conference of Catholic Bishops. The Congregation for Divine Worship and the Discipline of the Sacraments has approved the

Lectionary for Masses with Children for experimental use for a period of three years at which time the approval will be renewed or a definitive decree of confirmation will be granted.

The *Lectionary for Masses with Children* is principally intended for use at Masses which are primarily for children and not the ordinary Sunday Mass. "Proper balance and consideration for the entire assembly should be observed. Therefore, priest celebrants should not use this *Lectionary for Masses with Children* exclusively or even preferentially at Sunday Masses, even though large numbers of children are present" (Introduction, no. 13).

It is the hope of the Liturgy Committee that the *Lectionary for Masses with Children* will enable children to hear the word of God in a manner more suited to their age and ability to understand. In providing this lectionary it is our sincere desire to enable young children to come to Christ, from whom they have received new life in baptism and who gives them the joy of salvation.

\+ Wilton D. Gregory
Auxiliary Bishop of Chicago
Chairman, Committee on the Liturgy
National Conference of Catholic Bishops

INTRODUCTION

I. The Liturgical Celebration of the Word of God

Living Word of God

1. God speaks to us the Word, who has become flesh in Jesus Christ our Lord. Through him all things came to be and were made.[1] The many words spoken throughout history for our salvation have their origin and end in Christ Jesus.[2] In the liturgy we are called together that in the Spirit we may listen to and respond to the word of God in Christ. "That word constantly proclaimed in the liturgy is always, then, a living, active word through the power of the Holy Spirit. It expresses the Father's love that never fails in its effectiveness toward us."[3]

Word of God in the Assembly

2. The liturgical assembly is a gathering of God's holy People. Christ is present in the very act of gathering.[4] Christ is also present in the proclamation of the word of God.[5] This proclamation, if it is to promote a deeper experience of Christ's presence, must be understood in its most complete sense. It must be prepared for and experienced as the specific kind of event it is, namely, a ritual celebration composed of reading, dialogue in song, silence, and reflection, with the use of appropriate gestures and symbols. The ability to give assent to God's Good News is deeply influenced by the manner in which the word is proclaimed and celebrated in the liturgical assembly.[6] The Church's deepest calling is to praise God. Members of the Church do this by conforming their lives to the message of the Scriptures that they have heard and by bringing to the celebration of the liturgy all that they have done.[7]

God's Word in Story

3. Christian communities discover, express, and deepen their identity by sharing the stories of our salvation that we read in the Scriptures. The way we pass these biblical stories on to children will also influence the way in which the message of the Scriptures is communicated to the children.

Liturgy of the Word

4. One of the clearest aims and achievements of the liturgical reform after the Second Vatican Council has been the renewal of the scriptural elements of liturgical prayer and the wider opening of the Scriptures within the full cycle of liturgical seasons and celebrations.[8] Every sacramental rite, blessing, and hour of prayer calls for the proclamation of the word of God in the form of a liturgy of the word. The most effective realization of this proclamation is the eucharist, the visible word or sacrament of the paschal mystery into which we have been baptized. Full nourishment comes from the tables of God's word and eucharist.[9]

Liturgical Ministries

5. In its liturgy the Christian community acts in its capacity as an "ordered diversity of members" and ministries.[10] The liturgy is a dialogue between God and the Church. This dialogue is effected by the Spirit's

activity informing and inspiring the coordinated ministry of all who form the liturgical assembly (children as well as adults, including its bishops, presbyters, deacons, readers, musicians, and acolytes).[11]

II. The Celebration of the Word of God with Children

Scripture Never Omitted

6. The Directory for Masses with Children clearly sets forth the Church's desire that children, no less than other members of the community, be formed by the same word of God. Therefore, at Masses with adults in which children also participate and at Masses with children in which only a few adults participate "biblical reading should never be omitted."[12]

Separate Liturgy of the Word

7. In Masses with adults in which children also participate, "[s]ometimes, moreover, if the place itself and the nature of the community permit, it will be appropriate to celebrate the liturgy of the word, including a homily, with the children in a separate, but not too distant, room."[13]

8. When children are to participate in the liturgy of the word in a space separate from the main assembly, they first gather with the rest of the assembly to celebrate the introductory rites. At the conclusion of the opening prayer, but before the first reading is proclaimed, the presiding priest may formally send the children and their ministers to the place where they will celebrate their own liturgy of the word. This may be done by presenting the Lectionary to the one who will preside over the liturgy of the word with the children and/or by words of dismissal, such as the following:

A Receive this book of readings
and proclaim God's word faithfully
to the children entrusted to your care.

B My dear children,
you will now go to hear God's word,
to praise God in song,
and to reflect on the wonderful things God has done for us.
We will await your return
so that together we may celebrate the eucharist.

At the conclusion of their liturgy of the word, and before the liturgy of the eucharist begins, the children return to their families.

Weekday Masses with Children

9. Although children are always to be led toward the parish's Sunday celebration of the eucharist, nevertheless, during the week Masses with children in which only a few adults participate are recommended.[14]

Homily or Explanation of the Readings

10. Because the explanation of the Scripture readings is so important at Masses with children, a homily should always be given. However, in order that they may not be deprived of the riches of God's word, especially if the priest finds it difficult to adapt himself to the mentality of children, and

with the consent of the pastor or rector of the church, one of the adults participating in these celebrations may speak to the children after the gospel.[15]

III. The Lectionary for Masses with Children

A. One Lectionary

Purpose of Adaptation
11. This *Lectionary for Masses with Children* adheres as closely as possible to the selection and arrangement of readings for Sundays, solemnities, and feasts of the Lord in the *Lectionary for Mass*, while adapting them to the needs and capacities of children. In adapting the liturgy for use with children, the Church's goal is to nourish their faith and lead them to "active, conscious, and authentic" participation in the worship of the whole assembly,[16] but not to establish a different rite for children.[17]

Use of This Lectionary
12. In providing a lectionary for celebrations of the eucharist in which a considerable number of children are present, the Church intends to lead them into one community of faith, formed by the proclamation of the word of God. The scriptural readings contained in this Lectionary may be used at Sunday Masses when a large number of children are present along with adults, or when the children have a separate liturgy of the word, or for Masses at which most of the congregation consists of children (e.g., school Masses). The readings of this Lectionary are also a useful resource for those who wish to prepare other liturgical celebrations with children, and wish to do so within the context of the liturgical year.

13. Proper balance and consideration for the entire assembly should be observed. Therefore, priest celebrants should not use this *Lectionary for Masses with Children* exclusively or even preferentially at Sunday Masses, even though large numbers of children are present. In addition, this Lectionary may be used only when the liturgy of the word with the children is held in a place apart from the main assembly on Christmas Day, Epiphany, the Sundays of Lent, Easter Day, Ascension, and Pentecost. This is to ensure that on these days the Roman *Lectionary for Mass* will take precedence over the *Lectionary for Masses with Children* in the main assembly of the faithful.[18]

Family Preparation
14. Although the Church permits the liturgy of the word to be celebrated in a place apart from the main Sunday assembly,[19] it seeks to protect and foster the domestic church which is the Christian family.[20] This might be weakened if all the Scripture readings heard by parents were substantially different from those heard by their children on the same Sunday. This Lectionary is intended to encourage families to prepare together those readings which will be used in common both by the adults and the children for the celebration of the Sunday Mass (at least the gospel) and to reflect after the celebration on the word proclaimed there.

B. Adapted for Particular Hearers of the Word

Age Level
15. The hearers of the word for whom this work is primarily intended are children of elementary grades [preadolescents].[21]

Number of Readings
16. "If three or even two readings appointed on Sundays or weekdays can be understood by children only with difficulty, it is permissible to read two or only one of them, but the reading of the gospel should never be omitted."[22]

Omission of Readings
17. In the preparation of this Lectionary, readings from the *Lectionary for Mass* which were judged to be too abstract were eliminated or shortened.[23] Also omitted were passages of Scripture containing images that could confuse or disturb children, or readings children could perceive as anti-Semitic or racist.[24]

Length of Readings
18. Length was not the sole criterion for elimination or abridgment.[25] In particular cases longer or shorter forms of readings have been provided. Liturgical planners, with the consent of the priest celebrant, may further adapt particularly long readings by choosing to use only that part of the selection which presents a particular biblical image or is directly related to the other reading(s).

Replacement of Readings
19. When one of the first two readings for Sundays or solemnities or feasts of the Lord was judged inappropriate for children, it was omitted and not replaced with another. In cases where both of the two first readings in the Lectionary have been dropped, a replacement has been provided. The gospel selections appointed in the Roman *Lectionary for Mass* have been retained although in particular cases they have been shortened or otherwise adapted.

Responsorial Psalms
20. The responsorial psalms of the Lectionary have been adapted in order to foster the singing of these texts.[26] Some refrains and psalms have been shortened or replaced. For the most part, the responsorial psalms are related to the first reading.[27] To make it easier for the assembly to join in singing the responsorial psalm, some common texts have been provided for the liturgical seasons and for the commons of saints. These may be used in place of the assigned responsorial psalms when they are sung.[28]

C. That the Word of God Might Be Proclaimed in the Liturgical Celebration

Worthy Celebration
21. The liturgy has the power to form children and all believers in the paschal mystery. The worthy celebration of the liturgy itself is the best introduction to liturgy.[29]

Bodily Involvement

22. In order to engage children's authentic participation, liturgy must respect their need for physical involvement. They should be invited to participate in the actions of the liturgy whenever it is appropriate and possible.[30] Their internal life is still very much dependent upon what they experience through their senses. Therefore, ritual elements such as gestures and postures, processions, song, dialogue, silence, and the use of symbols are integral to their experience of the liturgy.

Ministers

23. Children imitate the behaviors and attitudes of adults. For this reason, adults who serve as ministers at liturgical celebrations where children are present should conduct the entire range of liturgical actions, gestures, and songs with dignity and care, yet without becoming distant or mechanical. All liturgical ministries are exercised for the sake of the prayer of the assembly. Therefore, ministers should be selected on the basis of liturgical competence. It should not be presumed that children should proclaim the word of God in the celebrations in which this Lectionary is used. Some younger children are able to read the Scriptures competently, but the witness of older children, teenagers, or adults, ministering graciously and reverently to young children engaged in liturgical prayer, is more conducive to the children's growing reverence for the word of God, than the peer ministry of embarrassed or ill-prepared children.[31]

Ritual Prayer

24. The Church's liturgy is first and foremost ritual prayer. The liturgy of the word is neither a catechetical session nor an introduction to biblical history. The liturgy celebrates the word of God in narrative and song, makes it visible in gesture and symbol and culminates in the celebration of the eucharist.

D. Throughout the Liturgical Year

Introduction: Calendars Express and Shape Identity

25. A calendar marks the celebrations which shape, carry on and expand a particular community's common life. This Lectionary, like the Roman *Lectionary for Mass* of which it is an adaptation, is based on the Church's calendar called the liturgical year. Its faithful observance is vital to Catholic identity. This is true for children no less than for adults. Faithful observance of the calendar promotes formation and participation in the life of the Church.

Paschal Mystery

26. The Sundays, seasons and feasts of the liturgical year celebrate many facets of a single mystery. Each of them expresses from a different perspective the one great mystery of Christ's dying and rising yesterday, today and for ever. The mystery of redemption effected by Christ's incarnation, death, and resurrection is grounded in historical events of the past, yet leads to a future glory not yet fully revealed. The entire mystery, however, is present: God is now creating and redeeming in Christ. Each day Christ's Church is dying and coming to new life in him through the indwelling of the Spirit given at baptism. In ritual prayer, past and future are caught up into God's

eternal present. Hence the liturgy is not an historical pageant trying to recreate a long-past event but rather is a true participation in Christ's death and resurrection, the paschal mystery. An understanding and appropriation of this mystery provides the essential starting point for preparing and celebrating the Church's liturgy.

Sunday

27. The shaping of time in the Church's tradition is related to the rhythms of nature, e.g., the relationship of morning and evening prayer to the daily rising and setting of the sun. The most fundamental shape of liturgical time, however, is the week. The first day of the week, Sunday, is the Lord's Day on which Christians assemble to celebrate the paschal mystery whose fullest expression is the celebration of the eucharist. Although it may be possible in appropriate ways to integrate a civil, diocesan, parochial, or domestic celebration within the Sunday liturgy, the full assembly's celebration of the Sunday eucharist must always take precedence over other special occasions. Fidelity to the Lectionary on Sundays, whether during the seasons or in Ordinary Time, is an indispensable element of Catholic formation. This Lectionary contains the readings for all the Sundays of the liturgical year in each year of the three-year cycle of readings.

Weekdays

28. In addition to the readings for Sunday, this Lectionary provides thirty-six sets of readings for the weekdays in Ordinary Time. All four gospels are represented in these weekday selections. The readings provided for the weekdays of each season are generally taken from the respective Sundays and weekdays of the *Lectionary for Mass* so that the images fundamental to the understanding and celebration of that season are adequately represented. Each set of readings has a heading which points out the dominant theme of the readings.

The Seasons: Easter Triduum, Season of Easter, and Season of Lent

29. The Triduum. The Easter Triduum or three days "begins with the evening Mass of the Lord's Supper on Holy Thursday, reaches its high point in the Easter Vigil, and closes with evening prayer on Easter Sunday."[32] The Sunday by Sunday celebration of our life in Christ finds its culmination in this annual celebration of Christ's passover from death to new life. These three days are best understood and celebrated as one liturgy which in its totality celebrates the paschal mystery. The liturgies of each day highlight the different facets of this mystery.

30. The duplication of the liturgies of Holy Thursday and Good Friday is permitted only with the permission of the Ordinary and, in the case of the Easter Vigil, is prohibited. These liturgies have a power and simplicity all of their own. No provision is made for a separate liturgy of the word for children on these occasions and this Lectionary has not provided adapted readings for these occasions. Nevertheless, care should be taken to ensure that participation by children in these celebrations is both encouraged and fostered.

31. The united proclamation of Christ's death and resurrection first sounds in the entrance song of the Evening Mass of the Lord's Supper: "We should glory in the cross of our Lord Jesus Christ, for he is our salvation, our life and our resurrection; through him we are saved and made free."[33] It intensifies in the antiphon at the veneration of the cross on Good Friday: "We worship you, Lord, we venerate your cross, we praise your resurrection. Through the cross you brought joy to the world." It climaxes in the Easter Vigil Preface: "We praise you with greater joy than ever on this Easter night when Christ became our paschal sacrifice." It echoes in the reading for Evening Prayer of Easter Sunday, the closing liturgy of the Triduum: "Christ has offered one single sacrifice for sins. . . . By virtue of that one single offering he has achieved the eternal perfection of all whom he is sanctifying."[34]

32. The Easter Triduum should reflect our deepest belief that Christ has died once for all and that Holy Thursday evening, Good Friday and Holy Saturday are as much celebrations of the Lord's paschal mystery as is Easter Sunday, although each of these days may focus upon a particular aspect of that mystery which cannot be separated from the others.

33. THE SEASON OF EASTER. Following ancient tradition, the Church celebrates Easter for fifty days, from Easter Sunday to Pentecost. These fifty days are understood to be and are celebrated as one "great Sunday."[35] The Scripture readings, liturgical texts, and rites of these fifty days take precedence over civil, school, diocesan, parochial, or domestic celebrations. These events may be integrated with the celebration of the season of Easter, but this should be done with great care.

34. The primacy of the celebration of the Sundays of Easter is rooted in the traditional character of this period as a time for ongoing catechesis, especially in regard to the sacraments of initiation (baptism, confirmation, and eucharist) and to the deeper spiritual meaning of the liturgical rites. This particular expression of the Church's formation process is called mystagogy.[36] Since most children have been baptized as infants and have received or soon will receive the eucharist, it is appropriate to draw out the meaning of these initiatory sacraments for the children during this season.

35. Throughout the season of Easter the first reading is from the Acts of the Apostles. In a three-year cycle of parallel and progressive selections, material is presented on the life of the primitive Church, its witness and growth.[37] For the second reading, passages are taken from I Peter in Year A, I John in Year B, the Revelation of John in Year C. "These are the texts that seem to fit in especially well with the spirit of joyous faith and sure hope proper to this season."[38] The gospel selections for the first three Sundays of Easter recount the appearances of the risen Christ. On the Fourth Sunday, the gospel is that of the Good Shepherd; on the Fifth, Sixth, and Seventh Sundays the Lord's discourse and prayer at the Last Supper are read. Eight sets of readings are provided for the weekdays of the Easter season.

36. THE SEASON OF LENT. Lent extends from Ash Wednesday until just before the Holy Thursday Mass of the Lord's Supper. This season is a period of preparation for the celebration of the Easter Triduum.

37. The season of Lent takes its shape and meaning from the process and rites of conversion which lead to baptism. The process of initiation gave birth to the forty days of Lent. The privileged nature of the Triduum and the joyous celebration of Easter for fifty days can be adequately understood and maintained in worship only if Lent has led the community to the realization that this season celebrates the very nature of Christian life. As catechumens are enrolled on the First Sunday of Lent for baptism at the Easter Vigil, the word of God calls all Christians—children as well as adults—back to a deeper appreciation of their own baptism.

38. The readings, prayers, and Lenten seasonal practices are ultimately to be interpreted and celebrated in the light of our baptism into Christ's dying and rising. The gospels for the first two Sundays of Lent in all three cycles recount the Lord's temptation and transfiguration. The readings of Year A for the Third, Fourth, and Fifth Sundays of Lent are of major importance to Christian initiation and are always used when the Scrutinies are celebrated and may also be used in Years B and C even when there are no catechumens in the parish. "The Old Testament readings are about the history of salvation, which is one of the themes proper to the catechesis of Lent. The series of texts for each year presents the main elements of salvation history from its beginning until the promise of the New Covenant."[39] For the season of Lent only three selections from the letters of the apostles are included in this Lectionary. As in the *Lectionary for Mass*, these selections correspond to the gospel. Nine sets of readings are provided for the weekdays of Lent.

THE SEASONS: ADVENT – CHRISTMAS

39. THE SEASON OF ADVENT. The first part of the Advent season extends from the First Sunday of Advent through December 16. The second part extends from December 17 through December 24.

40. The reign of God is already among us but is not yet made manifest in its fullness. As Christians, we celebrate what already is while standing in expectation of what is yet to be revealed. Though we cannot bring about the fullness of God's reign through our efforts alone we can cooperate with God's grace to be ready and vigilant for its advent (coming). The Advent season is one of vigilant waiting but not of Lenten penitence. The first part of the season of Advent directs the eyes of our faith to the fullness yet to be revealed when the Spirit-inspired vision of the prophets, especially Isaiah and John the Baptist, will become full reality. The second part prepares us to celebrate Christ's coming in the flesh at Bethlehem. This sense of vigilance and expectation should not be anticipated by civil, diocesan, parochial, or school celebrations of Christmas during the season of Advent.

41. The Sunday gospels in Advent treat the Lord's coming at the end of time (First Sunday of Advent), John the Baptist (Second and Third Sundays), and the events that immediately prepare for the Lord's birth (Fourth Sunday). The Old Testament readings, especially those from Isaiah, are prophecies about the Messiah and the Messianic age. The readings from the apostles serve as exhortations and as proclamations, in keeping with the different themes of Advent.[40] For the weekdays of Advent this Lectionary provides four sets of readings which reflect some of the major themes of the season.

42. The Season of Christmas. This season begins on the Vigil of Christmas and ends with the Feast of the Baptism of the Lord. The inauguration of the fullness we await was at long last disclosed in the incarnation and birth of Jesus (Christmas), born of Mary (Solemnity of Mary, Mother of God), who became a part of a human family (Feast of the Holy Family), was manifested to the nations (Epiphany), and revealed as God's own beloved child (Baptism of the Lord). The Christmas season celebrates the appearance of God among us in the birth, epiphany, and baptism of the Lord Jesus: the beginning of our salvation in Christ.

43. Christmas does not merely celebrate the birth of a child, rather this great feast celebrates the incarnation (birth) of the Lord of history in our world as God's own Word in our very flesh. It is the beginning of the paschal mystery and inevitably leads to his saving passion and resurrection from the dead. The full cycle of Christmas feasts, as surely as the celebration of the Easter Triduum, proclaims that God's "eternal Word has taken upon himself our human weakness."[41]

44. This is evident in the Gospel infancy narratives which, rather than being merely stories about the birth of a child, are anticipations of the acceptance and rejection which Jesus would meet throughout his ministry and unto his very death. Therefore Christmas is as integral to an adult understanding of faith as is Easter. Just as the Easter Triduum is one three-day celebration of Christ's paschal mystery, so the various feasts of the Christmas season are themselves celebrations of that same mystery made manifest in human history from the first moment of Jesus' birth. It is especially appropriate that the celebration of Christmas be prolonged throughout the Christmas season, rather than anticipating it as is so common in secular culture.

45. Only one set of readings for Christmas is provided in this Lectionary. These readings may be used for the Mass of the vigil, at midnight, at dawn, or during the day.

Ordinary Time

46. Ordinary Time comprises the thirty-three or thirty-four weeks of the liturgical year which follow the major seasons of Christmas and Easter. There are two periods of Ordinary Time: one which extends from the end of the Christmas season to the beginning of Lent; a longer one which extends from the end of the Easter season to the beginning of Advent. Ordinary Time is devoted to the mystery of Christ in all its aspects.[42] During these weeks the Gospel accounts of Jesus' ministry and teaching are proclaimed and celebrated. This Lectionary provides thirty-six sets of readings for use on the weekdays in Ordinary Time. All four gospels are represented in these weekday selections.

The Proper of Saints

47. Throughout the centuries the Church has kept holy the memory of Mary, Mother of God, the apostles, the martyrs, and all the saints. The liturgy presents these men and women to us as intercessors and models. The entire Church joins in the celebrations of saints of universal significance, whereas other saints may be commemorated with optional celebrations by local churches or religious families.

48. Children's openness to the power of stories makes them ready listeners when they hear stories of the saints, the examples of whose lives give them a deeper appreciation of the gospel. This is especially true in the stories of saints of our time and nation. This Lectionary provides readings for all solemnities and for many feasts. Common readings are provided for use on other feasts and memorials.

IV. Particular Issues

Place of Celebration

49. The place where the liturgy of the word is celebrated may influence how the children receive God's word. It should be chosen carefully. Sometimes a space outside the usual place of worship may need to be chosen.[43] Even when classrooms or other non-liturgical spaces must be used for celebrations of the word with children every care must be taken that these spaces be well prepared, and that the environment is suitable for the worship of God.

The Lectionary and Other Objects Used in the Celebration

50. By their beauty and by the reverent way in which they are carried and handled the books used for the celebration of the word of God should be eloquent witnesses to the Church's reverence for the Scriptures.[44] The proclamation of the word transcends the mere communication of information and becomes a community-building celebration of God's saving mystery especially when candles, incense, banners, and processions magnify the word's impact on eyes and ears, in hearts and minds.

Music

51. The eucharistic liturgy requires the full use of music which is integral to the whole celebration, including the proclamation of the word of God. The responsorial psalm is normally sung by a cantor with the assembly singing the refrain. The gospel acclamation must always be sung. A sung response to the petitions of the general intercessions can enhance participation.

Plays within the Liturgy of the Word

52. The Mass is not an historical reenactment of the events of salvation history and care should be taken not to give the impression that the liturgy of the word is a play. This is not to say that dramatic elements may not be used, e.g., the readings may at times be divided into parts distributed among the children;[45] however, the use of costumes, etc., is more appropriate in the context of other celebrations or services. Care should be taken especially at Christmas and during Holy Week and the Easter Triduum not to stage the various liturgies as plays. The Christmas Mass should not be presented as a birthday party for Jesus, nor should secular notions of Santa Claus be introduced into the Christmas liturgy.

Common Format

53. The preparation and celebration of liturgies for children begin with and flow from a clear desire to assist them to participate in the worship of the entire community. This is best accomplished when the basic shape of the ritual used with the children, its symbols, gestures, and language, is similar

to that of the full assembly. The children are thus enabled to celebrate the paschal mystery of Christ on their own level of understanding and are led to the celebration of those same mysteries in the full assembly of the faithful.

Conclusion

54. Christ's particular care for children teaches us that they are capable of welcoming God's call and responding to it. Children's human and, therefore, religious experience is complete and whole in itself and is not determined simply by their potential for adulthood. The fullest reality of the liturgical assembly is children and adults together — not separate celebrations which run the risk of diminishing the place of children in the liturgical assembly. It should be noted that the same thing can happen if inadequate attention is given to their presence in the full assembly. Nevertheless, there will be occasions when a particular assembly is constituted almost entirely of children and other occasions where their numbers are so significant that the adaptations suggested by the Directory for Masses with Children should be applied for the sake of good pastoral care. This adaptation of the *Lectionary for Mass* is intended further to help those ministering to children. For them it provides the opportunity for deeper conversion as they attend to these young hearers of the word. The way in which the word of God is proclaimed and celebrated in the lives of children today will shape the future life of the Church.

Notes

1 See John 1:1 – 3, 14.

2 See Hebrews 1:1 – 3.

3 Lectionary for Mass [=OLM], Introduction, no. 4.

4 See Matthew 18:19 – 20; see also Constitution on the Liturgy, *Sacrosanctum Concilium* [=SC], art. 7.

5 See SC, art. 7.

6 See Directory for Masses with Children [=DMC], no. 8.

7 See OLM, no. 6 and DMC, no. 15.

8 See SC, art. 24, 35, and 56.

9 See SC, art. 2; see also OLM, no. 10.

10 OLM, no. 8.

11 See DMC, nos. 22 – 24.

12 DMC, no. 41.

13 Ibid., no. 17.

14 See DMC, nos. 20 – 21.

15 DMC, no. 24.

16 Ibid., no. 12.

17 See DMC, nos. 3 and 21.

18 See letter of the Congregation for Divine Worship and the Discipline of the Sacraments granting permission for the experimental use of the *Lectionary for Masses with Children* (Prot. N. 1259/91).

19 See DMC, no. 17.

20 See DMC, no. 16.

21 See DMC, no. 6.

22 DMC, no. 42.

23 See DMC, nos. 42 – 43.

24 See DMC, no. 43.

25 See DMC, no. 44.

26 See DMC, no. 30.

27 See DMC, no. 46.

28 See OLM, Introduction, no. 9.

29 See DMC, no. 12.

30 See DMC, nos. 33 and 34.

31 See DMC, no. 24.

32 See General Norms for the Liturgical Year and the Calendar [=GNLYC], no. 19.

33 Galatians 6:14.

34 Hebrews 10:12 – 14.

35 See GNLYC, no. 22.

36 Rite of Christian Initiation of Adults, no. 247.

37 See OLM, no. 100.

38 OLM, no. 100.

39 OLM, no. 97.

40 See OLM, no. 93.

41 *Roman Missal (Sacramentary)*, Preface of Christmas III.

42 GNLYC, no. 43.

43 See DMC, no. 25.

44 See OLM, no. 35.

45 See DMC, no. 47.

Weekday Readings

SEASON OF ADVENT

FIRST READING

A reading from the book of the prophet Isaiah

Isaiah 30:19b–21

The LORD is kind,
and as soon as he hears you crying,
he will come to help you.

The Lord God will be gracious to you when he hears your cry.

The LORD has caused you trouble and sorrow
by not giving you enough bread and water.
But now you will see the LORD.
He is your guide,
and he will no longer be hidden from you.

Whether you turn to the right or to the left,
you will hear a voice saying,
"This is the road! Now follow it."

The word of the Lord.

Responsorial Psalm *R. To you, O Lord, I lift my soul.*

Psalm 25:4–5abc, 8–9, 10 and 14 (1)

Show me your paths
and teach me to follow;
guide me by your truth
and instruct me.
You keep me safe.

R. To you, O Lord, I lift my soul.

You are honest and merciful,
and you teach sinners
how to follow your path.
You lead humble people
to do what is right
and to stay on your path.

R. To you, O Lord, I lift my soul.

In everything you do,
you are kind and faithful
to everyone who keeps
our agreement with you.
Our LORD, *you are the friend*
of your worshipers,
and you make an agreement
with all of us.

R. To you, O Lord, I lift my soul.

Alleluia *R. Alleluia, alleluia.*

Psalm 85:8

Lord, show us your mercy and love,
and grant us your salvation.

R. Alleluia, alleluia.

GOSPEL **✚ A reading from the holy gospel according to Luke**

Luke 12:35–38

Jesus said to his disciples:
"Be ready and keep your lamps burning
just like those servants who wait up
for their master to return from a wedding feast.
As soon as he comes and knocks,
they open the door for him.

"Servants are fortunate
if their master finds them awake and ready
when he comes!

See that you are prepared.

I promise you that he will get ready
and have his servants sit down so he can serve them.
Those servants are really fortunate
if their master finds them ready,
even though he comes late at night or early in the morning."

The gospel of the Lord.

THE KINGDOM OF HEAVEN IS NEAR

FIRST READING

Isaiah 30:19, 23–24, 26

The Lord God will be gracious to you when he hears your cry.

A reading from the book of the prophet Isaiah

People of Jerusalem,
you don't need to cry anymore.
The LORD is kind,
and as soon as he hears you crying,
he will come to help you.

He will send rain to water the seeds you have planted,
and your fields will produce more crops than you need.
When that time comes,
your cattle will graze in open pastures.

Even the oxen and donkeys that plow your fields
will be fed grain that has been prepared in a special way.
And it will be placed there for them
with shovels and pitchforks.

On the day the LORD binds up his people's injuries
and heals the wounds he has caused,
the moon will be bright as the sun.
The light of the sun will be seven times brighter than usual,
and it will be like the light of seven days all at once.

The word of the Lord.

Responsorial Psalm

Psalm 147:1, 3–4, 5 and 7
(Isaiah 30:18)

R. Happy are all who long
for the coming of the Lord.

Shout praises to the LORD!
Our God is kind,
and it is right and good
to sing praises to him.

R. Happy are all who long
for the coming of the Lord.

He renews our hopes
and heals our bodies.
He decided how many stars
there would be in the sky
and gave each one a name.

R. Happy are all who long
for the coming of the Lord.

Our LORD is great and powerful!
He understands everything.
Celebrate and sing!
Play your harps
for the LORD our God.

R. Happy are all who long
for the coming of the Lord.

Alleluia

R. Alleluia, alleluia.

Psalm 85:8

Lord, show us your mercy and love,
and grant us your salvation.

R. Alleluia, alleluia.

GOSPEL

✚ A reading from the holy gospel according to Matthew

Matthew 9:35—10:1, 5a, 6–7

When Jesus saw the crowds, he felt sorry for them.

Jesus went to every town and village.
He taught in their meeting places
 and preached the good news about God's kingdom.
Jesus also healed every kind of disease and sickness.

When he saw the crowds,
he felt sorry for them.
They were confused and helpless,
like sheep without a shepherd.

He said to his disciples,
"A large crop is in the fields,
but there are only a few workers.
Ask the Lord in charge of the harvest
to send out workers to bring it in."

Jesus called together his twelve disciples.
He gave them the power to force out evil spirits
and to heal every kind of disease and sickness.

Jesus sent out the twelve apostles with these instructions:
"Go only to the people of Israel,
because they are like a flock of lost sheep.

"As you go,
announce that the kingdom of heaven will soon be here."

The gospel of the Lord.

FIRST READING

A reading from the book of the prophet Isaiah

Isaiah 40:25–26, 29–31

The Lord God is almighty and gives strength to the weary.

The Holy God asks,
"Who can compare with me?
Is anyone my equal?"

Look at the stars in the sky.
Who created all of these?
Who leads them like an army and gives them each a name?
The LORD is so strong and mighty
that none of the stars are missing.

The LORD gives strength to all who are weary.
Even young people tire out, then stumble and fall.
But all who trust the LORD will find new strength.
They will be strong like eagles that soar about on wings.
They will walk and run and not feel weary or tired.

The word of the Lord.

Responsorial Psalm

Psalm 33:4–5, 20 and 22 (22)

R. Lord, let your mercy be on us,
as we place our trust in you.

The LORD is truthful;
he can be trusted.
He loves justice and fairness,
and he is kind to everyone
everywhere on earth.

R. Lord, let your mercy be on us,
as we place our trust in you.

We depend on you, LORD,
to help and protect us.
Be kind and bless us!
We depend on you.

R. Lord, let your mercy be on us,
as we place our trust in you.

Alleluia *R. Alleluia, alleluia.*

Psalm 85:8

Lord, show us your mercy and love,
and grant us your salvation.

R. Alleluia, alleluia.

GOSPEL **✚ A reading from the holy gospel according to Luke**

Luke 7:17–26

Go back and tell John what you have seen and heard.

News about Jesus spread all over Judea
and everywhere else in that part of the country.

John's followers told John
everything that was being said about Jesus.
So he sent two of them to ask the Lord,
"Are you the one we should be looking for?
Or must we wait for someone else?"

When these messengers came to Jesus, they said,
"John the Baptist sent us to ask,
'Are you the one we should be looking for?
Or are we supposed to wait for someone else?'"

At that time Jesus was healing many people who were sick
or in pain or were troubled by evil spirits,
and he was giving sight to a lot of blind people.

Jesus said to the messengers sent by John,
"Go and tell John what you have seen and heard.
Blind people are now able to see,
and those who are lame can walk.
People who have leprosy are being healed,
and those who are deaf can now hear.
The dead are raised to life,
and the poor are hearing the good news.
God will bless everyone who does not reject me
because of what I do."

After John's messengers had gone,
Jesus began speaking to the crowds about John:

"What kind of person did you go out to the desert to see?
Was he like tall grass blown about by the wind?
What kind of man did you really go out to see?
Was he someone dressed in fine clothes?
People who wear expensive clothes and live in luxury
are in the king's palace.

"What then did you go out to see?
Was he a prophet?
He certainly was!
I tell you that he was more than a prophet."

The gospel of the Lord.

MY HEART PRAISES THE LORD

FIRST READING

A reading from the second letter of Paul to the Corinthians

2 Corinthians 1:3–4

Brothers and sisters:
Praise God, the Father of our Lord Jesus Christ!

Our merciful God always comforts us.

The Father is a merciful God,
who always gives us comfort.
He comforts us when we are in trouble,
so that we can share that same comfort
with others in trouble.

The word of the Lord.

Responsorial Psalm

R. Taste and see the goodness of the Lord.

Psalm 34:1–2, 3–4 (9a)

I will always praise the LORD.
With all my heart,
I will praise the LORD.
Let all who are helpless
listen and be glad.

R. Taste and see the goodness of the Lord.

Honor the LORD with me!
Celebrate his great name.
I asked the LORD for help,
and he saved me
from all my fears.

R. Taste and see the goodness of the Lord.

Alleluia *R. Alleluia, alleluia.*

Psalm 85:8 *Lord, show us your mercy and love,*
and grant us your salvation.

R. Alleluia, alleluia.

GOSPEL

Luke 1:46–56

✚ A reading from the holy gospel according to Luke

Mary said:
"With all my heart I praise the Lord,
and I am glad because of God my Savior.
He cares for me, his humble servant.
From now on, all people will say God has blessed me.
God All-Powerful has done great things for me,
and his name is holy.

The Almighty has done great things for me.

"He always shows mercy to everyone who worships him.
The Lord has used his powerful arm
to scatter those who are proud.
He drags strong rulers from their thrones
and puts humble people in places of power.
He gives the hungry good things to eat,
and he sends the rich away with nothing in their hands.
He helps his servant Israel
and is always merciful to his people.
He made this promise to our ancestors,
to Abraham and his family forever!"

Mary stayed with Elizabeth about three months.
Then she went back home.

The gospel of the Lord.

SEASON OF LENT

PRAY, FAST, AND SHARE

First Reading **A reading from the book of the prophet Isaiah**

Isaiah 58:6–9

The LORD says this:
I'll tell you what it really means
to worship the LORD.
Remove the chains of prisoners who are chained unjustly.
Free those who are abused!

Share your food with everyone who is hungry;
share your home with the poor and homeless.
Give clothes to those in need;
don't turn away your relatives.

Is this not the sort of fast that pleases me?

Then your light will shine like the dawning sun,
and you will quickly be healed.
Your honesty will protect you as you advance,
and the glory of the LORD will defend you from behind.
Then you will call for help,
and the LORD will answer, "Here I am!"

Don't oppress others or falsely accuse them
or say cruel things.

The word of the Lord.

Responsorial Psalm *R. The Lord is my light and my salvation.*

Psalm 27:1, 11ab and 13 (1a)

You, LORD, are the light
that keeps me safe.
I am not afraid of anyone.
You protect me,
and I have no fears.

R. The Lord is my light and my salvation.

Teach me to follow, LORD,
and lead me on the right path.
I know I will live
to see how kind you are.

R. The Lord is my light and my salvation.

Verse before the Gospel *R. Glory and praise to you,*
Lord Jesus Christ.

Matthew 4:17

Repent, says the Lord;
the kingdom of heaven is at hand.

R. Glory and praise to you,
Lord Jesus Christ.

ONE

GOSPEL ✚ **A reading from the holy gospel according to Matthew**

Matthew 6:1–6, 16–18

Jesus said to his disciples:
"When you do good deeds,
don't try to show off.
If you do, you won't get a reward
from your Father in heaven.

"When you give to the poor,
don't blow a loud horn.
That's what showoffs do in the meeting places
and on the street corners,
because they are always looking for praise.
I promise you that they already have their reward.

Your Father, who sees all that is done in secret, will reward you.

"When you give to the poor,
don't let anyone know about it.
Then your gift will be given in secret.
Your Father knows what is done in secret,
and he will reward you.

"When you pray,
don't be like those showoffs who love to stand up and pray
in the meeting places and on the street corners.
They do this just to look good.
I promise you that they already have their reward.

"When you pray,
go into a room alone and close the door.
Pray to your Father in private.
He knows what is done in private,
and he will reward you.

"When you go without eating,
don't try to look gloomy as those showoffs do
when they go without eating.
I promise you that they already have their reward.

"Instead, comb your hair and wash your face.
Then others won't know that you are going without eating.
But your Father sees what is done in private,
and he will reward you."

The gospel of the Lord.

OR

TWO

GOSPEL

✚ A reading from the holy gospel according to Matthew

Matthew 6:1–4

Jesus said to his disciples:
"When you do good deeds,
don't try to show off.
If you do, you won't get a reward
from your Father in heaven.

"When you give to the poor,
don't blow a loud horn.
That's what showoffs do in the meeting places
and on the street corners,
because they are always looking for praise.
I promise you that they already have their reward.

Your Father, who sees all that is done in secret, will reward you.

"When you give to the poor,
don't let anyone know about it.
Then your gift will be given in secret.
Your Father knows what is done in secret,
and he will reward you."

The gospel of the Lord.

OR

THREE

GOSPEL

✚ A reading from the holy gospel according to Matthew

Matthew 6:1, 5–6

Your Father, who sees all that is done in secret, will reward you.

Jesus said to his disciples:
"When you do good deeds,
don't try to show off.
If you do, you won't get a reward
from your Father in heaven.

"When you pray,
don't be like those showoffs who love to stand up and pray
in the meeting places and on the street corners.
They do this just to look good.
I promise you that they already have their reward.

"When you pray,
go into a room alone and close the door.
Pray to your Father in private.
He knows what is done in private,
and he will reward you."

The gospel of the Lord.

OR

FOUR

GOSPEL

Matthew 6:1, 16–18

Your Father, who sees all that is done in secret, will reward you.

✚ A reading from the holy gospel according to Matthew

Jesus said to his disciples:
"When you do good deeds,
don't try to show off.
If you do, you won't get a reward
from your Father in heaven.

"When you go without eating,
don't try to look gloomy as those showoffs do
when they go without eating.
I promise you that they already have their reward.

"Instead, comb your hair and wash your face.
Then others won't know that you are going without eating.
But your Father sees what is done in private,
and he will reward you."

The gospel of the Lord.

177

WHAT WE DO FOR OTHERS WE DO FOR JESUS

FIRST READING

A reading from the Acts of the Apostles

Acts 11:27–30

The disciples decided to send relief during the famine, each to contribute what they could afford, to the brothers and sisters living in Judea.

Some prophets from Jerusalem came to Antioch.
One of them was Agabus.
With the help of the Spirit,
he told that there would be a terrible famine
everywhere in the world.

And it happened when Claudius was Emperor.
The followers in Antioch
decided to send whatever help they could
to the followers in Judea.
So they had Barnabas and Saul take their gifts
to the church leaders in Jerusalem.

The word of the Lord.

Responsorial Psalm

Psalm 25:4–5ab, 5cd–6 (4a)

R. Teach me your ways, O Lord.

Show me your paths
and teach me to follow;
guide me by your truth
and instruct me.

R. Teach me your ways, O Lord.

You keep me safe,
and I always trust you.
Please, LORD, remember,
you have always been patient and kind.

R. Teach me your ways, O Lord.

Verse before the Gospel *R. Glory and praise to you,*
Lord Jesus Christ.

Matthew 4:17

Repent, says the Lord;
the kingdom of heaven is at hand.

R. Glory and praise to you,
Lord Jesus Christ.

GOSPEL **✚ A reading from the holy gospel according to Matthew**

Matthew 25:31–40

Whatever you have done to the very least of my brothers and sisters, you have done to me.

Jesus said to his disciples:
"When the Son of Man comes in his glory
with all of his angels,
he will sit on his royal throne.

"The people of all nations will be brought before him,
and he will separate them,
as shepherds separate their sheep from their goats.

"He will place the sheep on his right
and the goats on his left.
Then the king will say to those on his right,
'My father has blessed you!
Come and receive the kingdom that was prepared for you
before the world was created.

When I was hungry, you gave me something to eat,
and when I was thirsty, you gave me something to drink.
When I was a stranger, you welcomed me,
and when I was naked, you gave me clothes to wear.
When I was sick, you took care of me,
and when I was in jail, you visited me.'

"Then the ones who pleased the Lord will ask,
'When did we give you something to eat or drink?
When did we welcome you as a stranger
or give you clothes to wear
or visit you while you were sick or in jail?'

"The king will answer,
'Whenever you did it for any of my people,
no matter how unimportant they seemed,
you did it for me.'"

The gospel of the Lord.

FORGIVE ONE ANOTHER

FIRST READING

A reading from the letter of Paul to the Colossians

Colossians 3:12–14

Have charity, which is the bond of perfection.

Brothers and sisters:
God loves you and has chosen you as his own special people.
So be gentle, kind, humble, meek, and patient.
Put up with each other,
and forgive anyone who does you wrong,
just as Christ has forgiven you.
Love is more important than anything else.
It is what ties everything completely together.

The word of the Lord.

Responsorial Psalm

Psalm 51:1 and 10, 12 and 15 (see 3a)

*R. Be merciful, O Lord,
for we have sinned.*

*You are kind, God!
Please have pity on me.
You are always merciful!
Please wipe away my sins.
Create pure thoughts in me
and make me faithful again.*

*R. Be merciful, O Lord,
for we have sinned.*

*Make me as happy as you did
when you saved me;
make me want to obey!
Help me to speak,
and I will praise you, Lord.*

*R. Be merciful, O Lord,
for we have sinned.*

Verse before the Gospel

Matthew 4:17

R. Glory and praise to you,
Lord Jesus Christ.

Repent, says the Lord;
the kingdom of heaven is at hand.

R. Glory and praise to you,
Lord Jesus Christ.

GOSPEL

✚ A reading from the holy gospel according to Matthew

Matthew 6:7–15

This is how you should pray.

Jesus said to his disciples:
"When you pray,
don't talk on and on as people do who don't know God.
They think God likes to hear long prayers.
Don't be like them.
Your Father knows what you need before you ask.

"You should pray like this:

Our Father in heaven,
help us to honor your name.
Come and set up your kingdom,
so that everyone on earth will obey you,
as you are obeyed in heaven.
Give us our food for today.
Forgive our sins,
as we forgive others.
Keep us from being tempted and protect us from evil.

"If you forgive others for the wrongs they do to you,
your Father in heaven will forgive you.
But if you don't forgive others,
your Father will not forgive your sins."

The gospel of the Lord.

ASK AND YOU WILL RECEIVE

First Reading **A reading from the book of the prophet Isaiah**

Isaiah 12:4b–5

We will thank you because of your wonderful deeds.

When the LORD comes you will say,
"Our LORD, we are thankful,
and we worship only you.
We will tell the nations how glorious you are
and what you have done.
We will sing your praises everywhere
because of your wonderful deeds."

The word of the Lord.

Responsorial Psalm

Psalm 126:1–2ab, 2cde–3 (3)

R. The Lord has done great things for us;
we are filled with joy.

It seemed like a dream
when the LORD brought us back
to the city of Zion.
We celebrated with laughter
and joyful songs.

R. The Lord has done great things for us;
we are filled with joy.

In foreign nations it was said,
"The LORD has worked miracles
for his people."
And so we celebrated
because the LORD had indeed
worked miracles for us.

R. The Lord has done great things for us;
we are filled with joy.

Verse before the Gospel *R. Glory and praise to you,*
Lord Jesus Christ.

Matthew 4:17

Repent, says the Lord;
the kingdom of heaven is at hand.

R. Glory and praise to you,
Lord Jesus Christ.

GOSPEL

✚ A reading from the holy gospel according to Matthew

Matthew 7:7–11

Jesus said to his disciples:
"Ask, and you will receive.
Search, and you will find.
Knock, and the door will be opened for you.

"Everyone who asks will receive.
Everyone who searches will find.
And the door will be opened for everyone who knocks.

Ask and you will receive.

"Would any of you give your hungry child a stone,
if the child asked for some bread?
Would you give your child a snake
  if the child asked for a fish?
As bad as you are,
you still know how to give good gifts to your children.
But your heavenly Father is even more ready
  to give good things to people who ask."

The gospel of the Lord.

BE AT PEACE WITH EVERYONE

First Reading **A reading from the book of Genesis**

Genesis 50:15–21

After Jacob died,
Joseph's brothers said to each other,
"What if Joseph still hates us and wants to get even with us
for all the cruel things we did to him?"

So they sent a message to Joseph.
It said: "Before our father Jacob died, he told us,
'You did some cruel and terrible things to Joseph!
But you must ask him to forgive you.'"

Please forgive all the wrong we have done.

"Now we ask you to please forgive
all the terrible things we did.
After all, we serve the same God
that your father worshiped."

When Joseph heard this, he started crying.

Right then Joseph's brothers came
and bowed down to the ground in front of him.
They said, "We are your slaves."

But Joseph told them, "Don't be afraid!
I have no right to change what God has decided.
You tried to harm me,
but God made it turn out for the best,
so that he could save all these people, as he is now doing.
So then, don't be afraid.
I will take care of you and your children."

When Joseph said this, his brothers felt better.

The word of the Lord.

Responsorial Psalm

Psalm 122:1–2, 6–7, 8–9 (Sirach 36:18)

R. Give peace, O Lord,
to those who wait for you.

It made me glad
to hear them say,
"Let's go to the house
of the LORD!"
Jerusalem, we are standing
inside your gates.

R. Give peace, O Lord,
to those who wait for you.

Jerusalem, we pray
that you will have peace,
and that all will go well
for those who love you.
May there be peace
inside your city walls
and in your palaces.

R. Give peace, O Lord,
to those who wait for you.

Because of my friends
and my relatives,
I will pray for peace.
And because of the house
of the LORD our God,
I will work for your good.

R. Give peace, O Lord,
to those who wait for you.

Verse before the Gospel

Matthew 4:17

R. Glory and praise to you,
Lord Jesus Christ.

Repent, says the Lord;
the kingdom of heaven is at hand.

R. Glory and praise to you,
Lord Jesus Christ.

GOSPEL

✚ A reading from the holy gospel according to Matthew

Matthew 5:20–24

Those who are angry with their brother or sister will answer for it before the law.

Jesus said to his disciples:
"You must obey God's commands better than the Pharisees
and the teachers of the Law obey them.
If you don't,
I promise you that you will never get into the kingdom
of heaven.

"You know that our ancestors were told,
'Do not murder' and 'A murderer must be brought to trial.'
But I promise you that if you are angry with someone,
you will have to stand trial.

If you call someone a fool,
you will be taken to court.
And if you say that someone is worthless,
you will be in danger of the fires of hell.

"So if you are about to place your gift on the altar
and remember that someone is angry with you,
leave your gift there in front of the altar.
Make peace with that person,
then come back and offer your gift to God."

The gospel of the Lord.

181

LOVE EVERYONE

First Reading

Romans 12:17–18, 21

Do your best to live at peace with everyone.

A reading from the letter of Paul to the Romans

Brothers and sisters:
Don't mistreat someone who has mistreated you.
But try to earn the respect of others,
and do your best to live at peace with everyone.

Don't let evil defeat you,
but defeat evil with good.

The word of the Lord.

Responsorial Psalm

Psalm 85:8abc and 9, 10–11, 12–13 (8)

R. Lord, show us your mercy and love,
and grant us your salvation.

I will listen to you, LORD God,
because you promise peace
to those who are faithful.
You are ready to rescue
everyone who worships you,
so that you will live with us
in all of your glory.

R. Lord, show us your mercy and love,
and grant us your salvation.

Love and loyalty
will come together;
goodness and peace will unite.
Loyalty will sprout
from the ground;
justice will look down
from the sky above.

R. Lord, show us your mercy and love,
and grant us your salvation.

Our LORD, you will bless us;
our land will produce
wonderful crops.
Justice will march in front,
making a path
for you to follow.

R. Lord, show us your mercy and love,
and grant us your salvation.

Verse before the Gospel

Matthew 4:17

R. Glory and praise to you,
Lord Jesus Christ.

Repent, says the Lord;
the kingdom of heaven is at hand.

R. Glory and praise to you,
Lord Jesus Christ.

GOSPEL

Matthew 5:43–48

Be perfect as your heavenly Father is perfect.

✚ A reading from the holy gospel according to Matthew

Jesus said to his disciples:
"You have heard people say,
'Love your neighbors and hate your enemies.'
But I tell you to love your enemies
and pray for anyone who mistreats you.
Then you will be acting like your Father in heaven.

"He makes the sun rise on both good and bad people.
And he sends rain for the ones who do right
and for the ones who do wrong.

"If you love only those people who love you,
will God reward you for that?
Even tax collectors love their friends.
If you greet only your friends,
what's so great about that?
Don't even unbelievers do that?
But you must always act like your Father in heaven."

The gospel of the Lord.

LOVE OF GOD AND LOVE OF NEIGHBOR

FIRST READING

A reading from the book of Deuteronomy

Deuteronomy 10:12–14

The Lord wants you to serve him with all your heart and soul.

Moses told the people:
"People of Israel,
what does the LORD your God want from you?
The LORD wants you to worship and obey him
and to love and serve him with all your heart and soul.
For your own good you must obey his laws and commands
that I am teaching you today.

"Everything belongs to the LORD your God.
The highest heavens are his,
and so are the earth and everything on it."

The word of the Lord.

Responsorial Psalm

Psalm 19:7, 8ab and 9cd, 10 (9a)

R. The precepts of the Lord
give joy to the heart.

The Law of the LORD *is perfect;*
it gives us new life.
His teachings last forever,
and they give wisdom
to ordinary people.

R. The precepts of the Lord
give joy to the heart.

The LORD*'s instruction is right;*
it makes our hearts glad.
All of his decisions
are correct and fair.

R. The precepts of the Lord
give joy to the heart.

They are worth more
than the finest gold
and are sweeter than honey
from a honeycomb.

R. The precepts of the Lord
give joy to the heart.

Verse before the Gospel *R. Glory and praise to you,*
Lord Jesus Christ.

Matthew 4:17

Repent, says the Lord;
the kingdom of heaven is at hand.

R. Glory and praise to you,
Lord Jesus Christ.

GOSPEL

✚ A reading from the holy gospel according to Mark

Mark 12:28b–31

When one of the teachers of the Law of Moses
heard Jesus give a good answer, he asked him,
"What is the most important commandment?"

The Lord our God is one Lord and you shall love the Lord your God.

Jesus answered, "The most important one says:
'People of Israel, you have only one Lord and God.
You must love him with all your heart, soul, mind,
and strength.'
The second most important commandment says:
'Love others as much as you love yourself.'
No other commandment is more important than these."

The gospel of the Lord.

TRUST IN THE LORD

First Reading | **A reading from the book of Lamentations**

Lamentations 3:22–25

It is good to wait in silence for the Lord God to save.

We would have been destroyed,
if the LORD had not been kind.
But his mercy never fails.
The LORD can always be trusted to show mercy
each morning.

Deep in my heart I say,
"The LORD is all I need.
I can depend on him!"

The LORD is good to everyone who trusts and worships him.

The word of the Lord.

Responsorial Psalm

Psalm 33:1–2, 4–5, 21–22 (22)

R. Lord, let your mercy be on us,
as we place our trust in you.

You are the LORD's people.
Obey him and celebrate.
He deserves your praise.
Praise the LORD with harps!
Use harps with ten strings
to make music for him.

R. Lord, let your mercy be on us,
as we place our trust in you.

The LORD is truthful;
he can be trusted.
He loves justice and fairness,
and he is kind to everyone
everywhere on earth.

R. Lord, let your mercy be on us,
as we place our trust in you.

You make our hearts glad
because we trust you,
the only God.
Be kind and bless us!
We depend on you.

R. Lord, let your mercy be on us,
as we place our trust in you.

Verse before the Gospel *R. Glory and praise to you,*
Lord Jesus Christ.

Matthew 4:17

Repent, says the Lord;
the kingdom of heaven is at hand.

R. Glory and praise to you,
Lord Jesus Christ.

GOSPEL **✚ A reading from the holy gospel according to John**

John 4:46–53

While Jesus was in Galilee,
he returned to the village of Cana,
where he had turned the water into wine.

Go, your son will live.

There was an official in Capernaum whose son was sick.
And when the man heard that Jesus had come from Judea,
he went and begged him to keep his son from dying.

Jesus told the official,
"You won't have faith
unless you see miracles and wonders!"

The man replied, "Lord, please come before my son dies!"

Jesus then said, "Your son will live.
Go on home to him."

The man believed Jesus and started back home.

Some of the official's servants met him along the road
and told him,
"Your son is better!"

He asked them when the boy got better, and they answered,
"The fever left him yesterday at one o'clock."

The boy's father realized that at one o'clock the day before,
Jesus had told him,
"Your son will live!"

So the man and everyone in his family put their faith
in Jesus.

The gospel of the Lord.

JESUS BRINGS TOGETHER ALL PEOPLE

FIRST READING

A reading from the book of the prophet Ezekiel

Ezekiel 37:21–22, 24

I, the LORD God, will gather the people of Israel
and bring them back home
from the nations where they have gone.
I will make them into one nation on the hills of Israel.

I will make them into one nation.

Only one king will rule over them,
and they will never again be divided into two nations.
My servant David will be their king and only ruler,
and they will eagerly obey my laws and commands.

The word of the Lord.

Responsorial Psalm

Psalm 33:4–5, 12–13 and 14b, 20 and 22 (12b)

R. Happy the people
the Lord has chosen to be his own.

The LORD is truthful;
he can be trusted.
He loves justice and fairness,
and he is kind to everyone
everywhere on earth.

R. Happy the people
the Lord has chosen to be his own.

The LORD blesses each nation
that worships only him.
He blesses his chosen ones.
The LORD looks at the world,
and he watches us all.

R. Happy the people
the Lord has chosen to be his own.

We depend on you, LORD,
to help and protect us.
Be kind and bless us!
We depend on you.

R. Happy the people
the Lord has chosen to be his own.

Verse before the Gospel

Matthew 4:17

R. Glory and praise to you,
Lord Jesus Christ.

Repent, says the Lord;
the kingdom of heaven is at hand.

R. Glory and praise to you,
Lord Jesus Christ.

GOSPEL

✚ A reading from the holy gospel according to John

John 11:47–52

Jesus was going to die to gather together in unity the scattered children of God.

The chief priests and the Pharisees
called the council together and said,
"What should we do?
This man is working a lot of miracles.
If we don't stop him now,
everyone will put their faith in him.
Then the Romans will come and destroy our temple
and our nation."

One of the council members was Caiaphas,
who was also high priest that year.

He spoke up and said,
"You people don't have any sense at all!
Don't you know it is better
for one person to die for the people
than for our whole nation to be destroyed?"

Caiaphas did not say this on his own.
As high priest that year,
he was prophesying that Jesus would die for the nation.

Yet Jesus would not die just for the Jewish nation.
He would die to bring together all of God's scattered people.

The gospel of the Lord.

SEASON OF EASTER

185

WITNESSES OF THE RESURRECTION

FIRST READING — **A reading from the Acts of the Apostles**

Acts 2:32–33

God raised this man Jesus to life, and all of us are witnesses to it.

On the day of Pentecost Peter told the people:
"All of us can tell you that God has raised Jesus to life!

"Jesus was taken up to sit at the right side of God,
and he was given the Holy Spirit,
just as the Father had promised.

"Jesus is also the one who has given the Spirit to us,
and that is what you are now seeing and hearing."

The word of the Lord.

Responsorial Psalm

Psalm 96:1–2a, 2b–3, 11–12ab (3)

R. Proclaim God's marvelous deeds
to all the nations.

Sing a new song to the LORD!
Everyone on this earth,
sing praises to the LORD,
sing and praise his name.

R. Proclaim God's marvelous deeds
to all the nations.

Day after day announce,
"The LORD has saved us!"
Tell every nation on earth,
"The LORD is wonderful
and does marvelous things!"

R. Proclaim God's marvelous deeds
to all the nations.

Tell the heavens and the earth
to be glad and celebrate!
Command the ocean to roar
with all of its creatures
and the fields to rejoice
with all of their crops.

R. Proclaim God's marvelous deeds
to all the nations.

Alleluia *R. Alleluia, alleluia.*

See John 6:63c, 68c

Your words, Lord, are spirit and life:
you have the words of everlasting life.

R. Alleluia, alleluia.

GOSPEL **✚ A reading from the holy gospel according to John**

John 20:11–18

Mary Magdalene stood crying outside the tomb.
She was still weeping, when she stooped down
and saw two angels inside.
They were dressed in white
and were sitting where Jesus' body had been.
One was at the head and the other was at the foot.

I have seen the Lord and he said these things to me.

The angels asked Mary, "Why are you crying?"

She answered, "They have taken away my Lord's body!
I don't know where they have put him."

As soon as Mary said this,
she turned around and saw Jesus standing there.
But she did not know who he was.
Jesus asked her, "Why are you crying?
Who are you looking for?"

She thought he was the gardener and said,
"Sir, if you have taken his body away,
please tell me, so I can go and get him."

Then Jesus said to her, "Mary!"

She turned and said to him, "Rabboni."
The Aramaic word "Rabboni" means "Teacher."

Jesus told her, "Don't hold on to me!
I have not yet gone to the Father.
But tell my disciples that I am going to the one
who is my Father and my God,
as well as your Father and your God."
Mary Magdalene then went and told the disciples
that she had seen the Lord.
She also told them what he had said to her.

The gospel of the Lord.

THE POWER OF JESUS' NAME

First Reading

A reading from the Acts of the Apostles

Acts 3:1–10

At the time of prayer,
which was about three o'clock in the afternoon,
Peter and John were going into the temple.
A man who had been born lame was being carried
to the temple door.
Each day he was placed beside this door,
known as the Beautiful Gate.
He sat there and begged from the people who were going in.

What I have, I give you: in the name of Jesus stand up and walk.

The man saw Peter and John entering the temple,
and he asked them for money.
But they looked straight at him and said,
"Look up at us!"

The man stared at them
and thought he was going to get something.
But Peter said, "I don't have any silver or gold!
But I will give you what I do have.
In the name of Jesus Christ from Nazareth,
get up and start walking."
Peter then took him by the right hand and helped him up.

At once the man's feet and ankles became strong,
and he jumped up and started walking.
He went with Peter and John into the temple,
walking and jumping and praising God.

Everyone saw him walking around and praising God.
They knew that he was the beggar
who had been lying beside the Beautiful Gate,
and they were completely surprised.
They could not imagine what had happened to the man.

The word of the Lord.

Responsorial Psalm

Psalm 98:1, 2, 5–6 (3cd)

R. All the ends of the earth
have seen the saving power of God.

Sing a new song to the LORD!
He has worked miracles,
and with his own powerful arm,
he has won the victory.

R. All the ends of the earth
have seen the saving power of God.

The LORD has shown the nations
that he has the power to save
and to bring justice.

R. All the ends of the earth
have seen the saving power of God.

Make music for him on harps.
Play beautiful melodies!
Sound the trumpets and horns,
and celebrate with joyful songs
for our LORD and King!

R. All the ends of the earth
have seen the saving power of God.

Alleluia

See John 6:63c, 68c

R. Alleluia, alleluia.

Your words, Lord, are spirit and life:
you have the words of everlasting life.

R. Alleluia, alleluia.

GOSPEL

✚ A reading from the holy gospel according to John

John 14:12–14

If you have faith in me, you will do even greater things.

Jesus said to his disciples:
"I tell you for certain that if you have faith in me,
you will do the same things that I am doing.

"You will do even greater things,
now that I am going back to the Father.

"Ask me, and I will do whatever you ask.
This way the Son will bring honor to the Father.
I will do whatever you ask me to do."

The gospel of the Lord.

ONE IN CHRIST JESUS

First Reading **A reading from the Acts of the Apostles**

Acts 4:32–35

The followers of Jesus all felt the same way
about everything.
None of them claimed that their belongings were their own,
and they shared everything they had with each other.

The whole group of believers was united, heart and soul.

In a powerful way the apostles told everyone
that the Lord Jesus was now alive.

God greatly blessed his followers,
and no one went in need of anything.
Everyone who owned land or houses would sell them
and bring the money to the apostles.
Then they would give the money to anyone who needed it.

The word of the Lord.

Responsorial Psalm

Psalm 145:10–11, 15–16, 17–18 (18a)

R. The Lord is near
to all who call on him.

All creation will thank you,
and your loyal people
will praise you.
They will tell about
your marvelous kingdom
and your power.

R. The Lord is near
to all who call on him.

Everyone depends on you,
and when the time is right,
you provide them with food.
By your own hand you satisfy
the desires of all who live.

R. The Lord is near
to all who call on him.

Our LORD, *everything you do*
is kind and thoughtful,
and you are near to everyone
whose prayers are sincere.

R. The Lord is near
to all who call on him.

Alleluia

See John 6:63c, 68c

R. Alleluia, alleluia.

Your words, Lord, are spirit and life:
you have the words of everlasting life.

R. Alleluia, alleluia.

GOSPEL

✚ A reading from the holy gospel according to John

John 17:21–23

Jesus prayed to God:
"I want all of my followers to be one with each other,
just as I am one with you and you are one with me.
I also want them to be one with us.
Then the people of this world will believe that you sent me.

"I have honored my followers
in the same way that you honored me,
in order that they may be one with each other,
just as we are one.

May they be completely one.

"I am one with them,
and you are one with me,
so that they may become completely one.
Then this world's people will know that you sent me.
They will know that you love my followers
as much as you love me."

The gospel of the Lord.

FOLLOWERS OF JESUS

First Reading **A reading from the Acts of the Apostles**

Acts 5:17–21

The high priest and all the other Sadducees
who were with him became jealous.
They arrested the apostles and put them in the city jail.

Go and tell the people everything about this new life.

But that night an angel from the Lord opened the doors
of the jail and led the apostles out.
The angel said, "Go to the temple
and tell the people everything about this new life."
So they went into the temple before sunrise
and started teaching.

The word of the Lord.

Responsorial Psalm *R. The Lord hears the cry of the poor.*

Psalm 34:1–2, 3–4, 7–8 (7a)

I will always praise the LORD.
With all my heart,
I will praise the LORD.
Let all who are helpless
listen and be glad.

R. The Lord hears the cry of the poor.

Honor the LORD with me!
Celebrate his great name.
I asked the LORD for help,
and he saved me
from all my fears.

R. The Lord hears the cry of the poor.

If you honor the LORD,
his angel will protect you.
Discover for yourself
that the LORD is kind.
Come to him for protection,
and you will be glad.

R. The Lord hears the cry of the poor.

Alleluia *R. Alleluia, alleluia.*

See John 6:63c, 68c

Your words, Lord, are spirit and life:
you have the words of everlasting life.

R. Alleluia, alleluia.

GOSPEL **✚ A reading from the holy gospel according to John**

John 15:18–21

You do not belong to the world because I have chosen you out of it.

Jesus said to his disciples:
"If the people of this world hate you,
just remember that they hated me first.
If you belonged to the world,
its people would love you.
But you don't belong to the world.

"I have chosen you to leave the world behind,
and that is why its people hate you.

"Remember how I told you
    that servants are not greater than their master.
So if people mistreat me, they will mistreat you.
If they do what I say, they will do what you say.

"People will do to you exactly what they did to me.
They will do it because you belong to me,
and they don't know the one who sent me."

The gospel of the Lord.

OBEDIENCE TO GOD

First Reading **A reading from the Acts of the Apostles**

Acts 5:27–32

When the apostles were brought before the Jewish council,
the high priest said to them,
"We told you plainly not to teach in the name of Jesus.
But look what you have done!
You have been teaching all over Jerusalem,
and you are trying to blame us for his death."

Peter and the apostles replied:

We do not obey people. We obey God.

"We don't obey people. We obey God.
You killed Jesus by nailing him to a cross.
But the God our ancestors worshiped raised him to life
and made him our Leader and Savior.
Then God gave him a place at his right side,
so that the people of Israel would turn back to him
and be forgiven.
We are here to tell you about all this,
and so is the Holy Spirit,
who is God's gift to everyone who obeys God."

The word of the Lord.

Responsorial Psalm

Psalm 119:1–2, 7 and 24 (1b)

R. Happy are they
who follow the law of the Lord!

Our L*ORD, you bless everyone*
who lives right
and obeys your Law.
You bless all of those
who follow your commands
from deep in their hearts.

R. Happy are they
who follow the law of the Lord!

I will do right and praise you
by learning to respect
your perfect laws.
Your laws are my greatest joy!
I follow their advice.

R. Happy are they
who follow the law of the Lord!

Alleluia

See John 6:63c, 68c

R. Alleluia, alleluia.

Your words, Lord, are spirit and life:
you have the words of everlasting life.

R. Alleluia, alleluia.

GOSPEL

✚ A reading from the holy gospel according to John

John 14:21–26

Jesus said to his disciples:
"If you love me, you will do what I have said,
and my Father will love you.
I will also love you and show you what I am like."

If you love me you will obey me.

The other Judas, not Judas Iscariot, then spoke up and asked,
"Lord, what do you mean by saying
that you will show us what you are like,
but you will not show the people of this world?"

Jesus replied:
"If anyone loves me, they will obey me.
Then my Father will love them,
and we will come to them and live in them.
But anyone who doesn't love me,
won't obey me.
What they have heard me say doesn't really come from me,
but from the Father who sent me.

"I have told you these things while I am still with you.
But the Holy Spirit will come and help you,
because the Father will send the Spirit to take my place.
The Spirit will teach you everything
and will remind you of what I said while I was with you."

The gospel of the Lord.

First Reading **A reading from the Acts of the Apostles**

Acts 9:1–20

Saul kept on threatening to kill the Lord's followers.
He even went to the high priest
and asked for letters to the Jewish leaders in Damascus.
He did this because he wanted to arrest
and take to Jerusalem any man or woman
who had accepted the Lord's Way.

This man is my chosen instrument to bring my name before the Gentiles.

When Saul had almost reached Damascus,
a bright light from heaven suddenly flashed around him.
He fell to the ground and heard a voice that said,
"Saul! Saul! Why are you so cruel to me?"

"Who are you?" Saul asked.

"I am Jesus," the Lord answered.
"I am the one you are so cruel to.
Now get up and go into the city,
where you will be told what to do."

The men with Saul stood there speechless.
They had heard the voice,
but they had not seen anyone.
Saul got up from the ground,
and when he opened his eyes,
he could not see a thing.
Someone then led him by the hand to Damascus,
and for three days he was blind and did not eat or drink.

A follower named Ananias lived in Damascus,
and the Lord spoke to him in a vision.
Ananias answered, "Lord, here I am."

The Lord said to him,
"Get up and go to the house of Judas on Straight Street.
When you get there,
you will find a man named Saul from the city of Tarsus.

Saul is praying,
and he has seen a vision.
He saw a man named Ananias coming to him
  and putting his hands on him,
so that he could see again."

Ananias replied, "Lord, a lot of people have told me
  about the terrible things this man has done
  to your followers in Jerusalem.
Now the chief priests have given him the power
  to come here and arrest anyone who worships
  in your name."

The Lord said to Ananias, "Go!
I have chosen him to tell foreigners, kings,
  and the people of Israel about me.
I will show him how much he must suffer
  for worshiping in my name."

Ananias left and went into the house
  where Saul was staying.
Ananias placed his hands on him and said,
"Saul, the Lord Jesus has sent me.
He is the same one who appeared to you along the road.
He wants you to be able to see
  and to be filled with the Holy Spirit."

Suddenly something like fish scales fell from Saul's eyes,
and he could see.
He got up and was baptized.
Then he ate and felt much better.

For several days Saul stayed with the Lord's followers
  in Damascus.
Soon he went to the Jewish meeting places
  and started telling people that Jesus is the Son of God.

The word of the Lord.

Responsorial Psalm

Psalm 117:1, 2 (Mark 16:15)

R. Go out to all the world
and tell the good news.

All of you nations,
come praise the LORD!
Let everyone praise him.

R. Go out to all the world
and tell the good news.

His love for us is wonderful,
his faithfulness never ends.
Shout praises to the LORD!

R. Go out to all the world
and tell the good news.

Alleluia

See John 6:63c, 68c

R. Alleluia, alleluia.

Your words, Lord, are spirit and life:
you have the words of everlasting life.

R. Alleluia, alleluia.

GOSPEL

John 10:14–16

The good shepherd lays down his life for his sheep.

✚ A reading from the holy gospel according to John

Jesus said:
"I am the good shepherd.
I know my sheep, and they know me.
Just as the Father knows me,
I know the Father,
and I give up my life for my sheep.

"I have other sheep that are not in this sheep pen.
I must bring them together too,
when they hear my voice.
Then there will be one flock of sheep and one shepherd."

The gospel of the Lord.

BELIEVE IN JESUS

First Reading **A reading from the Acts of the Apostles**

Acts 11:19–22, 26c

The disciples preached to the Greeks, proclaiming the good news of the Lord Jesus.

Some of the Lord's followers had been scattered
because of the terrible trouble that started
when Stephen was killed.
They went as far as Phoenicia, Cyprus, and Antioch,
but they told the message only to the Jews.

Some of the followers from Cyprus and Cyrene
went to Antioch and started telling Gentiles
the good news about the Lord Jesus.
The Lord's power was with them,
and many people turned to the Lord
and put their faith in him.

News of what was happening reached the church
in Jerusalem.
Then they sent Barnabas to Antioch.

There in Antioch the Lord's followers
were first called Christians.

The word of the Lord.

Responsorial Psalm

Psalm 37:3–4, 5–6 (39a)

R. The salvation of the just
comes from the Lord.

Trust the LORD *and live right!*
The land will be yours,
and you will be safe.
Do what the LORD *wants,*
and he will give you
your heart's desire.

R. The salvation of the just
comes from the Lord.

Let the LORD *lead you*
and trust him to help.
Then it will be as clear
as the noonday sun
that you were right.

R. The salvation of the just
comes from the Lord.

Alleluia

R. Alleluia, alleluia.

See John 6:63, 68

Your words, Lord, are spirit and life:
you have the words of everlasting life.

R. Alleluia, alleluia.

GOSPEL

✚ A reading from the holy gospel according to John

John 15:26—16:1

The Spirit of truth will be my witness.

Jesus said to his disciples:
"I will send you the Spirit
who comes from the Father and shows what is true.
The Spirit will help you and will tell you about me.
Then you will also tell others about me,
because you have been with me from the beginning.

"I am telling you this to keep you from being afraid."

The gospel of the Lord.

PREACHING ABOUT JESUS

FIRST READING

A reading from the Acts of the Apostles

Acts 16:22–34

Believe in the Lord Jesus, and you will be saved, and your household too.

The crowd joined in the attack on Paul and Silas.
Then the officials tore the clothes off the two men
and ordered them to be beaten with a whip.

After they had been badly beaten,
they were put in jail,
and the jailer was told to guard them carefully.
The jailer did as he was told.
He put them deep inside the jail
and chained their feet to heavy blocks of wood.

About midnight Paul and Silas were praying
and singing praises to God,
while the other prisoners listened.
Suddenly a strong earthquake shook the jail
to its foundations.
The doors opened,
and the chains fell from all the prisoners.

When the jailer woke up and saw that the doors were open,
he thought that the prisoners had escaped.
He pulled out his sword and was about to kill himself.
But Paul shouted, "Don't harm yourself!
No one has escaped."

The jailer asked for a torch and went into the jail.

He was shaking all over as he kneeled down
in front of Paul and Silas.
After he had led them out of the jail, he asked,
"What must I do to be saved?"

They replied, "Have faith in the Lord Jesus
and you will be saved!
This is also true for everyone who lives in your home."
Then Paul and Silas told him and everyone else in his house
about the Lord.

While it was still night,
the jailer took them to a place
where he could wash their cuts and bruises.
Then he and everyone in his home were baptized.
They were very glad that they had put their faith in God.

After this, the jailer took Paul and Silas to his home
and gave them something to eat.

The word of the Lord.

Responsorial Psalm

Psalm 96:1–2, 3 and 10
(Mark 16:15)

R. Go out to all the world
and tell the good news.

Sing a new song to the LORD!
Everyone on this earth,
sing praises to the LORD,
sing and praise his name.
Day after day announce,
"The LORD has saved us!"

R. Go out to all the world
and tell the good news.

Tell every nation on earth,
"The LORD is wonderful
and does marvelous things!"
Announce to the nations,
"The LORD is King!
The world stands firm,
never to be shaken,
and he will judge its people
with fairness."

R. Go out to all the world
and tell the good news.

Alleluia

See John 6:63c, 68c

R. Alleluia, alleluia.

Your words, Lord, are spirit and life:
you have the words of everlasting life.

R. Alleluia, alleluia.

GOSPEL

Luke 9:1–6

Jesus sent them to proclaim the kingdom of God and to heal the sick.

✚ A reading from the holy gospel according to Luke

Jesus called together his twelve apostles
and gave them complete power over all demons
and diseases.
Then he sent them to tell about God's kingdom
and to heal the sick.

He told them, "Don't take anything with you!
Don't take a walking stick or a traveling bag or food
or money or even a change of clothes.
When you are welcomed into a home,
stay there until you leave that town.
If people won't welcome you,
leave the town and shake the dust from your feet
as a warning to them."

The apostles left and went from village to village,
telling the good news and healing people everywhere.

The gospel of the Lord.

In Ordinary Time the gospel acclamation is chosen from the texts given at no. 232 on pages 202–3.

LIGHT FOR THE WORLD

First Reading — **A reading from the letter of Paul to the Ephesians**

Ephesians 5:8–10

Act like people of the light and make your light shine.

Brothers and sisters:
You used to be like people living in the dark,
but now you are people of the light
because you belong to the Lord.
So act like people of the light
and make your light shine.
Be good and honest and truthful,
as you try to please the Lord.

The word of the Lord.

Responsorial Psalm — *R. The Lord is my light and my salvation.*

Psalm 27:1, 13–14 (1a)

You, Lord, are the light
that keeps me safe.
I am not afraid of anyone.
You protect me,
and I have no fears.

R. The Lord is my light and my salvation.

I know I will live
to see how kind you are.
Trust the LORD*!*
Be brave and strong
and trust the LORD*!*

R. The Lord is my light and my salvation.

GOSPEL

Matthew 5:14–16

You are the light of the world.

✚ A reading from the holy gospel according to Matthew

Jesus said to his disciples:
"You are like light for the whole world.
A city built on top of a hill cannot be hidden,
and no one would light a lamp and put it under a clay pot.
A lamp is placed on a lamp stand,
where it can give light to everyone in the house.
Make your light shine,
so that others will see the good that you do
and will praise your Father in heaven."

The gospel of the Lord.

194

LOVE EVERYONE

First Reading — **A reading from the first letter of Paul to the Corinthians**

1 Corinthians 13:4–7

Brothers and sisters:
Love is kind and patient,
never jealous, boastful, proud, or rude.
Love isn't selfish or quick tempered.
It doesn't keep a record of wrongs that others do.
Love rejoices in the truth, but not in evil.
Love is always supportive, loyal, hopeful, and trusting.
Love never fails!

Love is the greatest gift.

The word of the Lord.

Responsorial Psalm — *R. Now I will walk at your side.*

Psalm 116:5 and 7, 9 and 12 (9a)

You are kind, LORD,
so good and merciful.
You have treated me so kindly
that I don't need
to worry anymore.

R. Now I will walk at your side.

Now I will walk at your side
in this land of the living.
What must I give you, LORD,
for being so good to me?

R. Now I will walk at your side.

✚ A reading from the holy gospel according to Matthew

GOSPEL

Matthew 5:43–48

Be perfect as your heavenly Father is perfect.

Jesus said to his disciples:
"You have heard people say,
'Love your neighbors and hate your enemies.'
But I tell you to love your enemies
  and pray for anyone who mistreats you.
Then you will be acting like your Father in heaven.

"He makes the sun rise on both good and bad people.
And he sends rain for the ones who do right
  and for the ones who do wrong.

"If you love only those people who love you,
will God reward you for that?
Even tax collectors love their friends.
If you greet only your friends,
what's so great about that?
Don't even unbelievers do that?
But you must always act like your Father in heaven."

The gospel of the Lord.

THIS IS HOW YOU SHOULD PRAY

First Reading

A reading from the first letter of Paul to Timothy

1 Timothy 2:1–4

Let prayers be offered for everyone to God.

First of all,
I ask you to pray for everyone.
Ask God to help and bless them all,
and tell God how thankful you are for each of them.

Pray for kings and others in power,
so that we may live quiet and peaceful lives
as we worship and honor God.
This kind of prayer is good,
and it pleases God our Savior.

God wants everyone to be saved
and to know the whole truth.

The word of the Lord.

Responsorial Psalm

Psalm 25:1–2ab and 4, 5–6 (1)

R. To you, O Lord, I lift my soul.

I offer you my heart, LORD God,
and I trust you.
Don't make me ashamed.
Show me your paths
and teach me to follow.

R. To you, O Lord, I lift my soul.

Guide me by your truth
and instruct me.
You keep me safe,
and I always trust you.
Please, LORD, remember,
you have always
been patient and kind.

R. To you, O Lord, I lift my soul.

GOSPEL

Matthew 6:7–13

✚ A reading from the holy gospel according to Matthew

Jesus said to his disciples:
"When you pray,
don't talk on and on as people do who don't know God.
They think God likes to hear long prayers.
Don't be like them.
Your Father knows what you need before you ask.

"You should pray like this:

This is how you should pray.

Our Father in heaven,
help us to honor your name.
Come and set up your kingdom,
so that everyone on earth will obey you,
as you are obeyed in heaven.
Give us our food for today.
Forgive our sins,
as we forgive others.
Keep us from being tempted and protect us from evil."

The gospel of the Lord.

STORE UP RICHES IN HEAVEN

First Reading **A reading from the letter of Paul to the Colossians**

Colossians 3:1–2

Look for the things that are in heaven, where Christ is.

Brothers and sisters:
You have been raised to life with Christ.
Now set your heart on what is in heaven,
where Christ rules at God's right side.
Think about what is up there,
not about what is here on earth.

The word of the Lord.

Responsorial Psalm

Psalm 119:1–2, 14–15 (1b)

R. Happy are they who follow
the law of the Lord!

Our L*ORD, you bless everyone*
who lives right
and obeys your Law.
You bless all of those
who follow your commands
from deep in their hearts.

R. Happy are they who follow
the law of the Lord!

Obeying your instructions
brings as much happiness
as being rich.
I will study your teachings
and follow your footsteps.

R. Happy are they who follow
the law of the Lord!

GOSPEL

✚ A reading from the holy gospel according to Matthew

Matthew 6:19–21

Where your treasure is,
there will your heart be also.

Jesus said to his disciples:
"Don't store up treasures on earth!
Moths and rust can destroy them,
and thieves can break in and steal them.

"Instead, store up your treasures in heaven,
where moths and rust cannot destroy them,
and thieves cannot break in and steal them.

"Your heart will always be where your treasure is."

The gospel of the Lord.

197 I WILL TAKE CARE OF YOU

First Reading — **A reading from the book of the prophet Isaiah**

Isaiah 46:4

I will take care of you.

Even when you are old and gray,
I will still be the same,
and I will take care of you.

I created you,
and I will carry you and always keep you safe.

The word of the Lord.

Responsorial Psalm

Psalm 23:1–3a, 3b–4, 6 (1)

R. The Lord is my shepherd;
there is nothing I shall want.

You, LORD, are my shepherd.
I will never be in need.
You let me rest in fields
of green grass.
You lead me to streams
of peaceful water,
and you refresh my life.

R. The Lord is my shepherd;
there is nothing I shall want.

You are true to your name,
and you lead me
along the right paths.
I may walk through valleys
as dark as death,
but I won't be afraid.
You are with me,
and your shepherd's rod
makes me feel safe.

R. The Lord is my shepherd;
there is nothing I shall want.

Your kindness and love
will always be with me
each day of my life,
and I will live forever
in your house, LORD.

R. The Lord is my shepherd;
there is nothing I shall want.

GOSPEL ✚ **A reading from the holy gospel according to Matthew**

Matthew 6:25b–33

Jesus said to his disciples:
"Don't worry about having something to eat, drink, or wear.
Isn't life more than food or clothing?
Look at the birds in the sky!
They don't plant or harvest.
They don't even store grain in barns.
Yet your Father in heaven takes care of them.
Aren't you worth more than birds?

Do not worry about tomorrow.

"Can worry make you live longer?
Why worry about clothes?
Look how the wild flowers grow.
They don't work hard to make their clothes.
But I tell you that Solomon with all his wealth
was not as well clothed as one of them.
God gives such beauty to everything that grows in the fields,
even though it is here today
and thrown into a fire tomorrow.
He will surely do even more for you!
Why do you have such little faith?

"Don't worry and ask yourselves,
'Will we have anything to eat?
Will we have anything to drink?
Will we have clothes to wear?'
Only people who don't know God are always worrying
about such things.
Your Father in heaven knows that you need all of these.
But more than anything else,
put God's work first and do what he wants.
Then all the other things will be yours as well."

The gospel of the Lord.

198 FORGIVE AS THE LORD HAS FORGIVEN YOU

First Reading

A reading from the letter of Paul to the Colossians

Colossians 3:12–13

Forgive anyone who does you wrong, just as Christ has forgiven you.

Brothers and sisters:
God loves you and has chosen you as his own special people.
So be gentle, kind, humble, meek, and patient.
Put up with each other,
and forgive anyone who does you wrong,
just as Christ has forgiven you.

The word of the Lord.

Responsorial Psalm

R. The Lord is kind and merciful.

Psalm 103:1–2, 3 and 8, 11–12 (8a)

With all my heart
I praise the LORD,
and with all that I am
I praise his holy name!
With all my heart
I praise the LORD!
I will never forget
how kind he has been.

R. The Lord is kind and merciful.

The LORD forgives our sins,
heals us when we are sick.
The LORD is merciful!
He is kind and patient,
and his love never fails.

R. The Lord is kind and merciful.

How great is God's love for all
who worship him?
Greater than the distance
between heaven and earth!
How far has the LORD taken
our sins from us?
Farther than the distance
from east to west!

R. The Lord is kind and merciful.

GOSPEL

Matthew 7:1–5

Take the beam out of your own eye first.

✚ A reading from the holy gospel according to Matthew

Jesus said to his disciples:
"Don't condemn others,
and God will not condemn you.
God will be as hard on you as you are on others!
He will treat you exactly as you treat them.

"You can see the speck in your friend's eye,
but you don't notice the log in your own eye.
How can you say,
'My friend, let me take the speck out of your eye,'
when you don't see the log in your own eye?
You're nothing but showoffs!
First, take the log out of your own eye.
Then you can see how to take the speck out
of your friend's eye."

The gospel of the Lord.

199

MY BURDEN IS LIGHT

FIRST READING **A reading from the letter of Paul to the Philippians**

Philippians 4:8–9

Fill your minds with everything that is holy.

My friends,
keep your minds on whatever is true, pure, right,
holy, friendly, and proper.
Don't ever stop thinking about what is truly worthwhile
and worthy of praise.
You know the teachings I gave you,
and you know what you heard me say and saw me do.

So follow my example.
And God, who gives peace, will be with you.

The word of the Lord.

Responsorial Psalm *R. The precepts of the Lord give joy to the heart.*

Psalm 19:7, 8 (9a)

The Law of the LORD is perfect;
it gives us new life.
His teachings last forever,
and they give wisdom
to ordinary people.

R. The precepts of the Lord give joy
to the heart.

The LORD's instruction is right;
it makes our hearts glad.
His commands shine brightly,
and they give us light.

R. The precepts of the Lord give joy
to the heart.

GOSPEL

✚ A reading from the holy gospel according to Matthew

Matthew 11:29–30

I am gentle and humble of heart.

Jesus said to his disciples:
"Take the yoke I give you.
Put it on your shoulders and learn from me.
I am gentle and humble,
and you will find rest.
This yoke is easy to bear,
and this burden is light."

The gospel of the Lord.

TREASURES OF HEAVEN

First Reading — **A reading from the first letter of Peter**

1 Peter 1:3–4

God has something stored up for you in heaven.

Brothers and sisters:
Praise God, the Father of our Lord Jesus Christ.
God is so good,
and by raising Jesus from death,
he has given us new life and a hope that lives on.

God has something stored up for you in heaven,
where it will never decay or be ruined or disappear.

The word of the Lord.

Responsorial Psalm *R. Happy are those who fear the Lord.*

Psalm 112:1, 3, 4 (1a)

Shout praises to the LORD!
The LORD blesses everyone
who worships him and gladly
obeys his teachings.

R. Happy are those who fear the Lord.

They will get rich and prosper
and will always be remembered
for their fairness.

R. Happy are those who fear the Lord.

They will be so kind
and merciful and good,
that they will be like a light
in the dark for others
who do the right thing.

R. Happy are those who fear the Lord.

GOSPEL

Matthew 13:44–46

He sold all that he had and bought the field.

✚ A reading from the holy gospel according to Matthew

Jesus said to his disciples:
"The kingdom of heaven is like what happens
when someone finds treasure hidden in a field
and buries it again.
A person like that is happy and goes and sells everything
in order to buy that field.

"The kingdom of heaven is like what happens
when a shop owner is looking for fine pearls.
After finding a very valuable one,
the owner goes and sells everything
in order to buy that pearl."

The gospel of the Lord.

TRUST IN THE LORD

First Reading | **A reading from the book of the prophet Isaiah**

Isaiah 25:6–7, 9

We waited and waited and now the Lord is here.

On this mountain the LORD All-Powerful
 will prepare for all nations a feast of the finest foods.
Choice wines and the best meat will be served.
Here the LORD will strip away
 the funeral clothes that cover the nations.

On that day, people will say,
"The LORD God has saved us!
Let's celebrate.
We waited and waited, and now he is here."

The word of the Lord.

Responsorial Psalm *R. In you, my God, I place my trust.*

Psalm 91:1–2, 9 and 11 (see 2b)

Live under the protection
of God Most High
and stay in the shadow
of God All-Powerful.
Then you will say to the LORD,
"You are my fortress,
my place of safety;
you are my God,
and I trust you."

R. In you, my God, I place my trust.

The LORD Most High
is your fortress.
Run to him for safety.
God will command his angels
to protect you
wherever you go.

R. In you, my God, I place my trust.

GOSPEL **✚ A reading from the holy gospel according to Matthew**

Matthew 14:22–33

Order me to come to you across the water.

Jesus made his disciples get into a boat
and start back across the lake.
But he stayed until he had sent the crowds away.
Then he went up on a mountain
where he could be alone and pray.
Later that evening, he was still there.

By this time the boat was a long way from the shore.
It was going against the wind
and was being tossed around by the waves.
A little while before morning,
Jesus came walking on the water toward his disciples.
When they saw him, they thought he was a ghost.
They were terrified and started screaming.

At once Jesus said to them, "Don't worry!
I am Jesus. Don't be afraid."

Peter replied, "Lord, if it is really you,
tell me to come to you on the water."

"Come on!" Jesus said.
Peter then got out of the boat
and started walking on the water toward him.

But when Peter saw how strong the wind was,
he was afraid and started sinking.

"Lord, save me!" he shouted.

Right away Jesus reached out his hand.
He helped Peter up and said,
"You surely don't have much faith.
Why do you doubt?"

When Jesus and Peter got into the boat, the wind died down.
The men in the boat worshiped Jesus and said,
"You really are the Son of God!"

The gospel of the Lord.

GIFTS RECEIVED FROM GOD

First Reading **A reading from the first letter of Peter**

1 Peter 4:10–11

Brothers and sisters:
Each of you has been blessed
with one of God's many wonderful gifts
to be used in the service of others.
So use your gift well.

Each one of you has received a special gift; put yourselves at the service of others.

If you have the gift of speaking,
preach God's message.
If you have the gift of helping others,
do it with the strength that God supplies.

Everything should be done in a way
that will bring honor to God because of Jesus Christ,
who is glorious and powerful forever. Amen.

The word of the Lord.

Responsorial Psalm

Psalm 37:3 and 4, 5 and 26 (39a)

R. The salvation of the just
comes from the Lord.

Trust the LORD *and live right!*
The land will be yours,
and you will be safe.
Do what the LORD *wants,*
and he will give you
your heart's desire.

R. The salvation of the just
comes from the Lord.

Let the LORD *lead you*
and trust him to help.
Good people gladly give and lend,
and their children
turn out good.

R. The salvation of the just
comes from the Lord.

GOSPEL

✚ A reading from the holy gospel according to Matthew

Matthew 25:14–29

Jesus told his disciples this story about the kingdom of God:

"The kingdom is like what happened
when a man went away
and put his three servants in charge of all he owned.
The man knew what each servant could do.
So he handed five thousand coins to the first servant,
two thousand to the second,
and one thousand to the third.
Then he left the country.

Because you have been faithful in small matters, come into the joy of your master.

"As soon as the man had gone,
the servant with the five thousand coins
used them to earn five thousand more.
The servant who had two thousand coins did the same
with his money and earned two thousand more.
But the servant with one thousand coins dug a hole
and hid his master's money in the ground.

"Some time later the master of those servants returned.
He called them in and asked what they had done
with his money.
The servant who had been given five thousand coins
brought them in with the five thousand
that he had earned.
He said, 'Sir, you gave me five thousand coins,
and I have earned five thousand more.'

"'Wonderful!' his master replied.
'You are a good and faithful servant.
I left you in charge of only a little,
but now I will put you in charge of much more.
Come and share in my happiness!'

"Next, the servant who had been given two thousand coins
came in and said,
'Sir, you gave me two thousand coins,
and I have earned two thousand more.'

"'Wonderful!' his master replied.
'You are a good and faithful servant.
I left you in charge of only a little,
but now I will put you in charge of much more.
Come and share in my happiness!'

"The servant who had been given one thousand coins
then came in and said,
'Sir, I know that you are hard to get along with.
You harvest what you don't plant
and gather crops where you have not scattered seed.
I was frightened and went out and hid your money
in the ground.
Here is every single coin!'

"The master of the servant told him,
'You are lazy and good-for-nothing!
You know that I harvest what I don't plant
and gather crops where I have not scattered seed.
You could have at least put my money in the bank,
so that I could have earned interest on it.'

"Then the master said,
'Now your money will be taken away
and given to the servant with ten thousand coins!
Everyone who has something will be given more,
and they will have more than enough.
But everything will be taken from those
who don't have anything.'"

The gospel of the Lord.

203

THE WORD THAT I SPEAK

FIRST READING **A reading from the book of the prophet Isaiah**

Isaiah 55:10–11

My word carries out my will.

The rain and the snow fall from the sky.
But they don't return without watering the earth
  that produces seeds to plant and grain to eat.
And that's how it is with my words.
They don't return to me without doing everything
  I sent them to do.

The word of the Lord.

Responsorial Psalm

Psalm 65:9, 11–12, 13 (Luke 8:8)

R. The seed that falls on good ground
will yield a fruitful harvest.

Our God, you take care of the earth
and send rain to help the soil
grow all kinds of crops.
Your rivers never run dry,
and you prepare the earth
to produce much grain.

R. The seed that falls on good ground
will yield a fruitful harvest.

Wherever your footsteps
touch the earth,
a rich harvest is gathered.
Desert pastures blossom,
and mountains celebrate.

R. The seed that falls on good ground
will yield a fruitful harvest.

Meadows are filled
with sheep and goats;
valleys overflow with grain
and echo with joyful songs.

R. The seed that falls on good ground
will yield a fruitful harvest.

Gospel | **✚ A reading from the holy gospel according to Mark**

Mark 4:1–9

The next time Jesus taught beside Lake Galilee,
a big crowd gathered.
It was so large that he had to sit in a boat out on the lake,
while the people stood on the shore.
He used stories to teach them many things,
and this is part of what he taught:

The sower went out to sow seed.

"Now listen!
A farmer went out to scatter seed in a field.
While the farmer was scattering the seed,
some of it fell along the road and was eaten by birds.

"Other seeds fell on thin, rocky ground
  and quickly started growing
because the soil was not very deep.
But when the sun came up,
the plants were scorched and dried up,
because they did not have enough roots.

"Some other seeds fell where thorn bushes grew up
  and choked out the plants.
So they did not produce any grain.

"But a few seeds did fall on good ground
  where the plants grew and produced thirty or sixty
  or even a hundred times as much as was scattered."

Then Jesus said, "If you have ears, pay attention."

The gospel of the Lord.

I WILL HELP YOU

FIRST READING **A reading from the book of the prophet Isaiah**

Isaiah 41:14

The God of Israel saves and protects you.

The LORD says this:
"People of Israel, don't worry,
though others may say,
'Israel is only a worm!'
I am the holy God of Israel,
who saves and protects you."

The word of the Lord.

Responsorial Psalm

Psalm 90:1–2, 14 and 16 (1)

R. In every age, O Lord,
you have been our refuge.

Our LORD, in all generations
you have been our home.
You have always been God—
long before the birth
of the mountains,
even before you created
the earth and the world.

R. In every age, O Lord,
you have been our refuge.

When morning comes,
let your love satisfy
all our needs.
Then we can celebrate
and be glad for what time
we have left.
Do wonderful things for us,
your servants,
and show your mighty power
to our children.

R. In every age, O Lord,
you have been our refuge.

GOSPEL **✚ A reading from the holy gospel according to Mark**

Mark 4:35–41

Who can this be? Even the wind and the sea obey him.

Jesus said to his disciples, "Let's cross to the east side."
So they left the crowd,
and his disciples started across the lake with him
in the boat.

Some other boats followed along.
Suddenly a windstorm struck the lake.
Waves started splashing into the boat,
and it was about to sink.

Jesus was in the back of the boat with his head on a pillow,
and he was asleep.
His disciples woke him and said,
"Teacher, don't you care that we're about to drown?"

Jesus got up and ordered the wind and the waves to be quiet.
The wind stopped,
and everything was calm.

Jesus asked his disciples, "Why were you afraid?
Don't you have any faith?"

Now they were more afraid than ever and said to each other,
"Who is this?
Even the wind and the waves obey him!"

The gospel of the Lord.

205

THE LORD WILL HELP YOU

ONE

First Reading — **A reading from the book of the prophet Isaiah**

Isaiah 30:19–20, 23–24, 26

People of Jerusalem,
you don't need to cry anymore.
The LORD is kind,
and as soon as he hears your cries for help,
he will come.

The LORD has brought trouble and sorrow
by not giving you enough bread and water.
But now you will see the LORD, your teacher,
and he will guide you.

The Lord God will be gracious to you when he hears your cry.

The LORD will send rain
to water the seeds you have planted—
your fields will produce more crops than you need,
and your cattle will graze in open pastures.

Even the oxen and donkeys that plow your fields
will be fed the finest grain.

Then the LORD will bind up his people's injuries
and heal the wounds he has caused.
The moon will shine as bright as the sun,
and the sun will shine seven times brighter than usual.
It will be like the light of seven days all at once.

The word of the Lord.

OR

TWO

A reading from the letter of Paul to the Ephesians

First Reading

Ephesians 1:15–16a, 18–19a

My prayer is that you know about God's great power for us.

Brothers and sisters:
I have heard about your faith in the Lord Jesus
  and your love for all of God's people.
So I never stop being grateful for you.

My prayer is that light will flood your hearts
  and that you will understand the hope
  that was given to you when God chose you.
Then you will discover the glorious blessings
  that will be yours together with all of God's people.

I want you to know about the great and mighty power
  that God has for us followers.

The word of the Lord.

Responsorial Psalm

Psalm 121:1–2, 5–6, 7–8 (see 2)

R. Our help is from the Lord,
who made heaven and earth.

I look to the hills!
Where will I find help?
It will come from the LORD,
who created the heavens
and the earth.

continued

R. Our help is from the Lord,
who made heaven and earth.

The LORD is your protector,
there at your right side
to shade you from the sun.
You won't be harmed
by the sun during the day
or by the moon at night.

R. Our help is from the Lord,
who made heaven and earth.

The LORD will protect you
and keep you safe
from all dangers.
The LORD will protect you
now and always
wherever you are.

R. Our help is from the Lord,
who made heaven and earth.

GOSPEL **✚ A reading from the holy gospel according to Mark**

Mark 5:21–24, 35b–36, 38–42

Little girl, I say to you, arise.

Jesus got into the boat and crossed Lake Galilee.
Then as he stood on the shore,
a large crowd gathered around him.

The person in charge of the Jewish meeting place
was also there.
His name was Jairus,
and when he saw Jesus, he went over to him.

He kneeled at Jesus' feet and started begging him for help.
He said, "My daughter is about to die!
Please come and touch her,
so she will get well and live."

Jesus went with Jairus.
Many people followed along and kept crowding around.

Some men came from Jairus' home and said,
"Your daughter has died!
Why bother the teacher anymore?"

Jesus heard what they said,
and he said to Jairus,
"Don't worry. Just have faith!"

They went home with Jairus and saw the people
crying and making a lot of noise.

Then Jesus went inside and said to them,
"Why are you crying and carrying on like this?
The child is not dead.
She is just asleep."
But the people laughed at him.

After Jesus had sent them all out of the house,
he took the girl's father and mother and his three disciples
and went to where she was.
He took the twelve-year-old girl by the hand and said,

"Talitha, koum!"
which means, "Little girl, get up!"

The girl got right up and started walking around.

The gospel of the Lord.

WE ARE CALLED GOD'S CHILDREN

First Reading — **A reading from the first letter of John**

1 John 2:29b—3:1a

Beloved:
You know that everyone who does right is a child of God.

Whoever lives in God is a child of God.

Think how much the Father loves us.
He loves us so much that he lets us be called his children,
as we truly are.

The word of the Lord.

Responsorial Psalm — *R. Lord, let your face shine on me.*

Psalm 119:129–130, 133 and 135 (135a)

Your teachings are wonderful,
and I respect them all.
Understanding your word
brings light to the minds
of ordinary people.

R. Lord, let your face shine on me.

Keep your promise
and don't let me stumble
or let sin control my life.
Smile on me, your servant,
and teach me your laws.

R. Lord, let your face shine on me.

GOSPEL

Mark 9:33–37

Whenever you have accepted graciously a small child, you have accepted me.

✚ A reading from the holy gospel according to Mark

Jesus and his disciples went to his home in Capernaum.
After they were inside the house, Jesus asked them,
"What were you arguing about along the way?"
They had been arguing about which one of them
  was the greatest,
and so they did not answer.

After Jesus sat down and told the twelve disciples
  to gather around him,
he said, "If you want the place of honor,
you must become a slave and serve others!"

Then Jesus had a child stand near him.
He put his arm around the child and said,
"When you welcome even a child because of me,
  you welcome me.
And when you welcome me,
you welcome the one who sent me."

The gospel of the Lord.

JESUS BLESSED THE CHILDREN

FIRST READING

A reading from the book of the prophet Isaiah

Isaiah 41:10

I am your God; I will protect you.

The Lord says this:
Don't be afraid!
I am with you.
Don't tremble with fear.
I am your God.
I will help you to be strong,
as I protect you with my arm and give you victories.

The word of the Lord.

Responsorial Psalm

Psalm 17:1abc and 5, 6 and 8 (6b)

R. Lord, bend your ear
and hear my prayer.

I am innocent, LORD!
Won't you listen as I pray
and beg for help?
I have followed you,
without ever stumbling.

R. Lord, bend your ear
and hear my prayer.

I pray to you, God,
because you will help me.
Listen and answer my prayer!
Protect me as you would
your very own eyes;
hide me in the shadow
of your wings.

R. Lord, bend your ear
and hear my prayer.

GOSPEL

Mark 10:13–16

✚ A reading from the holy gospel according to Mark

Jesus blessed the children.

Some people brought their children to Jesus
so that he could bless them by placing his hands on them.
But his disciples told the people to stop bothering him.

When Jesus saw this, he became angry and said,
"Let the children come to me!
Don't try to stop them.
People who are like these little children
belong to the kingdom of God.
I promise you that you cannot get into God's kingdom,
unless you accept it the way a child does."

Then Jesus took the children in his arms
and blessed them by placing his hands on them.

The gospel of the Lord.

I WANT TO SEE AGAIN

FIRST READING

Isaiah 42:16

I will lead and guide those who are blind.

A reading from the book of the prophet Isaiah

The Lord says this:
I will lead the blind on roads they have never seen,
and I will guide them on paths they have never traveled.
Their road is dark and rough,
but I will give light and make the road smooth.
This is a promise I will never break.

The word of the Lord.

Responsorial Psalm

Psalm 27:1, 8 and 11ab (1)

R. The Lord is my light and my salvation.

You, LORD, are the light
that keeps me safe.
I am not afraid of anyone.
You protect me,
and I have no fears.

R. The Lord is my light and my salvation.

My heart tells me to pray.
I am eager to see your face.
Teach me to follow, LORD,
and lead me on the right path.

R. The Lord is my light and my salvation.

GOSPEL

Mark 10:46–52

Master, let me see again.

✚ A reading from the holy gospel according to Mark

Jesus and his disciples went to Jericho.
And as they were leaving,
they were followed by a large crowd.

A blind beggar by the name of Bartimaeus son of Timaeus
was sitting beside the road.
When he heard that it was Jesus from Nazareth,
he shouted, "Jesus, Son of David, have pity on me!"

Many people told the man to stop,
but he shouted even louder,
"Son of David, have pity on me!"

Jesus stopped and said, "Call him over!"

They called out to the blind man and said,
"Don't be afraid! Come on!
He is calling for you."

The man threw off his coat as he jumped up and ran to Jesus.
Jesus asked, "What do you want me to do for you?"

The blind man answered, "Master, I want to see!"

Jesus told him, "You may go.
Your eyes are healed because of your faith."

Right away the man could see,
and he went down the road with Jesus.

The gospel of the Lord.

209

THEY WERE EXTREMELY GENEROUS

FIRST READING **A reading from the second letter of Paul to the Corinthians**

2 Corinthians 8:1–3a, 12

My friends, we want you to know that the churches
in Macedonia have shown others how kind God is.
Although they were going through hard times
and were very poor,
they were glad to give generously.
They gave as much as they could afford and even more.

They were glad to give generously.

It doesn't matter how much you have.
What matters is how much you are willing to give
from what you have.

The word of the Lord.

Responsorial Psalm *R. The Lord is kind and merciful.*

Psalm 103:1–2, 5 and 11 (8a)

With all my heart
I praise the L*ORD,*
and with all that I am
I praise his holy name!
With all my heart
I praise the L*ORD!*
I will never forget
how kind he has been.

R. The Lord is kind and merciful.

Each day that we live,
he provides for our needs
and gives us the strength
of a young eagle.
How great is God's love for all
who worship him!
Greater than the distance
between heaven and earth!

R. The Lord is kind and merciful.

GOSPEL

✚ A reading from the holy gospel according to Mark

Mark 12:41–44

Jesus was sitting in the temple near the offering box
and watching people put in their gifts.
He noticed that many rich people
were giving a lot of money.

Finally, a poor widow came up
and put in two coins that were worth only a few pennies.

This poor widow has given more than all others.

Jesus told his disciples to gather around him.
Then he said:
"I tell you that this poor widow has put in more
than all the others.
Everyone else gave what they didn't need.
But she is very poor and gave everything she had.
Now she doesn't have a cent to live on."

The gospel of the Lord.

KIND IS THE LORD

FIRST READING **A reading from the book of the prophet Isaiah**

Isaiah 30:18

The Lord is waiting to show you how kind he is.

The LORD God is waiting to show you how kind he is
and to have pity on you.
The LORD always does right,
and he blesses everyone who trusts him.

The word of the Lord.

Responsorial Psalm

Psalm 33:1–2, 4–5, 21–22 (22)

R. Lord, let your mercy be on us,
as we place our trust in you.

You are the LORD*'s people.*
Obey him and celebrate!
He deserves your praise.
Praise the LORD *with harps!*
Use harps with ten strings
to make music for him.

R. Lord, let your mercy be on us,
as we place our trust in you.

The LORD *is truthful;*
he can be trusted.
He loves justice and fairness,
and he is kind to everyone
everywhere on earth.

R. Lord, let your mercy be on us,
as we place our trust in you.

You make our hearts glad
because we trust you,
the only God.
Be kind and bless us!
We depend on you.

R. Lord, let your mercy be on us,
as we place our trust in you.

GOSPEL ✚ **A reading from the holy gospel according to Luke**

Luke 7:1–10

After Jesus had finished teaching the people,
he went to Capernaum.
In that town an army officer's servant was sick
and about to die.
The officer liked this servant very much.
And when he heard about Jesus,
he sent some Jewish leaders
to ask him to come and heal the servant.

This man deserves your help.

The leaders went to Jesus and begged him to do something.
They said, "This man deserves your help!
He loves our nation and even built us a meeting place."
So Jesus went with them.

When Jesus was not far from the house,
the officer sent some friends to tell him,
"Lord, don't go to any trouble for me!
I am not good enough for you to come into my house.
And I am certainly not worthy to come to you.
Just say the word, and my servant will get well.
I have officers who give orders to me,
and I have soldiers who take orders from me.
I can say to one of them, 'Go!' and he goes.
I can say to another, 'Come!' and he comes.
I can say to my servant, 'Do this!'
and he will do it."

When Jesus heard this,
he was so surprised
 that he turned and said to the crowd following him,
"In all of Israel I've never found anyone
 with this much faith!"

The officer's friends returned and found the servant well.

The gospel of the Lord.

211

I WILL SAVE YOU

FIRST READING — **A reading from the book of the prophet Isaiah**

Isaiah 43:1–3a, 5

The LORD says this:
Descendants of Jacob,
I, the LORD, created you and formed your nation.

Israel, don't be afraid.
I will rescue you.
I have called you by name,
and you belong to me.

I will save you.

When you cross deep rivers,
I will be with you,
and you won't drown.
When you walk through fire,
you won't be burned or scorched by the flames.

I am the LORD, your God,
the Holy One of Israel,
the God who saves you.
Don't be afraid!
I am with you.

From the east and the west I will bring you together.

The word of the Lord.

Responsorial Psalm *R. Now I will walk at your side.*

Psalm 116:1–2, 5 and 12 (9a)

I love you, LORD!
You answered my prayers.
You paid attention to me,
and so I will pray to you
as long as I live.

R. Now I will walk at your side.

You are kind, LORD,
so good and merciful.
What must I give you, LORD,
for being so good to me?

R. Now I will walk at your side.

GOSPEL **✚ A reading from the holy gospel according to Luke**

Luke 7:11–17

Jesus and his disciples were on their way
to the town of Nain,
and a big crowd was going along with them.
As they came near the gate of the town,
they saw people carrying out the body of a widow's only son.
Many people from the town were walking along with her.

God has come to his people.

When the Lord saw the woman,
he felt sorry for her and said, "Don't cry!"

Jesus went over and touched the stretcher
on which the people were carrying the dead boy.
They stopped, and Jesus said,
"Young man, get up!"
The boy sat up and began to speak.
Jesus then gave him back to his mother.

Everyone was frightened and praised God.
They said, "A great prophet is here with us!
God has come to his people."

News about Jesus spread all over Judea
and everywhere else in that part of the country.

The gospel of the Lord.

212

GOD IS LOVE

First Reading **A reading from the first letter of John**

1 John 4:7–10

My dear friends, we must love each other.
Love comes from God,
and when we love each other,
it shows that we have been given new life.

We are now God's children, and we know him.

God is love.

God is love,
and anyone who doesn't love others has never known him.

God showed his love for us
when he sent his only Son into the world to give us life.

Real love is not our love for God, but his love for us.
God sent his Son to be the sacrifice
by which our sins are forgiven.

The word of the Lord.

Responsorial Psalm

Psalm 90:12 and 14, 16–17abc (14)

R. Fill us with your love, O Lord,
and we will sing for joy!

Teach us to use wisely
all the time we have.
When morning comes,
let your love satisfy
all our needs.
Then we can celebrate
and be glad for what time
we have left.

R. Fill us with your love, O Lord,
and we will sing for joy!

Do wonderful things for us,
your servants,
and show your mighty power
to our children.
Our Lord and our God,
treat us with kindness
and let all go well for us.

R. Fill us with your love, O Lord,
and we will sing for joy!

GOSPEL ✚ **A reading from the holy gospel according to Luke**

Luke 7:36–50

Her many sins were forgiven her, because she has shown great love.

A Pharisee invited Jesus to have dinner with him.
So Jesus went to the Pharisee's home and got ready to eat.

When a sinful woman in that town found out
that Jesus was there,
she bought an expensive bottle of perfume.
Then she came and stood behind Jesus.
She cried and started washing his feet with her tears
and drying them with her hair.
The woman kissed his feet and poured the perfume on them.

The Pharisee who had invited Jesus saw this
and said to himself,
"If this man really were a prophet,
he would know what kind of woman is touching him!
He would know that she is a sinner."

Jesus said to the Pharisee,
"Simon, I have something to say to you."

"Teacher, what is it?" Simon replied.

Jesus told him, "Two people were in debt to a moneylender.
One of them owed him five hundred silver coins,
and the other owed him fifty.
Since neither of them could pay him back,
the moneylender said
that they didn't have to pay him anything.
Which one of them will like him more?"

Simon answered,
"I suppose it would be the one who had owed more
and didn't have to pay it back."

"You are right," Jesus said.

He turned toward the woman and said to Simon,
"Have you noticed this woman?
When I came into your home,
you didn't give me any water so I could wash my feet.
But she has washed my feet with her tears
and dried them with her hair.

"You didn't greet me with a kiss,
but from the time I came in,
she has not stopped kissing my feet.

"You didn't even pour olive oil on my head,
but she has poured expensive perfume on my feet.

"So I tell you that all her sins are forgiven,
and that is why she has shown great love.
But anyone who has been forgiven only a little
will show only a little love."

Then Jesus said to the woman,
"Your sins are forgiven."

Some other guests started saying to one another,
"Who is this who dares to forgive sins?"

But Jesus told the woman,
"Because of your faith, you are now saved.
May God give you peace!"

The gospel of the Lord.

SENT TO PREACH THE KINGDOM OF GOD

First Reading **A reading from the book of the prophet Jeremiah**

Jeremiah 1:4–8

The LORD said to Jeremiah,
"Before I gave you life,
and before you were born,
I chose you to be a prophet to the nations."

Go now to those to whom I send you.

Jeremiah replied,
"LORD God, how can I speak for you? I'm too young."

The LORD answered, "Don't say you're too young.
Go to everyone I send you to
and tell them everything I command you.
Don't be afraid of them!
I, the LORD, will be with you to keep you safe."

The word of the Lord.

Responsorial Psalm

Psalm 96:1–2a, 2b–3, 7–8a (3)

*R. Proclaim God's marvelous deeds
to all the nations.*

*Sing a new song to the LORD!
Everyone on this earth,
sing praises to the LORD,
sing and praise his name.*

*R. Proclaim God's marvelous deeds
to all the nations.*

*Day after day announce,
"The LORD has saved us!"
Tell every nation on earth,
"The LORD is wonderful
and does marvelous things!"*

*R. Proclaim God's marvelous deeds
to all the nations.*

Tell everyone of every nation,
"Praise the glorious power
of the LORD.
He is wonderful! Praise him!"

R. Proclaim God's marvelous deeds
to all the nations.

GOSPEL

✚ A reading from the holy gospel according to Luke

Luke 9:1–6

Jesus sent them to proclaim the kingdom of God and to heal the sick.

Jesus called together his twelve apostles
and gave them complete power over all demons
and diseases.
Then he sent them to tell about God's kingdom
and to heal the sick.

He told them, "Don't take anything with you!
Don't take a walking stick or a traveling bag or food
or money or even a change of clothes.
When you are welcomed into a home,
stay there until you leave that town.
If people won't welcome you,
leave the town and shake the dust from your feet
as a warning to them."

The apostles left and went from village to village,
telling the good news and healing people everywhere.

The gospel of the Lord.

WHO IS MY NEIGHBOR?

FIRST READING **A reading from the first letter of John**

1 John 3:11, 18

We must love one another.

Beloved:
From the beginning you were told
that we must love each other.

Children, you show love for others by truly helping them,
and not merely by talking about it.

The word of the Lord.

Responsorial Psalm

Psalm 37:3 and 4, 5 and 26 (39a)

R. The salvation of the just
comes from the Lord.

Trust the LORD *and live right!*
The land will be yours,
and you will be safe.
Do what the LORD *wants,*
and he will give you
your heart's desire.

R. The salvation of the just
comes from the Lord.

Let the LORD *lead you*
and trust him to help.
Good people gladly give and lend,
and their children
turn out good.

R. The salvation of the just
comes from the Lord.

GOSPEL **✚ A reading from the holy gospel according to Luke**

Luke 10:25–37

An expert in the Law of Moses stood up
and asked Jesus a question to see what he would say.
"Teacher," he asked,
"What must I do to have eternal life?"

Jesus answered, "What is written in the Scriptures?
How do you understand them?"

Who is my neighbor!

The man replied, "The Scriptures say,
'Love the Lord your God with all your heart, soul,
strength, and mind.'
They also say, 'Love your neighbors as much
as you love yourself.' "

Jesus said, "You have given the right answer.
If you do this, you will have eternal life."

But the man wanted to show
that he knew what he was talking about.
So he asked Jesus, "Who are my neighbors?"

Jesus replied:
"As a man was going down from Jerusalem to Jericho,
robbers attacked him and grabbed everything he had.
They beat him up and ran off, leaving him half dead.

"A priest happened to be going down the same road.
But when he saw the man,
he walked by on the other side.
Later a temple helper came to the same place.
But when he saw the man who had been beaten up,
he also went by on the other side.

"A man from Samaria then came traveling along that road.
When he saw the man,
he felt sorry for him and went over to him.
He treated his wounds with olive oil and wine
and bandaged them.
Then he put him on his own donkey and took him to an inn,
where he took care of him.

"The next morning he gave the innkeeper
two silver coins and said,
'Please take care of the man.
If you spend more than this on him,
I will pay you when I return.'"

Then Jesus asked,
"Which of these three people was a real neighbor
to the man who was beaten up by robbers?"

The teacher answered, "The one who showed pity."
Jesus said, "Go and do the same!"

The gospel of the Lord.

ASK AND YOU WILL RECEIVE

FIRST READING

A reading from the letter of James

James 5:16c–18

Brothers and sisters:
The prayer of an innocent person is powerful,
and it can help a lot.

The prayer of the just has great power.

Elijah was just as human as we are,
and for three and a half years
his prayers kept the rain from falling.
But when he did pray for rain,
it fell from the skies and made the crops grow.

The word of the Lord.

Responsorial Psalm

Psalm 145:10–11, 15–16 (16)

R. You open your hand to feed us, Lord;
you answer all our needs.

All creation will thank you,
and your loyal people
will praise you.
They will tell about
your marvelous kingdom
and your power.

R. You open your hand to feed us, Lord;
you answer all our needs.

Everyone depends on you,
and when the time is right,
you provide them with food.
By your own hand you satisfy
the desires of all who live.

R. You open your hand to feed us, Lord;
you answer all our needs.

GOSPEL

Luke 11:5–10

Ask and you shall receive.

✚ A reading from the holy gospel according to Luke

Jesus said to his disciples:
"Suppose one of you goes to a friend in the middle
of the night and says,
'Let me borrow three loaves of bread.
A friend of mine has dropped in,
and I don't have a thing for him to eat.'
And suppose your friend answers, 'Don't bother me!
The door is bolted, and my children and I are in bed.
I cannot get up to give you something.'

"He may not get up and give you the bread,
just because you are his friend.
But he will get up and give you as much as you need,
simply because you are not ashamed to keep on asking.

"So I tell you to ask and you will receive,
search and you will find,
knock and the door will be opened for you.
Everyone who asks will receive,
everyone who searches will find,
and the door will be opened for everyone who knocks."

The gospel of the Lord.

BECOME STRONGER IN YOUR FAITH

FIRST READING **A reading from the letter of Paul to the Colossians**

Colossians 2:6–7

Brothers and sisters:
You have accepted Christ Jesus as your Lord.
Now keep on following him.
Plant your roots in Christ
and let him be the foundation for your life.

Be strong in your faith.

Be strong in your faith,
just as you were taught.
And be grateful.

The word of the Lord.

Responsorial Psalm *R. God is our help in times of trouble.*

Psalm 46:1–2, 7–8 (see 1)

God is our mighty fortress,
always ready to help
in times of trouble.
And so, we won't be afraid!
Let the earth tremble
and the mountains tumble
into the deepest sea.

R. God is our help in times of trouble.

The LORD All-Powerful
is with us.
The God of Jacob
is our fortress.
Come! See the fearsome things
the LORD has done on earth.

R. God is our help in times of trouble.

GOSPEL

✚ A reading from the holy gospel according to Luke

Luke 13:6–9

I will fertilize it to make it grow.

Jesus told the people this story:
"A man had a fig tree growing in his vineyard.
One day he went out to pick some figs,
but he didn't find any.
So he said to the gardener,
'For three years I have come looking for figs on this tree,
and I haven't found any yet.
Chop it down!
Why should it take up space?'

"The gardener answered,
'Master, leave it for another year.
I'll dig around it and put some manure on it to make it grow.
Maybe it will have figs on it next year.
If it doesn't, you can have it cut down.'"

The gospel of the Lord.

SHOW FAITH BY ACTIONS

First Reading

A reading from the letter of James

James 2:14–18

My friends,
what good is it to say you have faith,
when you don't do anything
to show that you really do have faith?
Can that kind of faith save you?

If you know someone who doesn't have any clothes or food,
you shouldn't just say, "I hope all goes well for you.
I hope you will be warm and have plenty to eat."

Faith without good works is dead.

What good is it to say this,
unless you do something to help?
Faith that doesn't lead us to do good deeds is all alone
and dead!

Suppose someone disagrees and says,
"It is possible to have faith without doing kind deeds."

I would answer, "Prove that you have faith
without doing kind deeds,
and I will prove that I have faith by doing them."

The word of the Lord.

Responsorial Psalm

Psalm 146:6d–7ab, 7c–9a (1b)

R. Praise the Lord, my soul!

God always keeps his word.
He gives justice to the poor
and food to the hungry.

R. Praise the Lord, my soul!

The LORD sets prisoners free
and heals blind eyes.
He gives a helping hand
to everyone who falls.
The LORD loves good people
and looks after strangers.

R. Praise the Lord, my soul!

GOSPEL

✚ A reading from the holy gospel according to Luke

Luke 14:12–14

Jesus said to the man who had invited him to dinner:
"When you give a dinner or a banquet,
don't invite your friends and family
and relatives and rich neighbors.
If you do, they will invite you in return,
and you will be paid back.
When you give a feast,
invite the poor, the crippled, the lame, and the blind.
They cannot pay you back.
But God will bless you and reward you
when his people rise from death."

Do not invite just your friends, but the poor and those who are crippled.

The gospel of the Lord.

THE GOOD SHEPHERD

ONE

First Reading — **A reading from the book of the prophet Isaiah**

Isaiah 40:10–11

Look!
The powerful Lord God is coming to rule
with his mighty arm.
He will reward some people and punish others.

The Lord cares for his nation as a shepherd cares for sheep.

The Lord cares for his nation,
as shepherds care for sheep.
He carries the lambs close to his chest,
while gently leading the mother sheep.

The word of the Lord.

OR

TWO

A reading from the book of the prophet Ezekiel

FIRST READING

Ezekiel 34:11–15

I will watch over my sheep and tend them.

The LORD says this:
"I, the LORD God, will look for my people
and take care of them myself.
As a shepherd looks for sheep that have wandered away,
I will search for my scattered people.
I will rescue them from all the places where they went
on that dark and gloomy day.
I will bring them back from the foreign countries
and protect them on the mountains,
in the valleys, and wherever they settle.

"My people will be like sheep grazing and resting
in good pastures and on Israel's mountains.
I, the LORD All-Powerful, will lead them there
and watch over them."

The word of the Lord.

Responsorial Psalm

Psalm 100:1–2, 3, 5
(3)

R. We are God's people:
the sheep of his flock.

Shout praises to the L*ORD,*
everyone on this earth.
Be joyful and sing
as you come in
to worship the L*ORD!*

R. We are God's people:
the sheep of his flock.

You know the L*ORD is God!*
He created us,
and we belong to him;
we are his people,
the sheep in his pasture.

R. We are God's people:
the sheep of his flock.

The L*ORD is good!*
His love and faithfulness
will last forever.

R. We are God's people:
the sheep of his flock.

GOSPEL

Luke 15:1–7

Share my joy: I have found my lost sheep!

✚ A reading from the holy gospel according to Luke

Tax collectors and sinners were all crowding around
to listen to Jesus.
So the Pharisees and the teachers
of the Law of Moses started grumbling,
"This man is friendly with sinners.
He even eats with them."

Then Jesus told them this story:

"If any of you has a hundred sheep,
and one of them gets lost,
what will you do?
Won't you leave the ninety-nine in the field
and go look for the lost sheep until you find it?
And when you find it,
you will be so glad
that you will put it on your shoulder and carry it home.
Then you will call in your friends and neighbors and say,
'Let's celebrate! I've found my lost sheep.'"

Jesus said,
"In the same way there is more happiness in heaven
because of one sinner who turns to God
than over ninety-nine good people who don't need to."

The gospel of the Lord.

GIVE THANKS TO GOD

First Reading **A reading from the first letter of Paul to the Thessalonians**

1 Thessalonians 5:16–18

Keep thanking God because of Jesus Christ.

Brothers and sisters:
Always be joyful and never stop praying.
Whatever happens, keep thanking God
because of Jesus Christ.
This is what God wants you to do.

The word of the Lord.

Responsorial Psalm

Psalm 138:1–2a, 2bcdef (2bc)

R. Lord, I thank you
for your faithfulness and love.

With all my heart
I praise you, LORD.
In the presence of angels
I sing your praises.
I worship at your holy temple.

R. Lord, I thank you
for your faithfulness and love.

I praise you for your love
and your faithfulness.
You were true to your word
and made yourself more famous
than ever before.

R. Lord, I thank you
for your faithfulness and love.

Gospel

Luke 17:11–19

✚ A reading from the holy gospel according to Luke

On his way to Jerusalem,
Jesus went along the border between Samaria and Galilee.
As he was going into a village,
ten men with leprosy came toward him.
They stood at a distance and shouted,
"Jesus, Master, have pity on us!"

Jesus looked at them and said,
"Go show yourselves to the priests."

It seems that no one has returned to give thanks to God.

On their way they were healed.
When one of them discovered that he was healed,
he came back, shouting praises to God.
He bowed down at the feet of Jesus and thanked him.
The man was from the country of Samaria.

Jesus asked, "Weren't ten men healed?
Where are the other nine?
Why was this foreigner the only one who came back
to thank God?"

Then Jesus told the man, "You may get up and go.
Your faith has made you well."

The gospel of the Lord.

PRAY ALWAYS

First Reading — **A reading from the letter of Paul to the Ephesians**

Ephesians 6:18b–19a, 20b

Pray always by the power of the Spirit.

Brothers and sisters:
Always pray by the power of the Spirit.
Stay alert and keep praying for God's people.

Pray that I will be given the message to speak.
And pray that I will be brave and will speak as I should.

The word of the Lord.

Responsorial Psalm — *R. To you, O Lord, I lift my soul.*

Psalm 25:1–2ab and 4, 5–6 (1)

I offer you my heart, LORD God,
and I trust you.
Don't make me ashamed.
Show me your paths
and teach me to follow.

R. To you, O Lord, I lift my soul.

Guide me by your truth
and instruct me.
You keep me safe,
and I always trust you.
Please, LORD, remember,
you have always
been patient and kind.

R. To you, O Lord, I lift my soul.

GOSPEL

Luke 18:1–8a

God will see justice done to his chosen who cry to him.

✚ A reading from the holy gospel according to Luke

Jesus told his disciples a story
about how they should keep on praying and never give up:

"In a town there was once a judge who didn't fear God
or care about people.
In that same town there was a widow
who kept going to the judge and saying,
'Make sure that I get fair treatment in court.'

"For a while the judge refused to do anything.
Finally, he said to himself,
'Even though I don't fear God or care about people,
I will help this widow
because she keeps on bothering me.
If I don't help her,
she will wear me out.'"

The Lord said:
"Think about what that crooked judge said.
Won't God protect his chosen ones
who pray to him day and night?
Won't he be concerned for them?
He will surely hurry and help them."

The gospel of the Lord.

GOD LOVES US

First Reading

A reading from the book of the prophet Hosea

Hosea 11:3–4

The Lord says this:
I took my people by the hand and taught them to walk.

The Lord was loving and kind to his people.

I was the one who healed them,
but they did not know it.
I was loving and kind,
and I made them want to come to me.
I freed them from slavery and tenderly fed them.

The word of the Lord.

Responsorial Psalm

Psalm 116:5 and 7, 9 and 12 (9a)

R. Now I will walk at your side.

You are kind, LORD,
so good and merciful.
You have treated me so kindly
that I don't need
to worry anymore.

R. Now I will walk at your side.

Now I will walk at your side
in this land of the living.
What must I give you, LORD,
for being so good to me?

R. Now I will walk at your side.

GOSPEL

John 3:16–17

God so loved the world
that he gave his only Son.

✚ A reading from the holy gospel according to John

Jesus told Nicodemus:
"God loved the people of this world so much
 that he gave his only Son,
so that everyone who has faith in him
 will have eternal life and never die.
God did not send his Son into the world
 to condemn its people.
He sent him to save them!"

The gospel of the Lord.

WE ARE THE PEOPLE OF GOD

ONE

First Reading

A reading from the book of the prophet Jeremiah

Jeremiah 31:33

They will be my people, says the Lord.

The LORD says this:
"This is the agreement that I, the LORD,
will make with the people of Israel:
I will write my laws on their hearts and minds.
I will be their God, and they will be my people."

The word of the Lord.

OR

TWO

First Reading

1 Peter 2:9–10

You are God's chosen people.

A reading from the first letter of Peter

Brothers and sisters:
You are God's chosen and special people.
You are a group of royal priests and a holy nation.
God has brought you out of darkness
  into his marvelous light.
Now you must tell all the wonderful things
  that he has done.

The Scriptures say, "Once you were nobody.
Now you are God's people.
At one time no one had pity on you.
Now God has treated you with kindness."

The word of the Lord.

Responsorial Psalm

Psalm 100:1–2, 3, 5 (3)

R. We are God's people:
the sheep of his flock.

Shout praises to the LORD,
everyone on this earth.
Be joyful and sing
as you come in
to worship the LORD!

R. We are God's people:
the sheep of his flock.

You know the LORD *is God!*
He created us,
and we belong to him;
we are his people,
the sheep in his pasture.

R. We are God's people:
the sheep of his flock.

The LORD *is good!*
His love and faithfulness
will last forever.

R. We are God's people:
the sheep of his flock.

GOSPEL

John 13:34–35

I give you a new commandment: love one another.

✚ A reading from the holy gospel according to John

Jesus said to his disciples:
"I am giving you a new command.
You must love each other,
just as I have loved you.
If you love each other,
everyone will know that you are my disciples."

The gospel of the Lord.

223

THE SPIRIT HAS GIVEN US LIFE

FIRST READING

A reading from the letter of Paul to the Galatians

Galatians 5:22–23, 25–26

Brothers and sisters:
God's Spirit makes us loving, happy, peaceful,
patient, kind, good, faithful,
gentle, and self-controlled.

The Spirit has given us life.

There is no law against behaving in any of these ways.

God's Spirit has given us life,
and so we should follow the Spirit.
But don't be conceited or make others jealous
by claiming to be better than they are.

The word of the Lord.

Responsorial Psalm

R. Lord, you will show us the path of life.

Psalm 16:1–2ab and 5, 7–8, 11 (11a)

Protect me, LORD God!
I run to you for safety,
and I have said,
"Only you are my Lord!"
You, LORD, are all I want!
You are my choice,
and you keep me safe.

R. Lord, you will show us the path of life.

I praise you, LORD,
for being my guide.
Even in the darkest night,
your teachings fill my mind.
I will always look to you,
as you stand beside me
and protect me from fear.

R. Lord, you will show us the path of life.

You have shown me
the path to life,
and you make me glad
by being near to me.
Sitting at your right side,
I will always be joyful.

R. Lord, you will show us the path of life.

GOSPEL

✚ A reading from the holy gospel according to John

John 14:15–17

The Holy Spirit will teach you all things.

Jesus said to his disciples:
"If you love me, you will do as I command.
Then I will ask the Father to send you the Holy Spirit
who will help you and always be with you.
The Spirit will show you what is true.

"The people of this world cannot accept the Spirit,
because they don't see or know him.
But you know the Spirit, who is with you
and will keep on living in you."

The gospel of the Lord.

PEACE I LEAVE WITH YOU

ONE

FIRST READING

A reading from the book of the prophet Isaiah

Isaiah 11:1b, 5–9

The LORD says this:
Someone from David's family will someday be king.
Honesty and fairness will be his royal robes.

Leopards and young goats, and wolves and lambs
will lie down and rest in the same field.
Calves and lions will eat together and be cared for by a child.
Cows and bears will share the same pasture,
and their young will rest side by side.
Lions will eat straw just like oxen.

All creation will be at peace.

Young children will play near snake holes.
They will stick their hands into dens of poisonous snakes
without being harmed.
No one will be hurt or killed on the LORD's holy mountain.

Just as water fills the sea,
the land will be filled with people who know
and honor the LORD.

The word of the Lord.

OR

TWO

A reading from the letter of Paul to the Colossians

FIRST READING

Colossians 3:15–16

Live in peace together, the peace that comes from Christ.

Brothers and sisters:
Each one of you is part of the body of Christ,
and you were chosen to live together in peace.
So let the peace that comes from Christ
control your thoughts.
And be grateful.

Let the message about Christ completely fill your lives,
while you use all your wisdom to teach
and instruct each other.
With thankful hearts,
sing psalms, hymns, and spiritual songs to God.

The word of the Lord.

Responsorial Psalm

Psalm 122:1–2, 8–9
(Sirach 36:18)

R. Give peace, O Lord,
to those who wait for you.

It made me glad
to hear them say,
"Let's go to the house
of the LORD!"
Jerusalem, we are standing
inside your gates.

R. Give peace, O Lord,
to those who wait for you.

Because of my friends
and my relatives,
I will pray for peace.
And because of the house
of the LORD our God,
I will work for your good.

R. Give peace, O Lord,
to those who wait for you.

GOSPEL

✚ A reading from the holy gospel according to John

John 14:27

My peace I give to you.

Jesus said to his disciples:
"I give you peace,
the kind of peace that only I can give.
It is not like the peace that this world can give.
So don't be worried or afraid."

The gospel of the Lord.

ONE WITH JESUS

First Reading **A reading from the first letter of Paul to the Corinthians**

1 Corinthians 12:12–13

Together you are Christ's body.

Brothers and sisters:
The body of Christ has many different parts,
just as any other body does.
Some of us are Jews,
and others are Gentiles.
Some of us are slaves,
and others are free.
But God's Spirit baptized each of us
and made us part of the body of Christ.
Now we each drink from that same Spirit.

The word of the Lord.

Responsorial Psalm

Psalm 80:8ab and 9–10ab, 14d–15ab and 19 (Isaiah 5:7a)

*R. The vineyard of the Lord
is the house of Israel.*

*We were like a grapevine
you brought out of Egypt.
You cleared the ground,
and we put our roots deep,
spreading over the land.
Shade from this vine
covered the mountains.*

*R. The vineyard of the Lord
is the house of Israel.*

See what's happening
to this vine.
With your own hands
you planted its roots.
LORD God All-Powerful,
make us strong again!
Smile on us and save us.

R. The vineyard of the Lord
is the house of Israel.

GOSPEL

✚ A reading from the holy gospel according to John

John 15:1–5

Jesus said to his disciples:
"I am the true vine,
and my Father is the gardener.
He cuts away every branch of mine
that does not produce fruit.
But he trims clean every branch that does produce fruit,
so that it will produce even more fruit.

"You are already clean because of what I have said to you.

Those who live in me,
and I in them,
will bear much fruit.

"Stay joined to me,
and I will stay joined to you.
Just as a branch cannot produce fruit
unless it stays joined to the vine,
you cannot produce fruit unless you stay joined to me.

"I am the vine, and you are the branches.
If you stay joined to me, and I stay joined to you,
then you will produce lots of fruit.
But you cannot do anything without me."

The gospel of the Lord.

MAY YOUR JOY BE COMPLETE

FIRST READING **A reading from the letter of Paul to the Romans**

Romans 5:10b–11

Brothers and sisters:
Now that we are at peace with God,
we will be saved by his Son's life.

We are happy because God sent Jesus Christ to make peace with us.

And in addition to everything else,
we are happy because God sent our Lord Jesus Christ
to make peace with us.

The word of the Lord.

Responsorial Psalm

Psalm 89:1–2, 15–16 (2a)

R. For ever I will sing the goodness of the Lord.

Our LORD, I will sing
of your love forever.
Everyone yet to be born
will hear me praise
your faithfulness.
I will tell them, "God's love
can always be trusted,
and his faithfulness lasts
as long as the heavens."

R. For ever I will sing the goodness of the Lord.

Our LORD, you bless those
who join in the festival
and walk in the brightness
of your presence.
We are happy all day
because of you,
and your saving power
brings honor to us.

R. For ever I will sing the goodness
of the Lord.

GOSPEL

✚ A reading from the holy gospel according to John

John 15:9–11

I have told you this to make you as happy as I am.

Jesus said to his disciples:
"I have loved you,
just as my Father has loved me.
So make sure that I keep on loving you.
If you obey me,
I will keep loving you,
just as my Father keeps loving me,
because I have obeyed him.

"I have told you this to make you as completely happy as I am."

The gospel of the Lord.

YOU ARE MY FRIENDS

FIRST READING

A reading from the first letter of John

1 John 3:1, 23

Beloved:
Think how much the Father loves us.
He loves us so much that he lets us be called his children,
as we truly are.
But since the people of this world
did not know who Christ is,
they don't know who we are.

We are called children of God, and that is what we are.

God wants us to have faith in his Son Jesus Christ
and to love each other.
This is also what Jesus taught us to do.

The word of the Lord.

Responsorial Psalm

Psalm 85:8, 9–10 (9b)

R. The Lord speaks of peace to his people.

I will listen to you, LORD God,
because you promise peace
to those who are faithful
and no longer foolish.

R. The Lord speaks of peace to his people.

You are ready to rescue
everyone who worships you,
so that you will live with us
in all of your glory.
Love and loyalty
will come together;
goodness and peace will unite.

R. The Lord speaks of peace to his people.

GOSPEL

John 15:12–15

You are my friends.

✚ A reading from the holy gospel according to John

Jesus said to his disciples:
"Now I tell you to love each other,
as I have loved you.
The greatest way to show love for friends is to die for them.
And you are my friends, if you obey me.

"Servants don't know what their master is doing,
and so I don't speak to you as my servants.
I speak to you as my friends,
and I have told you everything that my Father has told me."

The gospel of the Lord.

Last Weeks in Ordinary Time

First Reading

A reading from the letter of James

James 2:14–17

My friends,
what good is it to say you have faith,
when you don't do anything
to show that you really do have faith?
Can that kind of faith save you?

Faith without good works is dead.

If you know someone who doesn't have any clothes or food,
you shouldn't just say, "I hope all goes well for you.
I hope you will be warm and have plenty to eat."

What good is it to say this,
unless you do something to help?
Faith that doesn't lead us to do good deeds
is all alone and dead!

The word of the Lord.

Responsorial Psalm

Psalm 40:1 and 3ab, 8 and 11 (8a and 9a)

R. Here am I, Lord;
I come to do your will.

I patiently waited, LORD,
for you to hear my prayer.
You listened and you gave me
a new song,
a song of praise to you.

R. Here am I, Lord;
I come to do your will.

I enjoy pleasing you.
Your Law is in my heart.
You, LORD, never fail
to have pity on me;
your love and faithfulness
always keep me secure.

R. Here am I, Lord;
I come to do your will.

GOSPEL **✚ A reading from the holy gospel according to Matthew**

Matthew 7:21, 24–27

Jesus said to his disciples:
"Not everyone who calls me their Lord
will get into the kingdom of heaven.
Only the ones who obey my Father in heaven will get in.

Whoever does the will of the Father will enter the kingdom of heaven.

"Anyone who hears and obeys these teachings of mine
is like a wise person who built a house on solid rock.
Rain poured down, rivers flooded,
and winds beat against that house.
But it did not fall,
because it was built on solid rock.

"Anyone who hears my teachings and does not obey them
is like a foolish person who built a house on sand.
The rain poured down, the rivers flooded,
and the winds blew and beat against that house.
Finally, it fell with a crash."

The gospel of the Lord.

229 THE BANQUET OF THE KINGDOM

Last Weeks in Ordinary Time

First Reading **A reading from the book of the prophet Isaiah**

Isaiah 25:6, 9

The Lord will prepare a banquet for all nations.

On this mountain the LORD All-Powerful
will prepare for all nations a feast of the finest foods.
Choice wines and the best meat will be served.

On that day, people will say,
"The LORD God has saved us!
Let's celebrate.
We waited and waited, and now he is here."

The word of the Lord.

Responsorial Psalm *R. Taste and see the goodness of the Lord.*

Psalm 34:1–2, 3–4 (9a)

I will always praise the LORD.
With all my heart,
I will praise the LORD.
Let all who are helpless
listen and be glad.

R. Taste and see the goodness of the Lord.

Honor the LORD with me!
Celebrate his great name.
I asked the LORD for help,
and he saved me
from all my fears.

R. Taste and see the goodness of the Lord.

GOSPEL

Matthew 8:5–11

Many will come from the east and west and take their place in the kingdom of heaven.

✚ A reading from the holy gospel according to Matthew

When Jesus was going into the town of Capernaum,
an army officer came up to him and said,
"Lord, my servant is at home in such terrible pain
that he can't even move."

"I will go and heal him," Jesus replied.

But the officer said,
"Lord, I'm not good enough for you to come into my house.
Just give the order,
and my servant will get well.

"I have officers who give orders to me,
and I have soldiers who take orders from me.
I can say to one of them, 'Go!' and he goes.
I can say to another, 'Come!' and he comes.
I can say to my servant, 'Do this!' and he will do it."

When Jesus heard this,
he was so surprised that he turned and said to the crowd
following him,
"I tell you that in all of Israel
I've never found anyone with this much faith!
Many people will come from everywhere
to enjoy the feast in the kingdom of heaven
with Abraham, Isaac, and Jacob."

The gospel of the Lord.

THE LORD IS COMING SOON

Last Weeks in Ordinary Time

First Reading — **A reading from the letter of Paul to the Philippians**

Philippians 4:4–7

Brothers and sisters:
Always be glad because of the Lord!
I will say it again: Be glad.

Always be gentle with others.
The Lord will soon be here.
The Lord is near.
Don't worry about anything,
but pray about everything.

With thankful hearts offer up your prayers and requests to God.
Then, because you belong to Christ Jesus,
God will bless you with peace
that no one can completely understand.
And this peace will control the way you think and feel.

The word of the Lord.

Responsorial Psalm

Psalm 85:8abc and 9, 10–11 (8)

R. Lord, show us your mercy and love,
and grant us your salvation.

I will listen to you, LORD *God,*
because you promise peace
to those who are faithful.
You are ready to rescue
everyone who worships you,
so that you will live with us
in all of your glory.

R. Lord, show us your mercy and love,
and grant us your salvation.

Love and loyalty
will come together;
goodness and peace will unite.
Loyalty will sprout
from the ground;
justice will look down
from the sky above.

R. Lord, show us your mercy and love,
and grant us your salvation.

GOSPEL **✚ A reading from the holy gospel according to Luke**

Luke 12:35–40

Jesus said to his disciples:
"Be ready and keep your lamps burning
just like those servants who wait up
for their master to return from a wedding feast.
As soon as he comes and knocks,
they open the door for him.

"Servants are fortunate
Be prepared.
if their master finds them awake and ready
when he comes!
I promise you that he will get ready
and have his servants sit down so he can serve them.
Those servants are really fortunate if their master
finds them ready,
even though he comes late at night or early in the morning.

"You would surely not let a thief break into your home,
if you knew when the thief was coming.
So always be ready!
You don't know when the Son of Man will come."

The gospel of the Lord.

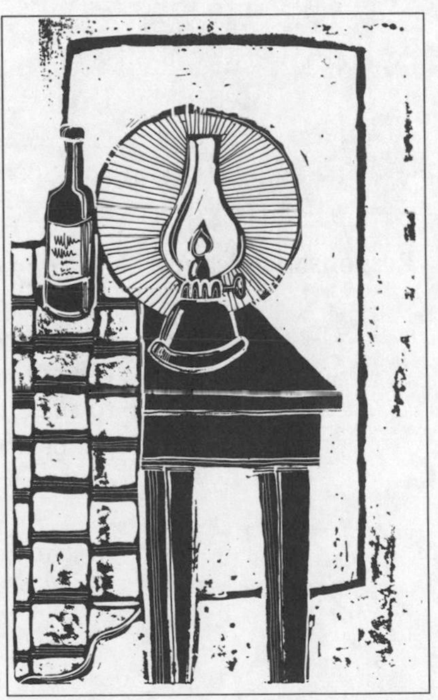

231

THE KINGDOM OF GOD IS AMONG YOU

Last Weeks in Ordinary Time

FIRST READING

A reading from the letter of Paul to the Ephesians

Ephesians 3:16b–17, 20–21

Christ's power is at work in our hearts.

Brothers and sisters:
I pray that God's Spirit will make you become
strong followers
and that Christ will live in your hearts because of your faith.
Stand firm and be deeply rooted in his love.

I pray that Christ Jesus and the church
will forever bring praise to God.
His power at work in us
can do far more than we dare ask or imagine. Amen.

The word of the Lord.

Responsorial Psalm

Psalm 126:1–2ab, 2cde–3 (3)

R. The Lord has done great things for us.

It seemed like a dream
when the LORD brought us back
to the city of Zion.
We celebrated with laughter
and joyful songs.

R. The Lord has done great things for us.

In foreign nations it was said,
"The LORD has worked miracles
for his people."
And so we celebrated
because the LORD had indeed
worked miracles for us.

R. The Lord has done great things for us.

GOSPEL

Luke 17:20–21

The kingdom of God is among you.

✚ A reading from the holy gospel according to Luke

Some Pharisees asked Jesus when God's kingdom
would come.

Jesus answered, "God's kingdom is not something
you can see.
There is no use saying, 'Look! Here it is,'
or 'Look! There it is.'
God's kingdom is here with you."

The gospel of the Lord.

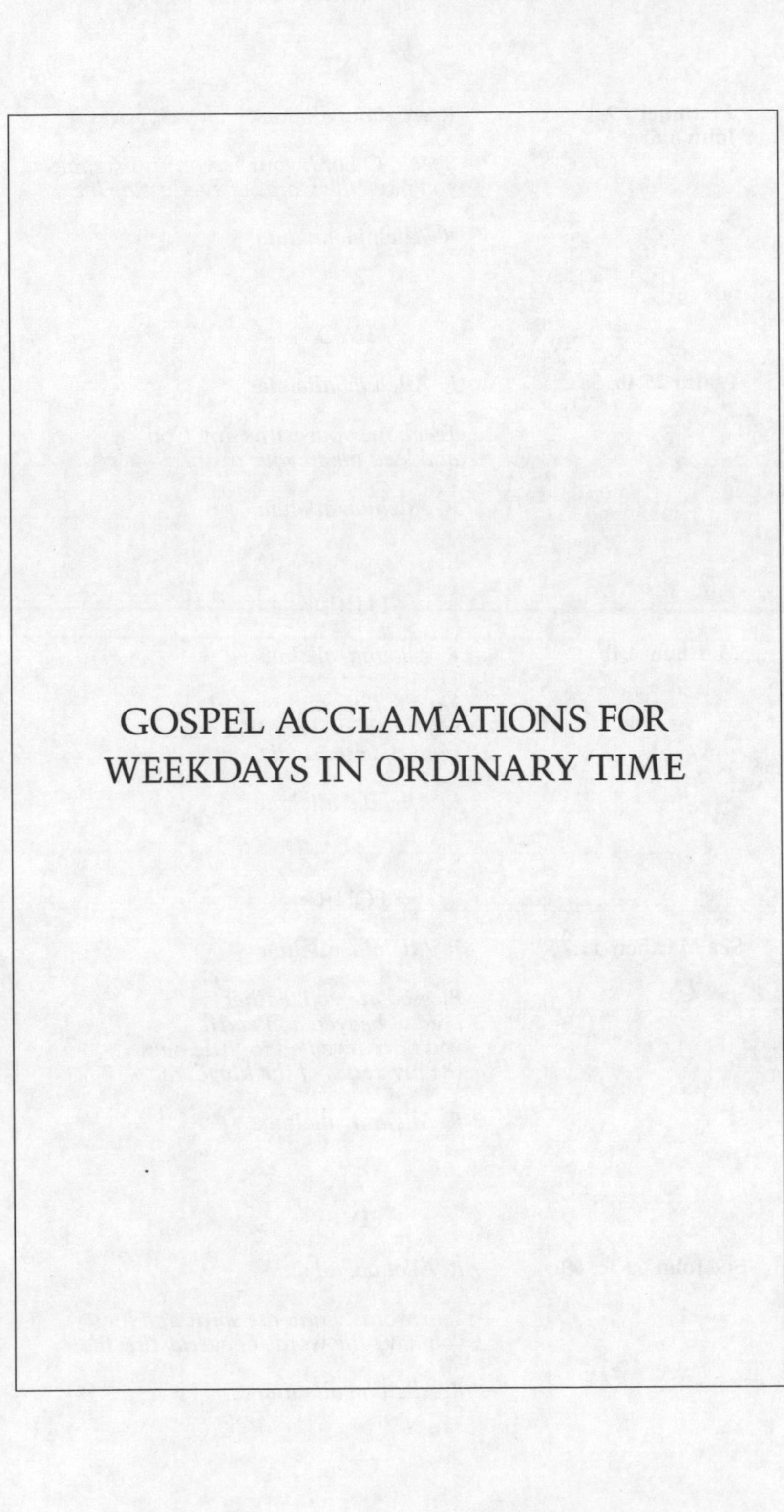

GOSPEL ACCLAMATIONS FOR WEEKDAYS IN ORDINARY TIME

232

Any of the following gospel acclamations may be chosen for use at weekday Masses during Ordinary Time.

ONE

1 Samuel 3:9; John 6:68c

R. Alleluia, alleluia.

Speak, O Lord, your servant is listening;
you have the words of everlasting life.

R. Alleluia, alleluia.

TWO

Psalm 25:4b, 5a

R. Alleluia, alleluia.

Teach me your paths, my God,
and lead me in your truth.

R. Alleluia, alleluia.

THREE

Matthew 4:4b

R. Alleluia, alleluia.

No one lives on bread alone,
but on every word that comes
from the mouth of God.

R. Alleluia, alleluia.

FOUR

See Matthew 11:25

R. Alleluia, alleluia.

Blessed are you, Father,
Lord of heaven and earth;
you have revealed to little ones
the mysteries of the kingdom.

R. Alleluia, alleluia.

FIVE

See John 6:63c, 68c

R. Alleluia, alleluia.

Your words, Lord, are spirit and life:
you have the words of everlasting life.

R. Alleluia, alleluia.

SIX

John 8:12

R. Alleluia, alleluia.

*I am the light of the world, says the Lord;
whoever follows me will have the light of life.*

R. Alleluia, alleluia.

SEVEN

John 14:6

R. Alleluia, alleluia.

*I am the way, the truth, and the life,
says the Lord;
no one comes to the Father, except through me.*

R. Alleluia, alleluia.

EIGHT

See Acts 16:14b

R. Alleluia, alleluia.

*Open our hearts, O Lord,
to listen to the words of your Son.*

R. Alleluia, alleluia.

NINE

1 John 2:5

R. Alleluia, alleluia.

*Whoever keeps the word of Christ
grows perfect in the love of God.*

R. Alleluia, alleluia.

Last Weeks of Ordinary Time

TEN

Matthew 24:42a, 44

R. Alleluia, alleluia.

*Be watchful and ready:
you know not when the Son of Man is coming.*

R. Alleluia, alleluia.

PROPER OF SAINTS

233 *For celebrations in honor of the saints, in addition to the texts referred to in individual cases, the readings given in the common of the saints may always be selected.*

▪ JANUARY ▪

234 January 1
Octave of Christmas
MARY, MOTHER OF GOD
Solemnity

See the Proper of Seasons, no. 15 [in volumes A, B and C].

235 January 2
BASIL THE GREAT AND GREGORY NAZIANZEN
bishops, doctors of the Church
Memorial

From the Common of Pastors or the Common of Doctors of the Church, p. 364 or 370.

236 January 4
ELIZABETH ANN SETON
married woman,
religious founder
Memorial

From the Common of Saints [For Religious], p. 376.

237 January 5
JOHN NEUMANN
bishop, religious, missionary
Memorial

From the Common of Pastors, p. 364.

238 January 6
BLESSED ANDRÉ BESSETTE
religious

From the Common of Saints [For Religious], p. 376.

239 January 7
RAYMOND OF PENYAFORT
presbyter, religious

From the Common of Pastors, p. 364.

240 January 13
HILARY
bishop, doctor of the Church

From the Common of Pastors or the Common of Doctors of the Church, p. 364 or 370.

241 January 17
ANTHONY
abbot
Memorial

From the Common of Saints [For Religious], p. 376.

242 January 20
FABIAN
pope, martyr

From the Common of Martyrs or the Common of Pastors [For a Pope], p. 358 or 364.

243 **SEBASTIAN**
martyr

From the Common of Martyrs, p. 358.

244 January 21
AGNES
virgin, martyr

Memorial

From the Common of Martyrs or the Common of Saints, p. 358 or 376.

245 January 22
VINCENT
deacon, martyr

From the Common of Martyrs, p. 358.

246 January 24
FRANCIS DE SALES
bishop, religious founder, doctor of the Church

Memorial

From the Common of Pastors or the Common of Doctors of the Church, p. 364 or 370.

247 January 25
THE CONVERSION OF PAUL
apostle

Feast

See p. 208.

248 January 26
TIMOTHY AND TITUS
bishops

Memorial

See p. 212.

249 January 27
ANGELA MERICI
virgin, religious founder

From the Common of Saints [For Educators], p. 376.

250 January 28
THOMAS AQUINAS
presbyter, religious, doctor of the Church

Memorial

From the Common of Doctors of the Church or the Common of Pastors, p. 370 or 364.

251 January 31
JOHN BOSCO
presbyter, religious founder

Memorial

From the Common of Pastors or the Common of Saints [For Educators], p. 364 or 376.

■

THE CONVERSION OF PAUL

First Reading **A reading from the Acts of the Apostles**

Acts 22:3–16

Paul told the people:
"I am a Jew, born and raised in the city of Tarsus in Cilicia.
I was a student of Gamaliel and was taught
to follow every single law of our ancestors.
In fact, I was just as eager to obey God
as any of you are today.

Rise and be baptized and wash away your sins, calling on the name of Jesus.

"I made trouble for everyone who followed the Lord's Way,
and I even had some of them killed.
I had others arrested and put in jail.
I didn't care if they were men or women.
The high priest and all the council members
can tell you that this is true.
They even gave me letters to the Jewish leaders
in Damascus,
so that I could arrest people there
and bring them to Jerusalem to be punished.

"One day about noon I was getting close to Damascus,
when a bright light from heaven suddenly flashed around.
I fell to the ground and heard a voice asking me,
'Saul, Saul, why are you so cruel to me?'

"'Who are you?' I answered.

"The Lord replied, 'I am Jesus from Nazareth!
I am the one you are so cruel to.'
The men who were traveling with me saw the light,
but did not hear the voice.

"I asked, 'Lord, what do you want me to do?'

"Then he told me, 'Get up and go to Damascus.
When you get there, you will be told what to do.'

"The light had been so bright that I couldn't see.
And the other men had to lead me by the hand to Damascus.

"In that city there was a man named Ananias,
who faithfully obeyed the Law of Moses
   and was well liked by all the Jewish people living there.
He came to me and said,
'Saul, my friend, you can now see again!'
At once I could see.

"Then Ananias told me,
'The God that our ancestors worshiped
   has chosen you to know what he wants done.
He has chosen you to see the One Who Obeys God
   and to hear his voice.
You must tell everyone what you have seen and heard.
What are you waiting for?
Get up! Be baptized,
and wash away your sins by praying to the Lord.'"

The word of the Lord.

Responsorial Psalm

Psalm 117:1, 2 (Mark 16:15)

R. Go out to all the world
and tell the good news.

All of you nations,
come praise the LORD!
Let everyone praise him.

R. Go out to all the world
and tell the good news.

His love for us is wonderful,
his faithfulness never ends.
Shout praises to the LORD!

R. Go out to all the world
and tell the good news.

Alleluia

See John 15:16

R. Alleluia, alleluia.

I have chosen you from the world,
says the Lord,
to go and bear fruit that will last.

R. Alleluia, alleluia.

GOSPEL

✚ A reading from the holy gospel according to Mark

Mark 16:15–18

Go out to all the world and tell the good news.

Jesus told his disciples:
"Go and preach the good news to everyone in the world.
Anyone who believes and is baptized will be saved.
But anyone who refuses to believe me will be condemned.

"Everyone who believes me will be able to do
wonderful things.
By using my name they will force out demons,
and they will speak new languages.
They will handle snakes and will drink poison
and not be hurt.
They will also heal sick people
by placing their hands on them."

The gospel of the Lord.

TIMOTHY AND TITUS

The first reading for this memorial is proper.
From the Common of Pastors, p. 364, except:

ONE

FIRST READING

A reading from the second letter of Paul to Timothy

2 Timothy 1:1–8

From Paul, an apostle of Christ Jesus.

God himself chose me to be an apostle,
and he gave me the promised life
that Jesus Christ makes possible.

I have in mind your faith, which is openly sincere.

Timothy, you are like a dear child to me.
I pray that God our Father and our Lord Christ Jesus
will be kind and merciful to you
and will bless you with peace.

Night and day I mention you in my prayers.
I am always grateful for you,
as I pray to the God
my ancestors and I have served with a clear conscience.

I remember how you cried, and I want to see you,
because that will make me truly happy.
I also remember the genuine faith of your mother Eunice.
Your grandmother Lois had the same sort of faith,
and I am sure that you have it as well.

So I ask you to make full use of the gift that God gave you
when I placed my hands on you.
Use it well.
God's Spirit does not make cowards out of us.
The Spirit gives us power, love, and self-control.

Don't be ashamed to speak for our Lord.
And don't be ashamed of me,
just because I am in jail for serving him.
Use the power that comes from God
and join with me in suffering for telling the good news.

The word of the Lord.

OR

TWO

A reading from the letter of Paul to Titus

FIRST READING

From Paul, a servant of God and an apostle of Jesus Christ.

Titus 1:1–5

I encourage God's own people to have more faith
  and to understand the truth about religion.
Then they will have the hope of eternal life
  that God promised long ago.
And God never tells a lie!

So, at the proper time,
God our Savior gave this message
  and told me to announce what he had said.

To Titus, my beloved son in a common faith.

Titus, because of our faith,
you are like a son to me.
I pray that God our Father and Christ Jesus our Savior
  will be kind to you and will bless you with peace!

I left you in Crete to do what had been left undone
  and to appoint leaders for the churches in each town.

The word of the Lord.

▪ FEBRUARY ▪

252 February 2

THE PRESENTATION OF THE LORD

Feast

See p. 216.

253 February 3

BLASE

bishop, martyr

From the Common of Martyrs or the Common of Pastors, p. 358 or 364.

254 **ANSGAR**

bishop, missionary

From the Common of Pastors [For Missionaries], p. 364.

255 February 5

AGATHA

virgin, martyr

Memorial

From the Common of Martyrs or the Common of Saints, p. 358 or 376.

256 February 6

PAUL MIKI

religious, missionary, martyr, and his **COMPANIONS,** martyrs

Memorial

From the Common of Martyrs, p. 358.

257 February 8

JEROME EMILIANI

presbyter, religious founder

From the Common of Saints [For Educators], p. 376.

258 February 10

SCHOLASTICA

virgin, religious

Memorial

From the Common of Saints [For Religious], p. 376.

259 February 11

OUR LADY OF LOURDES

From the Common of the Blessed Virgin Mary, p. 346.

260 February 14

CYRIL
religious, missionary, and
METHODIUS, bishop, missionary

Memorial

From the Common of Pastors [For Missionaries] or the Common of Saints, p. 364 or 376.

261 February 17

SEVEN FOUNDERS OF THE ORDER OF SERVITES
religious

From the Common of Saints [For Religious], p. 376.

262 February 21

PETER DAMIAN
bishop, religious, doctor of the Church

From the Common of Doctors of the Church or the Common of Pastors or the Common of Saints [For Religious], p. 370, or 364, or 376.

263 February 22

THE CHAIR OF THE APOSTLE PETER

Feast

See p. 220.

264 February 23

POLYCARP
bishop, martyr

Memorial

From the Common of Martyrs or the Common of Pastors, p. 358 or 364.

■

FIRST READING **A reading from the book of the prophet Malachi**

Malachi 3:1–2b

The Lord whom you seek will come to his temple.

The LORD All-Powerful says,
"I will send my messenger to prepare the way for me.
Then suddenly the LORD you are longing for
will come to his temple.
The messenger you are eagerly looking for
will come and announce my promise to you.
Who can face him on that day?
Who will be able to stand?"

The word of the Lord.

Responsorial Psalm

Psalm 24:7, 10 (10b)

R. The Lord of hosts: he is king of glory!

Open the ancient gates,
so that the glorious king
may come in.

R. The Lord of hosts: he is king of glory!

Who is this glorious king?
He is our LORD,
the All-Powerful!

R. The Lord of hosts: he is king of glory!

Alleluia *R. Alleluia, alleluia.*

Luke 2:32

This is the light of revelation
to the nations
and the glory of your people Israel.

R. Alleluia, alleluia.

GOSPEL ✚ **A reading from the holy gospel according to Luke**

Luke 2:22–32

The time came for Mary and Joseph to do
what the Law of Moses says a mother is supposed to do
after her baby is born.

They took Jesus to the temple in Jerusalem
and presented him to the Lord,
just as the Law of the Lord says,
"Each first-born baby boy belongs to the Lord."
The Law of the Lord also says
that parents have to offer a sacrifice,
giving at least a pair of doves or two young pigeons.
So that is what Mary and Joseph did.

My eyes have seen your saving power.

At this time a man named Simeon was living in Jerusalem.
Simeon was a good man.
He loved God and was waiting for God
to save the people of Israel.
God's Spirit came to him and told him that he would not die
until he had seen Christ the Lord.

When Mary and Joseph brought Jesus to the temple
to do what the Law of Moses says should be done
for a new baby,
the Spirit told Simeon to go into the temple.
Simeon took the baby Jesus in his arms
and praised God, saying,

"Lord, I am your servant,
and now I can die in peace,
because you have kept your promise to me.

"With my own eyes I have seen
what you have done to save your people,
and foreign nations will also see this.

"Your mighty power is a light for all nations,
and it will bring honor to your people Israel."

The gospel of the Lord.

263

THE CHAIR OF THE APOSTLE PETER

First Reading **A reading from the first letter of Peter**

1 Peter 5:1–4

Church leaders, I am writing to encourage you.
I too am a leader, as well as a witness of Christ's suffering,
and I will share in his glory when it is shown to us.

Just as shepherds watch over their sheep,
you must watch over everyone God has placed in your care.

I myself am one of your leaders and a witness to the sufferings of Christ.

Do it willingly in order to please God,
  and not simply because you think you must.
Let it be something you want to do,
  instead of something you do merely to make money.

Don't be bossy to those people who are in your care,
but set an example for them.
Then when Christ the Chief Shepherd returns,
you will be given a crown that will never lose its glory.

The word of the Lord.

Responsorial Psalm

Psalm 23:1–3a, 3b–4, 6
(1)

R. The Lord is my shepherd;
there is nothing I shall want.

You, LORD, are my shepherd.
I will never be in need.
You let me rest in fields
of green grass.
You lead me to streams
of peaceful water,
and you refresh my life.

R. The Lord is my shepherd;
there is nothing I shall want.

You are true to your name,
and you lead me
along the right paths.
I may walk through valleys
as dark as death,
but I won't be afraid.
You are with me,
and your shepherd's rod
makes me feel safe.

R. The Lord is my shepherd;
there is nothing I shall want.

Your kindness and love
will always be with me
each day of my life,
and I will live forever
in your house, LORD.

R. The Lord is my shepherd;
there is nothing I shall want.

Alleluia *R. Alleluia, alleluia.*

Matthew 16:18

You are Peter, the rock on which
I will build my Church;
the gates of hell
will not prevail against it.

R. Alleluia, alleluia.

GOSPEL ✚ **A reading from the holy gospel according to Matthew**

Matthew 16:13–19a

You are Peter; and to you I will give the keys of the kingdom of heaven.

When Jesus and his disciples were near the town
of Caesarea Philippi,
he asked them, "What do people say about the Son of Man?"

The disciples answered,
"Some people say you are John the Baptist
or maybe Elijah or Jeremiah or some other prophet."

Then Jesus asked them, "But who do you say I am?"

Simon Peter spoke up,
"You are the Messiah, the Son of the living God."

Jesus told him:
"Simon, son of Jonah, you are blessed!
You didn't discover this on your own.

It was shown to you by my Father in heaven.
So I will call you Peter, which means 'a rock.'
On this rock I will build my Church,
and death itself will not have any power over it.
I will give you the keys to the kingdom of heaven,
and God in heaven will allow whatever you allow on earth."

The gospel of the Lord.

▪ MARCH ▪

265 March 3

BLESSED KATHARINE DREXEL

virgin, religious founder

From the Common of Saints [For Religious; For Those Who Work for the Underprivileged], p. 376.

266 March 4

CASIMIR

From the Common of Saints, p. 376.

267 March 7

PERPETUA AND FELICITY

martyrs

Memorial

From the Common of Martyrs, p. 358.

268 March 8

JOHN OF GOD

religious founder

From the Common of Saints [For Religious; For Those Who Work for the Underprivileged], p. 376.

269 March 9

FRANCES OF ROME

married woman, religious founder

From the Common of Saints [For Religious], p. 376.

270 March 17

PATRICK

bishop, missionary

From the Common of Pastors [For Missionaries], p. 364.

271 March 18

CYRIL OF JERUSALEM

bishop, doctor of the Church

From the Common of Pastors or the Common of Doctors of the Church, p. 364 or 370.

272 March 19

JOSEPH, HUSBAND OF THE VIRGIN MARY

Solemnity

See p. 226.

273 March 23

TORIBIO DE MOGROVEJO
bishop

From the Common of Pastors, p. 364.

274 March 25

THE ANNUNCIATION OF THE LORD
Solemnity

See p. 230.

■

JOSEPH, HUSBAND OF THE VIRGIN MARY

First Reading **A reading from the second book of Samuel**

2 Samuel 7:4–5a, 12–14a, 16

One night, the Lord told Nathan to go to David
and give him this message:

"I'll choose one of your sons to be king
when you reach the end of your life
and are buried near your ancestors.

"I'll make him a strong ruler,
and no one will be able to take his kingdom away from him.

The Lord God will give to him the throne of his father, David (Luke 1:32).

"He will be the one to build a temple for me.
I will be his father,
and he will be my son.

"When he does wrong,
I'll see that he is corrected.
I will make sure that one of your descendants
will always be king."

The word of the Lord.

Responsorial Psalm *R. The son of David will live for ever.*

Psalm 89:1–2, 3–4 (37)

Our LORD, I will sing
of your love forever.
Everyone yet to be born
will hear me praise
your faithfulness.
I will tell them, "God's love
can always be trusted,
and his faithfulness lasts
as long as the heavens."

R. The son of David will live for ever.

You said, "David, my servant,
is my chosen one,
and this is the agreement
I made with him:
David, one of your descendants
will always be king."

R. The son of David will live for ever.

Verse before the Gospel *R. Glory and praise to you,*
Lord Jesus Christ.

Psalm 84:5

Blessed are they who dwell
in your house, O Lord;
they sing your praise without end!

R. Glory and praise to you,
Lord Jesus Christ.

ONE

GOSPEL

✚ A reading from the holy gospel according to Matthew

Matthew 1:16, 18–21, 24a

Jacob was the father of Joseph who was the husband of Mary.
She was the mother of Jesus, who is called the Messiah.

This is how Jesus Christ was born.
A young woman named Mary was engaged to Joseph
from King David's family.
But before they were married,
she learned that she was going to have a baby
by God's Holy Spirit.

Joseph did as the angel of the Lord commanded him.

Joseph was a good man and did not want to embarrass Mary
in front of everyone.
So he decided to quietly call off the wedding.

While Joseph was thinking about this,
an angel from the Lord came to him in a dream.
The angel said, "Joseph, the baby that Mary will have
is from the Holy Spirit.
Go ahead and marry her.
Then after her baby is born, name him Jesus,
because he will save his people from their sins."

After Joseph woke up, he and Mary were soon married.

The gospel of the Lord.

OR

TWO

GOSPEL

Luke 2:41–51

See how your father and I have been in sorrow seeking you.

✚ A reading from the holy gospel according to Luke

Every year Jesus' parents went to Jerusalem for Passover.
And when Jesus was twelve years old,
they all went there as usual for the celebration.

After Passover his parents left,
but they did not know that Jesus had stayed on in the city.
They thought he was traveling with some other people,
and they went a whole day
before they started looking for him.

When they could not find him
with their relatives and friends,
they went back to Jerusalem
and started looking for him there.

Three days later they found Jesus sitting in the temple,
listening to the teachers and asking them questions.
Everyone who heard him was surprised
at how much he knew and at the answers he gave.

When his parents found him, they were amazed.
His mother said, "Son, why have you done this to us?
Your father and I have been very worried,
and we have been searching for you!"

Jesus answered, "Why did you have to look for me?
Didn't you know that I would be in my Father's house?"
But they did not understand what he meant.

Jesus went back to Nazareth with his parents
and obeyed them.

The gospel of the Lord.

THE ANNUNCIATION OF THE LORD

FIRST READING

A reading from the letter of Paul to the Romans

Romans 1:1c–4

God appointed me to preach the good news about his Son, our Lord Jesus Christ.

Brothers and sisters:
God appointed me to preach the good news
that he promised long ago
by what his prophets said in the holy Scriptures.
This good news is about his Son, our Lord Jesus Christ!
As a human, he was from the family of David.
But the Holy Spirit proved
that Jesus is the powerful Son of God,
because he was raised from death.

The word of the Lord.

Responsorial Psalm

Psalm 40:7–8, 9 (8a and 9a)

R. Here am I, Lord;
I come to do your will.

I said, "I am here
to do what is written
about me in the book,
where it says,
'I enjoy pleasing you.
Your Law is in my heart.'"

R. Here am I, Lord;
I come to do your will.

When your people worshiped,
you know I told them,
"Our LORD always helps!"

R. Here am I, Lord;
I come to do your will.

Verse before the Gospel

John 1:14ab

R. Glory and praise to you,
Lord Jesus Christ.

The Word of God became flesh
and dwelt among us;
and we saw his glory.

R. Glory and praise to you,
Lord Jesus Christ.

GOSPEL **✚ A reading from the holy gospel according to Luke**

Luke 1:26–38

God sent the angel Gabriel to the town of Nazareth
in Galilee with a message for a virgin named Mary.
She was engaged to Joseph from the family of King David.
The angel greeted Mary and said,
"You are truly blessed! The Lord is with you."

Mary was confused by the angel's words
and wondered what they meant.

You will conceive and bear a son.

Then the angel told Mary, "Don't be afraid!
God is pleased with you, and you will have a son.
His name will be Jesus.
He will be great and will be called the Son of God.
The Lord God will make him king,
as his ancestor David was.
He will rule the people of Israel forever,
and his kingdom will never end."

Mary asked the angel, "How can this happen?
I am not married!"

The angel answered,
"The Holy Spirit will come down to you,
and God's power will come over you.
So your child will be called the holy Son of God.

"Your relative Elizabeth is also going to have a son,
even though she is old.
No one thought she could ever have a baby,
but in three months she will have a son.
Nothing is impossible for God!"

Mary said, "I am the Lord's servant!
Let it happen as you have said."

And the angel left her.

The gospel of the Lord.

▪ APRIL ▪

275 April 2

FRANCIS OF PAOLA

hermit, religious founder

From the Common of Saints [For Religious], p. 376.

276 April 4

ISIDORE OF SEVILLE

bishop, doctor of the Church

From the Common of Pastors or the Common of Doctors of the Church, p. 364 or 370.

277 April 5

VINCENT FERRER

presbyter, religious, missionary

From the Common of Pastors [For Missionaries], p. 364.

278 April 7

JOHN BAPTIST DE LA SALLE

presbyter, religious founder

Memorial

From the Common of Pastors or the Common of Saints [For Educators], p. 364 or 376.

279 April 11

STANISLAUS

bishop, martyr

Memorial

From the Common of Martyrs or the Common of Pastors, p. 358 or 364.

280 April 13

MARTIN I

pope, martyr

From the Common of Martyrs or the Common of Pastors [For a Pope], p. 358 or 364.

281 April 21

ANSELM

bishop, religious,
doctor of the Church

From the Common of Pastors or the Common of Doctors of the Church, p. 364 or 370.

282 April 23

GEORGE

martyr

From the Common of Martyrs, p. 358.

283 April 24

FIDELIS OF SIGMARINGEN

presbyter, religious, martyr

From the Common of Martyrs or the Common of Pastors, p. 358 or 364.

284 April 25

MARK

evangelist

Feast

See p. 236.

285 April 28

PETER CHANEL

presbyter, religious, missionary, martyr

From the Common of Martyrs or the Common of Pastors [For Missionaries], p. 358 or 364.

286 April 29

CATHERINE OF SIENA

virgin, doctor of the Church

Memorial

From the Common of Saints or the Common of Doctors of the Church, p. 376 or 370.

287 April 30

PIUS V

pope, religious

From the Common of Pastors [For a Pope], p. 364.

MARK

First Reading | **A reading from the first letter of Peter**

1 Peter 5:12–14

Brothers and sisters:
Silvanus helped me write this short letter,
and I consider him a faithful follower of the Lord.
I wanted to encourage you
and tell you how kind God really is,
so that you will keep on having faith in him.

My son, Mark, sends you greetings.

Greetings from the Lord's followers in Babylon.
They are God's chosen ones.

Mark, who is like a son to me, sends his greetings too.

Give each other a warm greeting.
I pray that God will give peace to everyone
who belongs to Christ.

The word of the Lord.

Responsorial Psalm

Psalm 89:1 and 5, 15–16 (2a)

R. For ever I will sing the goodness
of the Lord.

Our LORD, I will sing
of your love forever.
Everyone yet to be born
will hear me praise
your faithfulness.
Our LORD, let the heavens
now praise your miracles,
and let all of your angels
praise your faithfulness.

R. For ever I will sing the goodness
of the Lord.

Our LORD, you bless those
who join in the festival
and walk in the brightness
of your presence.
We are happy all day
because of you,
and your saving power
brings honor to us.

R. For ever I will sing the goodness
of the Lord.

Alleluia *R. Alleluia, alleluia.*

1 Corinthians 1:23a, 24b

We preach a Christ who was crucified;
he is the power and wisdom of God.

R. Alleluia, alleluia.

GOSPEL ✚ **A reading from the holy gospel according to Mark**

Mark 16:15–20

Jesus told his disciples:
"Go and preach the good news to everyone in the world.
Anyone who believes me and is baptized will be saved.
But anyone who refuses to believe me will be condemned.

"Everyone who believes me will be able
to do wonderful things.
By using my name they will force out demons,
and they will speak new languages.
They will handle snakes and will drink poison
and not be hurt.
They will also heal sick people
by placing their hands on them."

Tell the good news to all the world.

After the Lord Jesus had said these things to the disciples,
he was taken back up to heaven
where he sat down at the right side of God.
Then the disciples left and preached everywhere.
The Lord was with them,
and the miracles they worked
proved that their message was true.

The gospel of the Lord.

MARK

▪ MAY ▪

288 May 1

JOSEPH THE WORKER

See p. 242.

289 May 2

ATHANASIUS

bishop, doctor of the Church

Memorial

From the Common of Pastors or the Common of Doctors of the Church, p. 364 or 370.

290 May 3

PHILIP AND JAMES

apostles

Feast

From the Common of Apostles, p. 354.

291 May 12

NEREUS AND ACHILLEUS

martyrs

From the Common of Martyrs, p. 358.

292 **PANCRAS**

martyr

From the Common of Martyrs, p. 358.

293 May 14

MATTHIAS

apostle

Feast

See p. 246.

294 May 15

ISIDORE THE FARMER

married man

From the Common of Saints, p. 376.

295 May 18

JOHN I

pope, martyr

From the Common of Martyrs or the Common of Pastors [For a Pope], p. 358 or 364.

296 May 20

BERNARDINE OF SIENA

presbyter, religious, missionary

From the Common of Pastors [For Missionaries], p. 364.

297 May 25

BEDE THE VENERABLE

presbyter, religious,
doctor of the Church

From the Common of Pastors or the Common of Doctors of the Church, p. 364 or 370.

298 May 25, continued

GREGORY VII
pope, religious

From the Common of Pastors [For a Pope], p. 364.

299 **MARY MAGDALENE DE' PAZZI**
virgin, religious

From the Common of Saints [For Religious], p. 376.

300 May 26

PHILIP NERI
presbyter

Memorial

From the Common of Pastors or the Common of Saints [For Religious], p. 364 or 376.

301 May 27

AUGUSTINE OF CANTERBURY
bishop, religious, missionary

From the Common of Pastors [For Missionaries], p. 364.

302 May 31

THE VISIT OF THE VIRGIN MARY TO ELIZABETH

Feast

See p. 248.

303 (Saturday following the Second Sunday after Pentecost)

THE IMMACULATE HEART OF MARY

See p. 254.

JOSEPH THE WORKER

The gospel for this optional memorial is proper.

ONE

First Reading **A reading from the book of Genesis**

Genesis 1:26—2:3

God said, "Now we will make humans.
We will use ourselves as a pattern,
and they will be like us.
We will let them rule over fish, birds, animals,
and everything that crawls on the earth."

So God used himself as a pattern and made men and women.
He gave them his blessing and said, "Have a lot of children!
Fill the earth and subdue it. Fill the earth with people and bring it under your control.
Rule over the fish in the sea, the birds in the sky,
and all the living things that crawl on the earth."

God told the men and women,
"I have provided all kinds of grain and fruit for you to eat.
And I have given the green plants
as food for everything else that breathes.
These plants will be food for the wild animals, for the birds,
and for everything that crawls on the earth."

God looked at what he had done.
All of it was very good!

Evening and morning came,
and that was the end of the sixth day.

So heaven and earth and everything else was created.

On the seventh day God stopped working and rested.
God blessed the seventh day and made it special,
because on that day he had rested from all his work.

The word of the Lord.

OR

TWO

FIRST READING

Colossians 3:17, 23–24

Whatever the task,
do it with all your heart,
as serving the Lord
and not any human master.

A reading from the letter of Paul to the Colossians

Brothers and sisters:
Whatever you say or do should be done
in the name of the Lord Jesus,
as you give thanks to God the Father because of him.

Do your work willingly,
as though you were serving the Lord himself,
and not just your earthly master.
In fact, the Lord Christ is the one you are really serving,
and you know that he will reward you.

The word of the Lord.

Responsorial Psalm

Psalm 90:2, 14 and 16 (17c)

*R. Lord, give success to the work
of our hands.*

*Our Lord, you have always been God—
long before the birth
of the mountains,
even before you created
the earth and the world.*

*R. Lord, give success to the work
of our hands.*

*When morning comes,
let your love satisfy
all our needs.
Then we can celebrate
and be glad for what time
we have left.
Do wonderful things for us,
your servants,
and show your mighty power
to our children.*

*R. Lord, give success to the work
of our hands.*

Alleluia *R. Alleluia, alleluia.*

Psalm 68:20 *Blessed be the Lord day after day,*
the God who saves us
and bears our burdens.

R. Alleluia, alleluia.

✚ A reading from the holy gospel according to Matthew

GOSPEL

Matthew 13:54–58

Jesus went to his hometown.
He taught in their meeting place,
and the people were so amazed that they asked,

"Where does he get all this wisdom
and the power to work these miracles?
Isn't he the son of the carpenter?
Isn't Mary his mother,
and aren't James, Joseph, Simon, and Judas his brothers?
Don't his sisters still live here in our town?
How can he do all this?"

Is this not the son of the carpenter?

So the people were very unhappy
because of what he was doing.

But Jesus said, "Prophets are honored by everyone,
except the people of their hometown
and their own family."
And because the people did not have any faith,
Jesus did not work many miracles there.

The gospel of the Lord.

293

MATTHIAS

From the Common of Apostles, p. 354, except:

First Reading **A reading from the Acts of the Apostles**

Acts 1:15–17, 20a, 20c–26

The lot fell to Matthias, and he was numbered with the eleven apostles.

One day there were about a hundred and twenty
of the Lord's followers meeting together,
and Peter stood up to speak to them.

He said:
"My friends, long ago by the power of the Holy Spirit,
David said something about Judas,
and what he said has now happened.
Judas was one of us and had worked with us,
but he brought the mob to arrest Jesus.
In the book of Psalms David said,
'Leave his house empty.'

"It also says, 'Let someone else have his job.'

"So we need someone else to help us tell others
that Jesus has been raised from death.
He must also be one of the men
who was with us from the very beginning.
He must have been with us
from the time the Lord Jesus was baptized by John
until the day he was taken to heaven."

Two men were suggested:
One of them was Joseph Barsabbas, known as Justus,
and the other was Matthias.
Then they all prayed,
"Lord, you know what everyone is like!
Show us the one you have chosen to be an apostle
and to serve in place of Judas,
who got what he deserved."
They drew names,
and Matthias was chosen to join the group
of the eleven apostles.

The word of the Lord.

ONE

FIRST READING

A reading from the book of the prophet Zephaniah

Zephaniah 3:17–18a

The Lord, the King of Israel, is among you.

The LORD your God wins victory after victory,
and he is with you.
He celebrates and rejoices because of you,
and he will silently show you his love.

The LORD has promised,
"Your festivals will no longer be a time of sorrow."

The word of the Lord.

OR

TWO

A reading from the letter of Paul to the Romans

FIRST READING

Romans 12:9–16b

Brothers and sisters:
Be sincere in your love for others.
Hate everything that is evil
and hold tight to everything that is good.
Love each other as brothers and sisters
and honor others more than you do yourself.

Never give up.
Eagerly follow the Holy Spirit and serve the Lord.
Let your hope make you glad.
Be patient in time of trouble and never stop praying.

Contribute to the needs of God's people, and practice hospitality.

Take care of God's needy people
and welcome strangers into your home.

Ask God to bless everyone who mistreats you.
Ask him to bless them and not to curse them.
When others are happy, be happy with them,
and when they are sad, be sad.
Be friendly with everyone.
Don't be proud and feel that you are smarter than others.

The word of the Lord.

Responsorial Psalm

Isaiah 12:2, 4, 5–6 (6b)

R. Among you is the great
and Holy One of Israel.

I trust the LORD *to save me,*
and I won't be afraid.
My power and my strength
come from the LORD *God,*
and he has saved me.

R. Among you is the great
and Holy One of Israel.

On that day you will say,
"Our LORD*, we are thankful,*
and we worship only you.
We will tell the nations
how glorious you are
and what you have done."

R. Among you is the great
and Holy One of Israel.

"We will sing your praises everywhere
because of your wonderful deeds."
People of Jerusalem, celebrate and sing.
The famous LORD *God of Israel*
is here with you.

R. Among you is the great
and Holy One of Israel.

Alleluia *R. Alleluia, alleluia.*

See Luke 1:45 *Blessed are you, O Virgin Mary,*
for your firm believing
that the promises of the Lord
would be fulfilled.

R. Alleluia, alleluia.

GOSPEL

✚ A reading from the holy gospel according to Luke

Luke 1:39–56

Mary hurried to a town in the hill country of Judea.
She went to Zechariah's home,
where she greeted Elizabeth.
When Elizabeth heard Mary's greeting,
her baby moved within her.

Why should I be honored with a visit from the mother of my Lord?

The Holy Spirit came upon Elizabeth.
Then in a loud voice she said to Mary:
"God has blessed you more than any other woman!
He has also blessed the child you will have.
Why should the mother of my Lord come to me?
As soon as I heard your greeting,
my baby became happy and moved within me.
The Lord has blessed you
because you believed that he will keep his promise."

continued

Mary said:
"With all my heart I praise the Lord,
and I am glad because of God my Savior.
He cares for me, his humble servant.
From now on, all people will say God has blessed me.
God All-Powerful has done great things for me,
and his name is holy.

"He always shows mercy to everyone who worships him.
The Lord has used his powerful arm
to scatter those who are proud.
He drags strong rulers from their thrones
and puts humble people in places of power.
He gives the hungry good things to eat,
and he sends the rich away with nothing in their hands.
He helps his servant Israel
and is always merciful to his people.
He made this promise to our ancestors,
to Abraham and his family forever!"

Mary stayed with Elizabeth about three months.
Then she went back home.

The gospel of the Lord.

303

THE IMMACULATE HEART OF MARY

The gospel for this optional memorial is proper.
From the Common of the Blessed Virgin Mary, p. 346, except:

GOSPEL

✚ A reading from the holy gospel according to Luke

Luke 2:41–51

Mary treasured all these things in her heart.

Every year Jesus' parents went to Jerusalem for Passover.
And when Jesus was twelve years old,
they all went there as usual for the celebration.

After Passover his parents left,
but they did not know that Jesus had stayed on in the city.
They thought he was traveling with some other people,
and they went a whole day
before they started looking for him.

When they could not find him
with their relatives and friends,
they went back to Jerusalem
and started looking for him there.

Three days later they found Jesus sitting in the temple,
listening to the teachers and asking them questions.
Everyone who heard him was surprised
at how much he knew and at the answers he gave.

When his parents found him, they were amazed.
His mother said, "Son, why have you done this to us?
Your father and I have been very worried,
and we have been searching for you!"

Jesus answered, "Why did you have to look for me?
Didn't you know that I would be in my Father's house?"
But they did not understand what he meant.

Jesus went back to Nazareth with his parents
and obeyed them.

The gospel of the Lord.

▪ JUNE ▪

304 June 1

JUSTIN

martyr

Memorial

From the Common of Martyrs, p. 358.

305 June 2

MARCELLINUS AND PETER

martyrs

From the Common of Martyrs, p. 358.

306 June 3

CHARLES LWANGA

catechist, martyr, and his

COMPANIONS, martyrs

Memorial

From the Common of Martyrs, p. 358.

307 June 5

BONIFACE

bishop, religious, missionary, martyr

Memorial

From the Common of Martyrs or the Common of Pastors [For Missionaries], p. 358 or 364.

308 June 6

NORBERT

bishop, religious founder

From the Common of Pastors or the Common of Saints [For Religious], p. 364 or 376.

309 June 9

EPHREM OF SYRIA

deacon, doctor of the Church

From the Common of Doctors of the Church, p. 370.

310 June 11

BARNABAS

apostle

Memorial

See p. 258.

311 June 13

ANTHONY OF PADUA

presbyter, religious, doctor of the Church

Memorial

From the Common of Pastors or the Common of Doctors of the Church or the Common of Saints [For Religious], p. 364, or 370, or 376.

312 June 19

ROMUALD

abbot, religious founder

From the Common of Saints [For Religious], p. 376.

313 June 21

ALOYSIUS GONZAGA

religious

Memorial

From the Common of Saints [For Religious], p. 376.

314 June 22

PAULINUS OF NOLA
bishop

From the Common of Pastors, p. 364.

315 **JOHN FISHER**
bishop, martyr, and **THOMAS MORE,** married man, martyr

From the Common of Martyrs, p. 358.

316 June 24

THE BIRTH OF JOHN THE BAPTIST

Solemnity

See p. 260.

317 June 27

CYRIL OF ALEXANDRIA
bishop, doctor of the Church

From the Common of Pastors or the Common of Doctors of the Church, p. 364 or 370.

318 June 28

IRENAEUS
bishop, martyr

Memorial

From the Common of Martyrs or the Common of Doctors of the Church, p. 358 or 370.

319 June 29

PETER AND PAUL
apostles

Solemnity

See p. 264.

320 June 30

FIRST MARTYRS OF THE CHURCH OF ROME

From the Common of Martyrs, p. 358.

■

BARNABAS

The first reading for this memorial is proper.
From the Common of Apostles, p. 354, except:

First Reading **A reading from the Acts of the Apostles**

Acts 11:21–26; 13:1–3

The Lord's power was with the followers of Jesus,
and many people turned to the Lord
and put their faith in him.

News of what was happening reached the church
in Jerusalem.
Then they sent Barnabas to Antioch.

Barnabas was a good man, filled with the Holy Spirit and with faith.

When Barnabas got there
and saw what God had been kind enough to do for them,
he was very glad.
So he begged them to remain faithful to the Lord
with all their hearts.

Barnabas was a good man of great faith,
and he was filled with the Holy Spirit.
Many more people turned to the Lord.

Barnabas went to Tarsus to look for Saul.
He found Saul and brought him to Antioch,
where they met with the church for a whole year
and taught many of its people.
There in Antioch the Lord's followers
were first called Christians.

The church at Antioch had several prophets and teachers.
They were Barnabas, Simeon, also called Niger,
Lucius from Cyrene,
Manaen, who was Herod's close friend, and Saul.

While they were worshiping the Lord
and going without eating,
the Holy Spirit told them,
"Appoint Barnabas and Saul to do the work
for which I have chosen them."

Everyone prayed and went without eating for a while longer.
Next, they placed their hands on Barnabas and Saul
to show that they had been appointed to this work.
Then everyone sent them on their way.

The word of the Lord.

THE BIRTH OF JOHN THE BAPTIST

FIRST READING

A reading from the book of the prophet Jeremiah

Jeremiah 1:4–8

The LORD said to Jeremiah,
"Before I gave you life,
and before you were born,
I chose you to be a prophet to the nations."

Before I formed you in the womb, I knew you.

Jeremiah replied,
"LORD God, how can I speak for you? I'm too young."

The LORD answered, "Don't say you're too young.
Go to everyone I send you to
and tell them everything I command you.
Don't be afraid of them!
I, the LORD, will be with you to keep you safe."

The word of the Lord.

Responsorial Psalm

Psalm 139:1–3, 13–14abc, 14de–15 (14a)

R. I praise you
for I am wonderfully made.

You have looked deep
into my heart, LORD,
and you know all about me.
You know when I am resting
or when I am working,
and from heaven
you discover my thoughts.
You notice everything I do
and everywhere I go.

R. I praise you
for I am wonderfully made.

You are the one
who put me together
inside my mother's body,
and I praise you
because of the wonderful way
you created me.

R. I praise you
for I am wonderfully made.

Everything you do is marvelous!
Of this I have no doubt.
Nothing about me
is hidden from you!
I was secretly woven together
deep in the earth below.

R. I praise you
for I am wonderfully made.

Alleluia

R. Alleluia, alleluia.

See Luke 1:76

You, child, shall be called
the prophet of the Most High,
for you will go before the Lord
to prepare his way.

R. Alleluia, alleluia.

GOSPEL

✠ A reading from the holy gospel according to Luke

Luke 1:5–17

A son is born to you and you will name him John.

When Herod was king of Judea,
there was a priest by the name of Zechariah
from the priestly group of Abijah.
His wife Elizabeth was from the family of Aaron.
Both of them were good people and pleased the Lord God
by obeying all that he had commanded.
But they did not have children.
Elizabeth could not have any,
and both Zechariah and Elizabeth were already old.

One day Zechariah's group of priests were on duty,
and he was serving God as a priest.
According to the custom of the priests,
he had been chosen to go into the Lord's temple that day
and to burn incense,
while the people stood outside praying.

All at once an angel from the Lord came
and appeared to Zechariah at the right side of the altar.
Zechariah was confused and afraid when he saw the angel.
But the angel told him: "Don't be afraid, Zechariah!
God has heard your prayers.
Your wife Elizabeth will have a son,
and you must name him John.
His birth will make you very happy,
and many people will be glad.
Your son will be a great servant of the Lord.
He must never drink wine or beer,
and the power of the Holy Spirit will be with him
from the time he is born.

"John will lead many people in Israel
to turn back to the Lord their God.
He will go ahead of the Lord
with the same power and spirit that Elijah had.
And because of John,
parents will be more thoughtful of their children.
And people who now disobey God
will begin to think as they ought to.
That is how John will get people ready for the Lord."

The gospel of the Lord.

PETER AND PAUL

FIRST READING **A reading from the Acts of the Apostles**

Acts 12:1–11

Now I know it is indeed true: the Lord has saved me from the power of Herod.

King Herod caused terrible suffering for some members of the church.
He ordered soldiers to cut off the head of James, the brother of John.
When Herod saw that this pleased the Jewish people,
he had Peter arrested during the Feast of Thin Bread.
He put Peter in jail and ordered four squads of soldiers to guard him.
Herod planned to put him on trial in public after the feast.

While Peter was being kept in jail,
the church never stopped praying to God for him.

The night before Peter was to be put on trial,
he was asleep and bound by two chains.
A soldier was guarding him on each side,
and two other soldiers were guarding the entrance to the jail.
Suddenly an angel from the Lord appeared,
and light flashed around in the cell.
The angel poked Peter in the side and woke him up.
Then he said, "Quick! Get up!"

The chains fell off his hands, and the angel said,
"Get dressed and put on your sandals."
Peter did what he was told.
Then the angel said, "Now put on your coat and follow me."
Peter left with the angel,
but he thought everything was only a dream.
They went past the two groups of soldiers,
and when they came to the iron gate to the city,
it opened by itself.
They went out and were going along the street,
when all at once the angel disappeared.

Peter now realized what had happened, and he said,
"I am certain that the Lord sent his angel
to rescue me from Herod
and from everything the Jewish leaders planned
to do to me."

The word of the Lord.

Responsorial Psalm

Psalm 34:3–4, 5–6, 7–8 (5b)

R. The Lord set me free from all my fears.

Honor the LORD with me!
Celebrate his great name.
I asked the LORD for help,
and he saved me
from all my fears.

R. The Lord set me free from all my fears.

Keep your eyes on the LORD!
You will shine like the sun
and never blush with shame.
I was a nobody, but I prayed,
and the LORD saved me
from all my troubles.

R. The Lord set me free from all my fears.

If you honor the LORD,
his angel will protect you.
Discover for yourself
that the LORD is kind.
Come to him for protection,
and you will be glad.

R. The Lord set me free from all my fears.

SECOND READING

A reading from the second letter of Paul to Timothy

2 Timothy 4:17–18

The Lord will bring me safely into his heavenly kingdom.

The Lord stood beside me.
He gave me the strength to tell his full message,
so that all Gentiles would hear it.
And I was kept safe from hungry lions.

The Lord will always keep me from being harmed by evil,
and he will bring me safely into his heavenly kingdom.
Praise him forever and ever! Amen.

The word of the Lord.

Alleluia *R. Alleluia, alleluia.*

Matthew 16:18

You are Peter, the rock on which
I will build my Church;
the gates of hell
will not prevail against it.

R. Alleluia, alleluia.

Gospel

Matthew 16:13–19

You are Peter; to you I will give the keys of the kingdom of heaven.

✚ A reading from the holy gospel according to Matthew

When Jesus and his disciples were near the town
of Caesarea Philippi,
he asked them, "What do people say about the Son of Man?"

The disciples answered,
"Some people say you are John the Baptist
or maybe Elijah or Jeremiah or some other prophet."

Then Jesus asked them, "But who do you say I am?"

Simon Peter spoke up,
"You are the Messiah, the Son of the living God."

Jesus told him:
"Simon, son of Jonah, you are blessed!
You didn't discover this on your own.
It was shown to you by my Father in heaven.
So I will call you Peter, which means 'a rock.'
On this rock I will build my Church,
and death itself will not have any power over it.
I will give you the keys to the kingdom of heaven,
and God in heaven will allow whatever you allow on earth.
But he will not allow anything that you don't allow."

The gospel of the Lord.

▪ JULY ▪

321 July 1
BLESSED JUNÍPERO SERRA
presbyter, religious, missionary

From the Common of Pastors [For Missionaries] or the Common of Saints [For Religious], p. 364 or 376.

322 July 3
THOMAS
apostle

Feast

See p. 270.

323 July 4
ELIZABETH OF PORTUGAL
married woman

From the Common of Saints [For Those Who Work for the Underprivileged], p. 376.

324 **INDEPENDENCE DAY**

Mass For Peace and Justice, p. 458.

325 July 5
ANTHONY MARY ZACCARIA
presbyter, religious founder

From the Common of Pastors or the Common of Saints [For Educators or For Religious], p. 364 or 376.

326 July 6
MARIA GORETTI
virgin, martyr

From the Common of Martyrs or the Common of Saints, p. 358 or 376.

327 July 11
BENEDICT
abbot, religious founder

Memorial

From the Common of Saints [For Religious], p. 376.

328 July 13
HENRY
married man

From the Common of Saints, p. 376.

329 July 14
BLESSED KATERI TEKAKWITHA
virgin

Memorial

From the Common of Saints, p. 376.

330 July 15
BONAVENTURE
bishop, religious, doctor of the Church

Memorial

From the Common of Pastors or the Common of Doctors of the Church, p. 364 or 370.

331 July 16

OUR LADY OF MOUNT CARMEL

From the Common of the Blessed Virgin Mary, p. 346.

332 July 21

LAWRENCE OF BRINDISI

presbyter, religious, doctor of the Church

From the Common of Pastors or the Common of Doctors of the Church, p. 364 or 370.

333 July 22

MARY MAGDALENE

disciple of the Lord

Memorial

See p. 272.

334 July 23

BRIDGET OF SWEDEN

married woman, religious founder

From the Common of Saints [For Religious], p. 376.

335 July 25

JAMES

apostle

From the Common of Apostles, p. 354.

336 July 26

JOACHIM AND ANN

parents of the Virgin Mary

Memorial

From the Common of Saints, p. 376.

337 July 29

MARTHA

disciple of the Lord

Memorial

See p. 274.

338 July 30

PETER CHRYSOLOGUS

bishop, doctor of the Church

From the Common of Pastors or the Common of Doctors of the Church, p. 364 or 370.

339 July 31

IGNATIUS OF LOYOLA

presbyter, religious founder

Memorial

From the Common of Pastors or the Common of Saints [For Religious], p. 364 or 376.

■

THOMAS

From the Common of Apostles, p. 354, except:

GOSPEL **✚ A reading from the holy gospel according to John**

John 20:24–29

Although Thomas the Twin was one of the twelve disciples,
he was not with the others when Jesus appeared to them.
So they told him, "We have seen the Lord!"

But Thomas said, "First, I must see the nail scars
in his hands and touch them with my finger.
I must put my hand where the spear went into his side.
I won't believe unless I do this!"

My Lord and my God.

A week later the disciples were together again.
This time Thomas was with them.
Jesus came in while the doors were still locked
and stood in the middle of the group.
He greeted his disciples and said to Thomas,
"Put your finger here and look at my hands!
Put your hand into my side.
Stop doubting and have faith!"

Thomas replied, "You are my Lord and my God!"

Jesus said, "Thomas, do you have faith
because you have seen me?
The people who have faith in me without seeing me
are the ones who are really blessed!"

The gospel of the Lord.

333

MARY MAGDALENE

The gospel for this memorial is proper.
From the Common of Saints, p. 376, except:

GOSPEL

✚ A reading from the holy gospel according to John

John 20:1–2, 11–18

On Sunday morning while it was still dark,
Mary Magdalene went to the tomb
and saw that the stone had been rolled away
from the entrance.
She ran to Simon Peter and to Jesus' favorite disciple
and said,
"They have taken the Lord from the tomb!
We don't know where they have put him."

Woman, why are you weeping? Whom are you seeking?

Mary Magdalene stood crying outside the tomb.
She was still weeping, when she stooped down
and saw two angels inside.
They were dressed in white
and were sitting where Jesus' body had been.
One was at the head and the other was at the foot.

The angels asked Mary, "Why are you crying?"

She answered, "They have taken away my Lord's body!
I don't know where they have put him."

As soon as Mary said this,
she turned around and saw Jesus standing there.
But she did not know who he was.
Jesus asked her, "Why are you crying?
Who are you looking for?"

She thought he was the gardener and said,
"Sir, if you have taken his body away,
please tell me, so I can go and get him."

Then Jesus said to her, "Mary!"

She turned and said to him, "Rabboni."
The Aramaic word "Rabboni" means "Teacher."

Jesus told her, "Don't hold on to me!
I have not yet gone to the Father.
But tell my disciples that I am going to the one
  who is my Father and my God,
  as well as your Father and your God."
Mary Magdalene then went and told the disciples
  that she had seen the Lord.
She also told them what he had said to her.

The gospel of the Lord.

337

MARTHA

The gospel for this memorial is proper.
From the Common of Saints, p. 376, except:

GOSPEL **✚ A reading from the holy gospel according to John**

John 11:17–27

When Jesus got to Bethany,
he found that Lazarus had already been in the tomb
four days.
Bethany was only about two miles from Jerusalem,
and many people had come from the city
to comfort Martha and Mary
because their brother had died.

I believed that you are the Christ, the Son of the living God.

When Martha had heard that Jesus had arrived,
she went out to meet him,
but Mary stayed in the house.
Martha said to Jesus, "Lord, if you had been here,
my brother would not have died.
Yet even now I know that God will do anything you ask."

Jesus told her, "Your brother will live again!"

Martha answered,
"I know that he will be raised to life on the last day,
when all the dead are raised."

Jesus then said,
"I am the one who raises the dead to life!
Everyone who has faith in me will live,
even if they die.
And everyone who lives because of faith in me
will never die.
Do you believe this?"

"Yes, Lord!" she replied.
"I believe that you are Christ, the Son of God.
You are the one we hoped would come into the world."

The gospel of the Lord.

▪ AUGUST ▪

340 August 1

ALPHONSUS LIGOURI

bishop, religious founder, doctor of the Church

Memorial

From the Common of Pastors or the Common of Doctors of the Church, p. 364 or 370.

341 August 2

EUSEBIUS OF VERCELLI

bishop

From the Common of Pastors, p. 364.

342 August 4

JOHN MARY VIANNEY

presbyter

Memorial

From the Common of Pastors, p. 364.

343 August 5

THE DEDICATION OF THE BASILICA OF SAINT MARY IN ROME

From the Common of the Blessed Virgin Mary, p. 346.

344 August 6

THE TRANSFIGURATION OF THE LORD

Feast

See p. 280.

345 August 7

SIXTUS II,

pope, martyr, and his

COMPANIONS, martyrs

From the Common of Martyrs, p. 358.

346 **CAJETAN**

presbyter, religious founder

From the Common of Pastors or the Common of Saints [For Religious], p. 364 or 376.

347 August 8

DOMINIC

presbyter, religious founder

Memorial

From the Common of Pastors [For Missionaries] or the Common of Saints [For Religious], p. 364 or 376.

348 August 10
LAWRENCE
deacon, martyr
Feast

From the Common of Martyrs, p. 358.

349 August 11
CLARE
virgin, religious founder
Memorial

From the Common of Saints [For Religious], p. 376.

350 August 13
PONTIAN,
pope, martyr, and
HIPPOLYTUS,
presbyter, martyr

From the Common of Martyrs or the Common of Pastors, p. 358 or 364.

351 August 14
MAXIMILIAN MARY KOLBE
presbyter, religious, martyr
Memorial

From the Common of Martyrs or the Common of Pastors, p. 358 or 364.

352 August 15
THE ASSUMPTION OF THE VIRGIN MARY INTO HEAVEN
Solemnity

See p. 286.

353 August 16
STEPHEN OF HUNGARY
married man

From the Common of Saints, p. 376.

354 August 18
JANE FRANCES DE CHANTAL
married woman, religious founder

From the Common of Saints [For Religious], p. 376.

355 August 19
JOHN EUDES
presbyter, religious founder

From the Common of Pastors or the Common of Saints, p. 364 or 376.

356 August 20

BERNARD

abbot, doctor of the Church

Memorial

From the Common of Doctors of the Church or the Common of Saints [For Religious], p. 370 or 376.

357 August 21

PIUS X

pope

Memorial

From the Common of Pastors [For a Pope], p. 364.

358 August 22

THE QUEENSHIP OF THE VIRGIN MARY

Memorial

From the Common of the Blessed Virgin Mary, p. 346.

359 August 23

ROSE OF LIMA

virgin

From the Common of Saints [For Religious], p. 376.

360 August 24

BARTHOLOMEW

apostle

Feast

From the Common of Apostles, p. 354.

361 August 25

LOUIS OF FRANCE

married man

From the Common of Saints, p. 376.

362 **JOSEPH CALASANZ**

presbyter, religious founder

From the Common of Pastors or the Common of Saints [For Religious], p. 364 or 376.

363 August 27

MONICA

married woman

Memorial

From the Common of Saints, p. 376.

364 August 28

AUGUSTINE
bishop, doctor of the Church

Memorial

From the Common of Pastors or the Common of Doctors of the Church, p. 364 or 370.

365 August 29

THE MARTYRDOM OF JOHN THE BAPTIST

Memorial

See p. 288.

■

THE TRANSFIGURATION OF THE LORD

FIRST READING **A reading from the second letter of Peter**

2 Peter 1:16–19

Brothers and sisters:
When we told you about the power
and the return of our Lord Jesus Christ,
we were not telling clever stories
that someone had made up.
But with our own eyes we saw his true greatness.

We heard this voice from out of heaven.

God, our great and wonderful Father,
truly honored him by saying,
"This is my own dear Son, and I am pleased with him."
We were there with Jesus on the holy mountain
and heard this voice speak from heaven.

All of this makes us even more certain
that what the prophets said is true.
So you should pay close attention to their message,
as you would to a lamp shining in some dark place.
You must keep on paying attention until daylight comes
and the morning star rises in your hearts.

The word of the Lord.

Responsorial Psalm

Psalm 97:1–2, 5–6, 9 (1a and 9a)

R. The Lord is king,
the most high over all the earth.

The LORD is King!
Tell the earth to celebrate
and all islands to shout.
Dark clouds surround him,
and his throne is supported
by justice and fairness.

R. The Lord is king,
the most high over all the earth.

Mountains melt away like wax
in the presence of the LORD
of all the earth.
The heavens announce,
"The LORD brings justice!"
Everyone sees God's glory.

R. The Lord is king,
the most high over all the earth.

The LORD rules the whole earth,
and he is more glorious
than all the false gods.

R. The Lord is king,
the most high over all the earth.

Alleluia

Matthew 17:5c

R. Alleluia, alleluia.

This is my beloved Son,
in whom is all my delight;
hear him.

R. Alleluia, alleluia.

YEAR A

GOSPEL ✚ **A reading from the holy gospel according to Matthew**

Matthew 17:1–9

Jesus took Peter and the brothers James and John with him.
They went up on a very high mountain
where they could be alone.
There in front of the disciples Jesus was completely changed.
His face was shining like the sun,
and his clothes became white as light.

Jesus' face shone like the sun.

All at once Moses and Elijah were there talking with Jesus.
So Peter said to him, "Lord, it is good for us to be here!
Let us make three shelters,
one for you, one for Moses, and one for Elijah."

While Peter was still speaking,
the shadow of a bright cloud passed over them.
From the cloud a voice said,
"This is my own dear Son, and I am pleased with him.
Listen to what he says!"

When the disciples heard the voice,
they were so afraid that they fell flat on the ground.
But Jesus came over and touched them.
He said, "Get up and don't be afraid!"
When they opened their eyes, they saw only Jesus.

On their way down from the mountain,
Jesus warned his disciples not to tell anyone
what they had seen
until after the Son of Man had been raised from death.

The gospel of the Lord.

YEAR B

✚ A reading from the holy gospel according to Mark

GOSPEL

Mark 9:2–10

Jesus took Peter, James, and John with him.
They went up on a high mountain,
  where they could be alone.
There in front of the disciples,
Jesus was completely changed.
And his clothes became much whiter
  than any bleach on earth could make them.
Then Moses and Elijah were there talking with Jesus.

This is my beloved Son.

Peter said to Jesus, "Teacher, it is good for us to be here!
Let us make three shelters,
  one for you, one for Moses, and one for Elijah."
But Peter and the others were terribly frightened,
and he did not know what he was talking about.

The shadow of a cloud passed over and covered them.
From the cloud a voice said, "This is my Son, and I love him.
Listen to what he says!"
At once the disciples looked around,
but they saw only Jesus.

As Jesus and his disciples were coming down the mountain,
he told them not to say a word about what they had seen,
until the Son of Man had been raised from death.
So they kept it to themselves.
But they wondered what he meant by the words
  "raised from death."

The gospel of the Lord.

YEAR C

GOSPEL **✚ A reading from the holy gospel according to Luke**

Luke 9:28b–36

Jesus took Peter, John, and James with him
and went up on a mountain to pray.
While he was praying,
his face changed, and his clothes became shining white.
Suddenly Moses and Elijah were there speaking with him.
They appeared in heavenly glory
and talked about all that Jesus' death
in Jerusalem would mean.

As he prayed the appearance of his face was changed.

Peter and the other two disciples had been sound asleep.
All at once they woke up and saw how glorious Jesus was.
They also saw the two men who were with him.

Moses and Elijah were about to leave,
when Peter said to Jesus,
"Master, it is good for us to be here!
Let us make three shelters,
one for you, one for Moses, and one for Elijah."
But Peter did not know what he was talking about.

While Peter was still speaking,
a shadow from a cloud passed over them,
and they were frightened as the cloud covered them.
From the cloud a voice spoke, "This is my chosen Son.
Listen to what he says!"

After the voice had spoken,
Peter, John, and James saw only Jesus.
For some time they kept quiet
and did not say anything about what they had seen.

The gospel of the Lord.

352

THE ASSUMPTION OF THE VIRGIN MARY INTO HEAVEN

From the Common of the Blessed Virgin Mary, p. 346, except:

GOSPEL

✚ A reading from the holy gospel according to Luke

Luke 1:39–56

Mary hurried to a town in the hill country of Judea.
She went into Zechariah's home,
where she greeted Elizabeth.
When Elizabeth heard Mary's greeting,
her baby moved within her.

The Holy Spirit came upon Elizabeth.
Then in a loud voice she said to Mary:
"God has blessed you more than any other woman!
He has also blessed the child you will have.
Why should the mother of my Lord come to me?
As soon as I heard your greeting,
my baby became happy and moved within me.
The Lord has blessed you
because you believed that he will keep his promise."

The Almighty has done great things for me; the Lord has lifted up the lowly.

Mary said:
"With all my heart I praise the Lord,
and I am glad because of God my Savior.
He cares for me, his humble servant.
From now on, all people will say God has blessed me.
God All-Powerful has done great things for me,
and his name is holy.

"He always shows mercy to everyone who worships him.
The Lord has used his powerful arm to scatter
those who are proud.
He drags strong rulers from their thrones
and puts humble people in places of power.
He gives the hungry good things to eat,
and he sends the rich away with nothing in their hands.
He helps his servant Israel and is always merciful
to his people.
He made this promise to our ancestors,
to Abraham and his family forever!"

Mary stayed with Elizabeth about three months.
Then she went back home.

The gospel of the Lord.

THE MARTYRDOM OF JOHN THE BAPTIST

The gospel for this memorial is proper.
From the Common of Martyrs, p. 358, except:

GOSPEL

✚ A reading from the holy gospel according to Mark

Mark 6:17–29

I want you to give me the head of John the Baptist on a dish.

Herod had earlier married Herodias,
the wife of his brother Philip.
But John had told him,
"It isn't right for you to take your brother's wife!"
So, in order to please Herodias,
Herod arrested John and put him in prison.

Herodias had a grudge against John and wanted to kill him.
But she could not do it
because Herod was afraid of John and protected him.

He knew that John was a good and holy man.
Even though Herod was confused by what John said,
he was glad to listen to him.
And he often did.

Finally, Herodias got her chance
when Herod gave a great birthday celebration for himself
and invited his officials, his army officers,
and the leaders of Galilee.

The daughter of Herodias came in
and danced for Herod and his guests.
She pleased them so much that Herod said,
"Ask for anything, and it's yours!
I swear that I will give you as much as half of my kingdom,
if you want it."

The girl left and asked her mother,
"What do you think I should ask for?"

Her mother answered, "The head of John the Baptist!"

The girl hurried back and told Herod,
"Right now on a platter I want the head of John the Baptist!"

The king was very sorry for what he had said.
But he did not want to break the promise he had made
in front of his guests.
At once he ordered a guard to cut off John's head
there in prison.
The guard put the head on a platter and took it to the girl.
Then she gave it to her mother.

When John's followers learned that he had been killed,
they took his body and put it in a tomb.

The gospel of the Lord.

▪ SEPTEMBER ▪

366 September 3

GREGORY THE GREAT
pope, religious,
doctor of the Church

Memorial

From the Common of Pastors [For a Pope] or the Common of Doctors of the Church, p. 364 or 370.

367 September 8

THE BIRTH OF THE VIRGIN MARY

Feast

From the Common of the Blessed Virgin Mary, p. 346.

368 September 9

PETER CLAVER
presbyter, religious, missionary

Memorial

From the Common of Pastors or the Common of Saints [For Those Who Work for the Underprivileged], p. 364 or 376.

369 September 13

JOHN CHRYSOSTOM
bishop, doctor of the Church

Memorial

From the Common of Pastors or the Common of Doctors of the Church, p. 364 or 370.

370 September 14

THE HOLY CROSS

Feast

See p. 292.

371 September 15

OUR LADY OF SORROWS

Memorial

See p. 296.

372 September 16

CORNELIUS, pope, martyr, and
CYPRIAN, bishop, martyr

Memorial

From the Common of Martyrs or the Common of Pastors, p. 358 or 364.

373 September 17

ROBERT BELLARMINE
bishop, religious,
doctor of the Church

From the Common of Pastors or the Common of Doctors of the Church, p. 364 or 370.

374 September 19

JANUARIUS
bishop, martyr

From the Common of Martyrs or the Common of Pastors, p. 358 or 364.

375 September 20

ANDREW KIM TAEGON,
presbyter, martyr, **PAUL CHONG HASANG,** martyr, and
their **COMPANIONS,** martyrs

Memorial

From the Common of Martyrs, p. 358.

376 September 21

MATTHEW

apostle, evangelist

Feast

See p. 298.

377 September 26

COSMAS AND DAMIAN

martyrs

From the Common of Martyrs, p. 358.

378 September 27

VINCENT DE PAUL

presbyter, religious founder

Memorial

From the Common of Pastors [For Missionaries] or the Common of Saints [For Those Who Work for the Underprivileged], p. 364 or 376.

379 September 28

WENCESLAUS

martyr

From the Common of Martyrs, p. 358.

380 **LAWRENCE RUIZ,**

married man, martyr, and his

COMPANIONS, martyrs

From the Common of Martyrs, p. 358.

381 September 29

MICHAEL, GABRIEL, AND RAPHAEL

archangels

Feast

See p. 300.

382 September 30

JEROME

presbyter, doctor of the Church

Memorial

From the Common of Pastors or the Common of Doctors of the Church, p. 364 or 370.

■

THE HOLY CROSS

FIRST READING **A reading from the book of Numbers**

Numbers 21:4b–9

One day the people of Israel got angry
and started insulting Moses and God.
They said, "Did you bring us out of Egypt
just to let us die in the desert?
There's no bread or water in this place.
We are sick of this awful food!"

When those that were afflicted looked upon the serpent, they were healed.

So the LORD sent poisonous snakes to attack the people,
and many of them were bitten and died.

The others came to Moses and said,
"We were wrong to insult you and the LORD.
Please pray for the LORD to take these snakes away."

Moses prayed for the people.
Then the LORD said,
"Make a snake out of bronze and put it on a pole.
The people who are bitten can look at the snake,
and they won't die."
So Moses made a bronze snake and put it on a pole.
Everyone who looked at the snake lived,
even after being bitten by a poisonous snake.

The word of the Lord.

Responsorial Psalm *R. Our Lord and God, you keep me safe.*

Psalm 88:4–5, 14–15abc (7a)

LORD God, I am as good as dead
and completely helpless.
I am no better off
than those in the grave,
those you have forgotten
and no longer help.

R. Our Lord and God, you keep me safe.

Why do you reject me?
Why do you turn from me?
Ever since I was a child,
I have been sick
and close to death.

R. Our Lord and God, you keep me safe.

Alleluia *R. Alleluia, alleluia.*

We adore you, O Christ,
and we praise you,
because by your cross
you have redeemed the world.

R. Alleluia, alleluia.

GOSPEL **✚ A reading from the holy gospel according to John**

John 3:13–17

Jesus told Nicodemus:
"No one has gone up to heaven except the Son of Man,
who came down from there.
And the Son of Man must be lifted up,
just as that metal snake was lifted up by Moses in the desert.
Then everyone who has faith in the Son of Man
will have eternal life.

The Son of Man must be lifted up.

"God loved the people of this world so much
that he gave his only Son,
so that everyone who has faith in him
will have eternal life and never die.
God did not send his Son into the world
to condemn its people.
He sent him to save them!"

The gospel of the Lord.

371

OUR LADY OF SORROWS

The gospel for this memorial is proper.
From the Common of the Blessed Virgin Mary, p. 346, except:

GOSPEL

✚ A reading from the holy gospel according to John

John 19:25–27

Jesus' mother stood beside his cross
with her sister and Mary the wife of Clopas.
Mary Magdalene was standing there too.

How that loving mother was pierced with grief and anguish when she saw the sufferings of her son (Stabat Mater).

When Jesus saw his mother
and his favorite disciple with her,
he said to his mother,
"This man is now your son."
Then he said to the disciple,
"She is now your mother."

From then on, that disciple took her into his own home.

The gospel of the Lord.

MATTHEW

From the Common of Apostles, p. 354, except:

GOSPEL ✚ **A reading from the holy gospel according to Matthew**

Matthew 9:9–13

Follow me. And standing up, Matthew followed Jesus.

As Jesus was leaving Capernaum,
he saw a tax collector named Matthew
sitting at the place for paying taxes.
Jesus said to him, "Come with me."
Matthew got up and went with him.

Later, Jesus and his disciples were having dinner
at Matthew's house.
Many tax collectors and other sinners were also there.
Some Pharisees asked Jesus' disciples,
"Why does your teacher eat with tax collectors
and other sinners?"

Jesus heard them and answered,
"Healthy people don't need a doctor,
but sick people do.
Go and learn what the Scriptures mean when they say,
'Instead of offering sacrifices to me,
I want you to be merciful to others.'
I didn't come to invite good people to be my followers.
I came to invite sinners."

The gospel of the Lord.

MATTHEW

MICHAEL, GABRIEL, AND RAPHAEL

FIRST READING

A reading from the book of Revelation

Revelation 12:7–12a

A war broke out in heaven.
Michael and his angels were fighting against the dragon
and its angels.

But the dragon lost the battle.
It and its angels were forced out of their places in heaven
and were thrown down to the earth.
Yes, that old snake and his angels
were thrown out of heaven!

Michael and his angels battled with the dragon.

That snake, who fools everyone on earth,
is known as the devil and Satan.

Then I, John, heard a voice from heaven shout,
"Our God has shown his saving power,
and his kingdom has come!
God's own Chosen One has shown his authority.
Satan accused our people in the presence of God
day and night.
Now he has been thrown out!

"Our people defeated Satan because of the blood of the Lamb
and the message of God.
They were willing to give up their lives.

"The heavens should rejoice,
together with everyone who lives there.
But pity the earth and the sea,
because the devil was thrown down to the earth."

The word of the Lord.

Responsorial Psalm

Psalm 138:1–2ab, 2c–3, 4–5 (1c)

R. In the sight of the angels
I will sing your praises, Lord.

With all my heart
I praise you, LORD.
In the presence of angels
I sing your praises.
I worship at your holy temple
and praise you for your love.

R. In the sight of the angels
I will sing your praises, Lord.

I praise you for your faithfulness.
You were true to your word
and made yourself more famous
than ever before.
When I asked for your help,
you answered my prayer
and gave me courage.

R. In the sight of the angels
I will sing your praises, Lord.

All kings on earth
have heard your promises, LORD,
and they will praise you.
You are so famous
that they will sing about
the things you have done.

R. In the sight of the angels
I will sing your praises, Lord.

Alleluia *R. Alleluia, alleluia.*

Psalm 103:21

Bless the Lord, all you angels,
you ministers who do God's will.

R. Alleluia, alleluia.

GOSPEL **✚ A reading from the holy gospel according to John**

John 1:47–51

When Jesus saw Nathanael coming toward him, he said,
"Here is a true descendant of our ancestor Israel.
And he is not deceitful."

"How do you know me?" Nathanael asked.

Above the Son of Man you will see the angels of God ascending and descending.

Jesus answered, "Before Philip called you,
I saw you under the fig tree."

Nathanael said, "Rabbi, you are the Son of God
and the King of Israel!"

Jesus answered, "Did you believe me
just because I said that I saw you under the fig tree?
You will see something even greater.
I tell you for certain that you will see heaven open
and God's angels going up and coming down
on the Son of Man."

The gospel of the Lord.

MI
CH
ÆL
GABRIEL
RA
PHA
EL

▪ OCTOBER ▪

383 October 1

THÉRÈSE OF THE CHILD JESUS
virgin, religious

Memorial

From the Common of Saints [For Religious], p. 376.

384 October 2

THE GUARDIAN ANGELS

Memorial

See p. 306.

385 October 4

FRANCIS OF ASSISI
religious founder

Memorial

From the Common of Saints [For Religious], p. 376.

386 October 6

BRUNO
presbyter, hermit,
religious founder

From the Common of Pastors or the Common of Saints [For Religious], p. 364 or 376.

387 **BLESSED MARIE-ROSE DUROCHER**
virgin, religious founder

From the Common of Saints [For Religious], p. 376.

388 October 7

OUR LADY OF THE ROSARY

Memorial

From the Common of the Blessed Virgin Mary, p. 346.

389 October 9

DENIS, bishop, martyr, and his **COMPANIONS,** martyrs

From the Common of Martyrs, p. 358.

390 **JOHN LEONARDI**
presbyter, religious founder

From the Common of Pastors or the Common of Saints [For Those Who Work for the Underprivileged], p. 364 or 376.

391 October 14

CALLISTUS I
pope, martyr

From the Common of Martyrs or the Common of Pastors [For a Pope], p. 358 or 364.

392 October 15

TERESA OF JESUS
virgin, religious,
doctor of the Church

Memorial

From the Common of Saints [For Religious] or the Common of Doctors of the Church, p. 376 or 370.

393 October 16

HEDWIG
married woman, religious

From the Common of Saints [For Religious], p. 376.

394 **MARGARET MARY ALACOQUE**
virgin, religious

From the Common of Saints [For Religious], p. 376.

395 October 17

IGNATIUS OF ANTIOCH
bishop, martyr

Memorial

From the Common of Martyrs or the Common of Pastors, p. 358 or 364.

396 October 18

LUKE
evangelist

Feast

See p. 310.

397 October 19

ISAAC JOGUES AND JOHN DE BRÉBEUF, presbyters, religious, missionaries, martyrs, and their **COMPANIONS,** martyrs

Memorial

From the Common of Martyrs or the Common of Pastors [For Missionaries], p. 358 or 364.

398 October 20

PAUL OF THE CROSS
presbyter, religious founder

From the Common of Pastors or the Common of Saints [For Religious], p. 364 or 376.

399 October 23

JOHN OF CAPISTRANO
presbyter, religious founder

From the Common of Pastors [For Missionaries], p. 364.

400 October 24

ANTHONY MARY CLARET
bishop, religious founder

From the Common of Pastors [For Missionaries], p. 364.

401 October 28

SIMON AND JUDE
apostles

Feast

From the Common of Apostles, p. 354.

■

THE GUARDIAN ANGELS

The gospel for this memorial is proper.

First Reading **A reading from the book of Exodus**

Exodus 23:20–21a

My angel will go before you.

The Lord told Moses:
"I am sending an angel ahead of you.
The angel will protect you as you travel
and will bring you to the place I have made ready.
But you must obey him and do what he says."

The word of the Lord.

Responsorial Psalm

Psalm 91:1–2, 3–4, 5–6, 10–11 (11)

R. The Lord has put angels in charge of you,
to guard you in all your ways.

Live under the protection
of God Most High
and stay in the shadow
of God All-Powerful.
Then you will say to the LORD,
"You are my fortress,
my place of safety;
you are my God,
and I trust you."

R. The Lord has put angels in charge of you,
to guard you in all your ways.

The Lord will keep you safe
from secret traps
and deadly diseases.
He will spread his wings over you
and keep you secure.
His faithfulness is like
a shield or a city wall.

R. The Lord has put angels in charge of you,
to guard you in all your ways.

You won't need to worry
about dangers at night
or arrows during the day.
And you won't fear diseases
that strike in the dark
or sudden disaster at noon.

R. The Lord has put angels in charge of you,
to guard you in all your ways.

No terrible disasters
will strike you
or your home.
God will command his angels
to protect you
wherever you go.

R. The Lord has put angels in charge of you,
to guard you in all your ways.

Alleluia *R. Alleluia, alleluia.*

Psalm 103:21

Bless the Lord, all you angels,
you ministers who do God's will.

R. Alleluia, alleluia.

GOSPEL **✚ A reading from the holy gospel according to Matthew**

Matthew 18:1–5, 10

Their angels in heaven are always in the presence of my Father, who is in heaven.

The disciples came to Jesus and asked him
who would be the greatest in the kingdom of heaven.
Jesus called a child over and had the child stand near him.

Then he said: "I promise you this.
If you don't change and become like this child,
you will never get into the kingdom of heaven.
But if you are as humble as this child,
you are the greatest in the kingdom of heaven.
And when you welcome one of these children
because of me,
you welcome me.

"Don't be cruel to any of these little ones!
I promise you that their angels are always with my Father
in heaven."

The gospel of the Lord.

LUKE

From the Common of Apostles, p. 354, except:

GOSPEL

✚ A reading from the holy gospel according to Luke

Luke 10:1–9

The Lord chose seventy-two other followers
and sent them out two by two to every town and village
where he was about to go.

He said to them:
"A large crop is in the fields,
but there are only a few workers.
Ask the Lord in charge of the harvest
to send out workers to bring it in.
Now go,
but remember, I am sending you like lambs
into a pack of wolves.
Don't take along a moneybag or a traveling bag or sandals.
And don't waste time greeting people on the road.

The harvest is rich, but the laborers are few.

"As soon as you enter a home, say,
'God bless this home with peace.'
If the people living there are peace-loving,
your prayer for peace will bless them.
But if they are not peace-loving,
your prayer will return to you.

"Stay with the same family,
eating and drinking whatever they give you,
because workers are worth what they earn.
Don't move around from house to house.

"If the people of a town welcome you,
eat whatever they offer you.
Heal their sick and say,
'God's kingdom will soon be here!'"

The gospel of the Lord.

LUKE

▪ NOVEMBER ▪

402 November 1

ALL SAINTS

Solemnity

See p. 316.

403 November 2

THE COMMEMORATION OF ALL THE FAITHFUL DEPARTED (ALL SOULS)

From the Masses for the Dead, p. 476.

404 November 3

MARTIN DE PORRES

religious

From the Common of Saints [For Religious], p. 376.

405 November 4

CHARLES BORROMEO

bishop

Memorial

From the Common of Pastors, p. 364.

406 November 9

THE DEDICATION OF THE LATERAN BASILICA IN ROME

Feast

From the Common of the Dedication of a Church, p. 340.

407 November 10

LEO THE GREAT

pope, doctor of the Church

Memorial

From the Common of Pastors [For a Pope] or the Common of Doctors of the Church, p. 364 or 370.

408 November 11

MARTIN OF TOURS

bishop

Memorial

From the Common of Pastors or the Common of Saints [For Religious], p. 364 or 376.

409 November 12

JOSAPHAT

bishop, religious, martyr

Memorial

From the Common of Martyrs or the Common of Pastors, p. 358 or 364.

410 November 13

FRANCES XAVIER CABRINI

virgin, religious, missionary

Memorial

From the Common of Saints [For Religious], p. 376.

411 November 15

ALBERT THE GREAT

bishop, religious, doctor of the Church

From the Common of Pastors or the Common of Doctors of the Church, p. 364 or 370.

412 November 16

MARGARET OF SCOTLAND

married woman

From the Common of Saints [For Those Who Work for the Underprivileged], p. 376.

413 **GERTRUDE THE GREAT**

virgin, religious

From the Common of Saints [For Religious], p. 376.

414 November 17

ELIZABETH OF HUNGARY

married woman, religious

Memorial

From the Common of Saints [For Those Who Work for the Underprivileged], p. 376.

415 November 18

THE DEDICATION OF THE BASILICAS OF THE APOSTLES PETER AND PAUL IN ROME

See p. 320.

416 **ROSE PHILIPPINE DUCHESNE**

virgin, religious, missionary

From the Common of Saints [For Religious], p. 376.

417 November 21

THE PRESENTATION OF THE VIRGIN MARY

Memorial

From the Common of the Blessed Virgin Mary, p. 346.

418 November 22

CECILIA

virgin, martyr

Memorial

From the Common of Martyrs or the Common of Saints, p. 358 or 376.

419 November 23

CLEMENT I

pope, martyr

From the Common of Martyrs or the Common of Pastors [For a Pope], p. 358 or 364.

420 **COLUMBAN**

abbot, missionary

From the Common of Pastors [For Missionaries] or the Common of Saints [For Religious], p. 364 or 376.

421 **BLESSED MIGUEL AGUSTÍN PRO**

presbyter, religious, martyr

From the Common of Martyrs or the Common of Pastors, p. 358 or 364.

422 November 24

ANDREW DUNG-LAC

presbyter, martyr, and his

COMPANIONS, martyrs

Memorial

From the Common of Martyrs, p. 358.

423 November 30

ANDREW

apostle

Feast

See p. 324.

424 Fourth Thursday in November

THANKSGIVING DAY

Mass in Thanksgiving, p. 440.

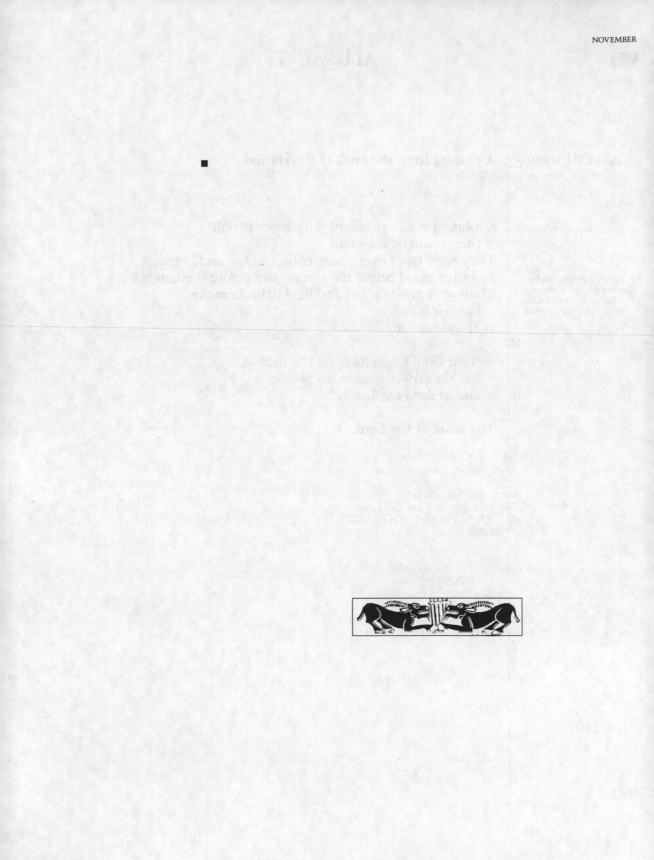

ALL SAINTS

First Reading **A reading from the book of Revelation**

Revelation 7:9–10

I saw an immense crowd, beyond hope of counting, of people from every nation, race, tribe, and language.

I, John, saw a large crowd with more people
than could be counted.
They were from every race, tribe, nation, and language,
and they stood before the throne and before the Lamb.
They wore white robes and held palm branches
in their hands,
as they shouted,

"Our God, who sits upon the throne,
has the power to save his people,
and so does the Lamb."

The word of the Lord.

Responsorial Psalm

Psalm 24:1–2, 3–4, 5–6 (see 6)

R. Lord, this is the people that longs
to see your face.

The earth and everything on it
belong to the LORD.
The world and its people
belong to him.
The LORD placed it all
on the oceans and rivers.

R. Lord, this is the people that longs
to see your face.

Who may climb the LORD's hill
or stand in his holy temple?
Only those who do right
for the right reasons,
and don't worship idols
or tell lies under oath.

R. Lord, this is the people that longs
to see your face.

The LORD God, who saves them,
will bless and reward them,
because they worship and serve
the God of Jacob.

R. Lord, this is the people that longs
to see your face.

Alleluia *R. Alleluia, alleluia.*

Matthew 11:28

Come to me, all you that labor
and are burdened,
and I will give you rest, says the Lord.

R. Alleluia, alleluia.

GOSPEL **✚ A reading from the holy gospel according to Matthew**

Matthew 5:1–12ab

When Jesus saw the crowds,
he went up on the side of a mountain and sat down.

Jesus' disciples gathered around him, and he taught them:

"God blesses those people who depend only on him.
They belong to the kingdom of heaven!

Rejoice and be glad, for your reward will be great in heaven.

"God blesses those people who grieve.
They will find comfort!

"God blesses those people who are humble.
The earth will belong to them!

"God blesses those people who want to obey him
more than to eat or drink.
They will be given what they want!

"God blesses those people who are merciful.
They will be treated with mercy!

"God blesses those people whose hearts are pure.
They will see him!

"God blesses those people who make peace.
They will be called his children!

"God blesses those people who are treated badly
for doing right.
They belong to the kingdom of heaven.

"God will bless you when people insult you, mistreat you,
and tell all kinds of evil lies about you because of me.
Be happy and excited!
You will have a great reward in heaven."

The gospel of the Lord.

415

THE DEDICATION OF THE BASILICAS OF THE APOSTLES PETER AND PAUL IN ROME

The readings for this optional memorial are proper.

FIRST READING **A reading from the Acts of the Apostles**

Acts 28:11–16

Three months after reaching Malta
we sailed in a ship that had been docked there
for the winter.
The ship was from Alexandria in Egypt
and was known as "The Twin Gods."
We arrived in Syracuse and stayed for three days.
From there we sailed to Rhegium.

So we came to Rome.

The next day a south wind began to blow,
and two days later we arrived in Puteoli.
There we found some of the Lord's followers,
who begged us to stay with them.
A week later we left for the city of Rome.

Some of the followers in Rome heard about us
and came to meet us at the Market of Appius
and at the Three Inns.
When Paul saw them,
he thanked God and was encouraged.

We arrived in Rome,
and Paul was allowed to live in a house by himself
with a soldier to guard him.

The word of the Lord.

Responsorial Psalm

Psalm 98:1, 2–3, 4–6
(see 2b)

*R. The Lord has revealed
to the nations his saving power.*

*Sing a new song to the LORD!
He has worked miracles,
and with his own powerful arm,
he has won the victory.*

*R. The Lord has revealed
to the nations his saving power.*

*The LORD has shown the nations
that he has the power to save
and to bring justice.
God has been faithful
in his love for Israel,
and his saving power is seen
everywhere on earth.*

*R. The Lord has revealed
to the nations his saving power.*

*Tell everyone on this earth
to sing happy songs
in praise of the LORD.
Make music for him on harps.
Play beautiful melodies!
Sound the trumpets and horns
and celebrate with joyful songs
for our LORD and King!*

*R. The Lord has revealed
to the nations his saving power.*

Alleluia

R. Alleluia, alleluia.

*We praise you, O God;
we acclaim you as Lord;
the glorious company
of apostles praise you.*

R. Alleluia, alleluia.

GOSPEL

✚ A reading from the holy gospel according to Matthew

Matthew 14:22–33

Jesus made his disciples get into a boat
and start back across the lake.
But he stayed until he had sent the crowds away.
Then he went up on a mountain
where he could be alone and pray.
Later that evening, he was still there.

Order me to come to you across the water.

By this time the boat was a long way from the shore.
It was going against the wind
and was being tossed around by the waves.
A little while before morning,
Jesus came walking on the water toward his disciples.
When they saw him, they thought he was a ghost.
They were terrified and started screaming.

At once Jesus said to them, "Don't worry!
I am Jesus. Don't be afraid."

Peter replied, "Lord, if it is really you,
tell me to come to you on the water."

"Come on!" Jesus said.
Peter then got out of the boat
and started walking on the water toward him.

But when Peter saw how strong the wind was,
he was afraid and started sinking.

"Lord, save me!" he shouted.

Right away Jesus reached out his hand.
He helped Peter up and said,
"You surely don't have much faith.
Why do you doubt?"

When Jesus and Peter got into the boat, the wind died down.
The men in the boat worshiped Jesus and said,
"You really are the Son of God!"

The gospel of the Lord.

ANDREW

From the Common of Apostles, p. 354, except:

GOSPEL

✚ A reading from the holy gospel according to Matthew

Matthew 4:18–22

Immediately they left their nets and followed Jesus.

While Jesus was walking along the shore of Lake Galilee,
he saw two brothers.
One was Simon, also known as Peter,
and the other was Andrew.
They were fishermen, and they were casting their net
into the lake.

Jesus said to them, "Come with me!
I will teach you how to bring in people instead of fish."
Right then the two brothers dropped their nets
and went with him.

Jesus walked on until he saw James and John,
the sons of Zebedee.
They were in a boat with their father, mending their nets.
Jesus asked them to come with him too.
Right away they left the boat and their father
and went with Jesus.

Jesus went all over Galilee,
teaching in the Jewish meeting places
and preaching the good news about God's kingdom.

The gospel of the Lord.

AND-
REW

▪ DECEMBER ▪

425 December 3

FRANCIS XAVIER

presbyter, religious, missionary

Memorial

From the Common of Pastors [For Missionaries], p. 364.

426 December 4

JOHN OF DAMASCUS

presbyter, doctor of the Church

From the Common of Pastors or the Common of Doctors of the Church, p. 364 or 370.

427 December 6

NICHOLAS

bishop

From the Common of Pastors, p. 364.

428 December 7

AMBROSE

bishop, doctor of the Church

Memorial

From the Common of Pastors or the Common of Doctors of the Church, p. 364 or 370.

429 December 8

THE IMMACULATE CONCEPTION OF THE VIRGIN MARY

Solemnity

See p. 328.

430 December 9

BLESSED JUAN DIEGO (CUATITLATOATZIN)

hermit

From the Common of Saints, p. 376.

431 December 11

DAMASUS I

pope

From the Common of Pastors [For a Pope], p. 364.

432 December 12

OUR LADY OF GUADALUPE

Feast

From the Common of the Blessed Virgin Mary, p. 346.

433 December 13

LUCY

virgin, martyr

Memorial

From the Common of Martyrs or the Common of Saints, p. 358 or 376.

434 December 14

JOHN OF THE CROSS

presbyter, doctor of the Church

Memorial

From the Common of Pastors or the Common of Doctors of the Church, p. 364 or 370.

435 December 21

PETER CANISIUS

presbyter, religious, doctor of the Church

From the Common of Pastors or the Common of Doctors of the Church, p. 364 or 370.

436 December 23

JOHN OF KANTY

presbyter

From the Common of Pastors, p. 364.

437 December 26

STEPHEN

first martyr

Feast

See p. 332.

438 December 27

JOHN

apostle, evangelist

Feast

See p. 334.

439 December 28

THE HOLY INNOCENTS

martyrs

Feast

See p. 336.

440 December 29

THOMAS BECKET

bishop, martyr

From the Common of Martyrs or the Common of Pastors, p. 358 or 364.

441 December 31

SYLVESTER I

pope

From the Common of Pastors [For a Pope], p. 364.

■

429

THE IMMACULATE CONCEPTION OF THE VIRGIN MARY

First Reading

Genesis 3:9–15, 20

I will put enmity between your offspring and her offspring.

A reading from the book of Genesis

The LORD called out to Adam and asked, "Where are you?"

Adam answered, "I was naked,
and when I heard you walking through the garden,
I was afraid and hid!"

"How did you know you were naked?" God asked.
"Did you eat from the tree I told you not to?"

Adam said, "It was that woman you put here with me!
She gave me some of the fruit, and I ate it."

The LORD God then asked her, "What have you done?"

The woman answered,
"The snake tricked me into eating some of that fruit."

The LORD God said to the snake:
"Because of what you have done,
you will suffer a greater curse than the cattle
and the wild animals.
For as long as you live,
you will crawl on your stomach
and eat dirt from the ground.
You and this woman will hate each other.
Your descendants and hers will always be enemies.
One of them will crush your head,
and you will bite him on the heel."

Adam named his wife Eve,
because she would become the mother of all people.

The word of the Lord.

Responsorial Psalm

Psalm 98:1, 2–3ab, 3cd–4
(1a)

R. Sing to the Lord a new song,
for he has done marvelous deeds.

Sing a new song to the LORD!
He has worked miracles,
and with his own powerful arm,
he has won the victory.

R. Sing to the Lord a new song,
for he has done marvelous deeds.

The LORD has shown the nations
that he has the power to save
and to bring justice.
God has been faithful
in his love for Israel.

R. Sing to the Lord a new song,
for he has done marvelous deeds.

His saving power is seen
everywhere on earth.
Tell everyone on this earth
to sing happy songs
in praise of the LORD.

R. Sing to the Lord a new song,
for he has done marvelous deeds.

Alleluia *R. Alleluia, alleluia.*

See Luke 1:28

*Hail, Mary, full of grace,
the Lord is with you;
blessed are you among women.*

R. Alleluia, alleluia.

GOSPEL **✚ A reading from the holy gospel according to Luke**

Luke 1:26–38

God sent the angel Gabriel to the town of Nazareth
in Galilee with a message for a virgin named Mary.
She was engaged to Joseph from the family of King David.
The angel greeted Mary and said,
"You are truly blessed! The Lord is with you."

Mary was confused by the angel's words
and wondered what they meant.

Rejoice, favored one, the Lord is with you.

Then the angel told Mary, "Don't be afraid!
God is pleased with you, and you will have a son.
His name will be Jesus.
He will be great
and will be called the Son of God Most High.
The Lord God will make him king,
as his ancestor David was.
He will rule the people of Israel forever,
and his kingdom will never end."

Mary asked the angel, "How can this happen?
I am not married!"

The angel answered,
"The Holy Spirit will come down to you,
and God's power will come over you.
So your child will be called the holy Son of God.

"Your relative Elizabeth is also going to have a son,
even though she is old.
No one thought she could ever have a baby,
but in three months she will have a son.
Nothing is impossible for God!"

Mary said, "I am the Lord's servant!
Let it happen as you have said."

And the angel left her.

The gospel of the Lord.

437

STEPHEN

From the Common of Martyrs, p. 358, except:

First Reading

A reading from the Acts of the Apostles

Acts 6:8–10; 7:54–60

I can see heaven thrown open.

God gave Stephen
the power to work great miracles and wonders
among the people.
But some Jews from Cyrene and Alexandria
were members of a group who called themselves
"Free Men."
They started arguing with Stephen.
Some others from Cilicia and Asia also argued with him.
But they were no match for Stephen,
who spoke with the great wisdom that the Spirit gave him.

Those who heard Stephen's speech were angry and furious.
But Stephen was filled with the Holy Spirit.
He looked toward heaven,
where he saw our glorious God
and Jesus standing at his right side.
Then Stephen said, "I see heaven open
and the Son of Man standing at the right side of God!"

The council members shouted and covered their ears.
At once they all attacked Stephen
and dragged him out of the city.
Then they started throwing stones at him.
The men who had brought charges against him
put their coats at the feet of a young man named Saul.

As Stephen was being stoned to death, he called out,
"Lord Jesus, please welcome me!"
He kneeled down and shouted,
"Lord, don't blame them for what they have done."
Then he died.

The word of the Lord.

STEPHEN

JOHN

From the Common of Apostles, p. 354, except:

GOSPEL ✚ **A reading from the holy gospel according to John**

John 20:2–8

On Sunday morning Mary Magdalene ran to Simon Peter
and to Jesus' favorite disciple and said,
"They have taken the Lord from the tomb!
We don't know where they have put him."

Peter and the other disciple started for the tomb.
They ran side by side,
until the other disciple ran faster than Peter
and got there first.
He bent over and saw the strips of linen cloth
lying inside the tomb,
but he did not go in.

The other disciple outran Peter and came first to the tomb.

When Simon Peter got there,
he went into the tomb and saw the strips of cloth.
He also saw the piece of cloth
that had been used to cover Jesus' face.
It was rolled up and in a place by itself.
The disciple who got there first then went into the tomb,
and when he saw it, he believed.

The gospel of the Lord.

JOHN

THE HOLY INNOCENTS

From the Common of Martyrs, p. 358, except:

GOSPEL

✚ A reading from the holy gospel according to Matthew

Matthew 2:13–18

After the wise men had gone,
an angel from the Lord appeared to Joseph in a dream.
The angel said, "Get up!
Hurry and take the child and his mother to Egypt!
Stay there until I tell you to return,
because Herod is looking for the child
 and wants to kill him."

Herod killed all the male children who were in Bethlehem.

That night Joseph got up
 and took his wife and the child to Egypt,
where they stayed until Herod died.
So the Lord's promise came true,
 just as the prophet had said,
"I called my son out of Egypt."

When Herod found out that the wise men from the east
 had tricked him,
he was very angry.
He gave orders for his men to kill
 all the boys who lived in or near Bethlehem
 and were two years old and younger.

So the Lord's promise came true,
just as the prophet Jeremiah had said,
"In Ramah a voice was heard crying and weeping loudly.
Rachel was mourning for her children,
and she refused to be comforted,
because they were dead."

The gospel of the Lord.

Commons

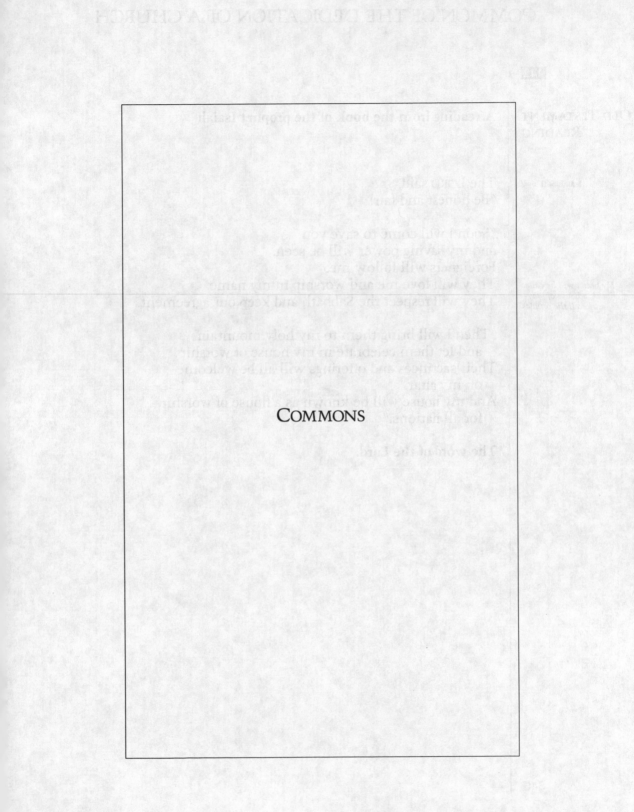

442

OLD TESTAMENT READING

A reading from the book of the prophet Isaiah

Isaiah 56:1, 6–7

The LORD said,
"Be honest and fair!

"Soon I will come to save you,
and my saving power will be seen.
Foreigners will follow me.
They will love me and worship in my name.
They will respect the Sabbath and keep our agreement.

My house will be called a house of prayer for all the peoples.

"Then I will bring them to my holy mountain
and let them celebrate in my house of worship.
Their sacrifices and offerings will all be welcome
on my altar.
And my house will be known as a house of worship
for all nations."

The word of the Lord.

443

ONE

A reading from the letter of Paul to the Ephesians

NEW TESTAMENT READING

Ephesians 2:20–22

Through the Lord, the whole building is bound together as one holy temple.

Brothers and sisters:
You are like a building with the apostles and prophets
as the foundation and with Christ
as the most important stone.
Christ is the one who holds the building together
and makes it grow into a holy temple for the Lord.
And you are part of that building Christ has built
as a place for God's own Spirit to live.

The word of the Lord.

TWO

NEW TESTAMENT READING

A reading from the book of Revelation

Revelation 21:1–4

I, John, saw a new heaven and a new earth.
The first heaven and the first earth had disappeared,
and so had the sea.
Then I saw New Jerusalem, that holy city,
coming down from God in heaven.
It was like a bride dressed in her wedding gown
and ready to meet her husband.

Behold, the home of God is among his people.

I heard a loud voice shout from the throne:
"God's home is now with his people.
He will live with them,
and they will be his own.
Yes, God will make his home among his people.
He will wipe all tears from their eyes,
and there will be no more death, suffering, crying, or pain.
These things of the past are gone forever."

The word of the Lord.

444

Responsorial Psalm

Psalm 84:2, 3, 4–5, 10 (2) (Revelation 21:3b)

R. How lovely is your dwelling place,
Lord, mighty God!
or:
R. Here God lives among his people.

Deep in my heart I long
for your temple,
and with all that I am
I sing joyful songs to you.

R. How lovely is your dwelling place,
Lord, mighty God!
or:
R. Here God lives among his people.

LORD God All-Powerful,
my King and my God,
sparrows find a home
near your altars;
swallows build nests there
to raise their young.

R. How lovely is your dwelling place,
Lord, mighty God!
or:
R. Here God lives among his people.

You bless everyone
who lives in your house,
and they sing your praises.
You bless all who depend
on you for their strength
and all who deeply desire
to visit your temple.

R. How lovely is your dwelling place,
Lord, mighty God!
or:
R. Here God lives among his people.

continued

One day in your temple
is better than a thousand
anywhere else.
I would rather serve
in your house,
than live in the homes
of the wicked.

R. How lovely is your dwelling place,
Lord, mighty God!
or:
R. Here God lives among his people.

445

Alleluia Verse and Verse before the Gospel

See Matthew 7:8

In my house, says the Lord,
everyone who asks will receive;
whoever seeks shall find;
and to those who knock
it shall be opened.

446

GOSPEL

✚ A reading from the holy gospel according to Luke

Luke 19:1–10

Today salvation has come to this house.

Jesus was going through Jericho,
where a man named Zacchaeus lived.
He was in charge of collecting taxes and was very rich.

Jesus was heading his way,
and Zacchaeus wanted to see what he was like.
But Zacchaeus was a short man and could not see
over the crowd.
So he ran ahead and climbed up into a sycamore tree.

When Jesus got there, he looked up and said,
"Zacchaeus, hurry down!
I want to stay with you today."

Zacchaeus hurried down and gladly welcomed Jesus.

Everyone who saw this started grumbling,
"This man Zacchaeus is a sinner!
And Jesus is going home to eat with him."

Later that day Zacchaeus stood up and said to the Lord,
"I will give half of my property to the poor.
And I will now pay back four times as much
to everyone I have ever cheated."

Jesus said to Zacchaeus,
"Today you and your family have been saved,
because you are a true son of Abraham.
The Son of Man came to look for and to save
people who are lost."

The gospel of the Lord.

COMMON OF THE BLESSED VIRGIN MARY

447

ONE

OLD TESTAMENT READING

Isaiah 9:2–3a, 6–7a

A reading from the book of the prophet Isaiah

Those who walked in the dark have see a bright light.
And it shines upon everyone who lives
in the land of darkest shadows.

Our LORD, you have made your nation stronger.
Because of you, its people are glad and celebrate.

A son is given to us.

For us a child has been born.
A son has been given to us,
and he will be our ruler.
His names will be:
Wonderful Adviser and Mighty God,
Eternal Father and Prince of Peace.

His power will never end,
and peace will last forever.

The word of the Lord.

TWO

OLD TESTAMENT READING

Zechariah 2:14–15

A reading from the book of the prophet Zechariah

The LORD said, "Everyone in Jerusalem, celebrate and shout!
I am coming to live with you."

Rejoice, daughter of Zion, for I am coming.

Many nations will turn to the LORD and become his people,
and he will live with all of you.
Then you will know
that the LORD All-Powerful has sent me.

The word of the Lord.

448

ONE

A reading from the Acts of the Apostles

NEW TESTAMENT READING

Acts 1:12–13a, 14

They all joined in continuous prayer together with Mary, the mother of Jesus.

The apostles returned to Jerusalem
from the Mount of Olives,
which was about a half mile from Jerusalem.
Then they went upstairs to the room
where they had been staying.
The apostles often met together
and prayed with a single purpose in mind.
The women and Mary the mother of Jesus would meet
with them,
and so would his brothers.

The word of the Lord.

TWO

A reading from the letter of Paul to the Ephesians

NEW TESTAMENT READING

Ephesians 1:3–6

Before the world was made, God chose us in Christ.

Brothers and sisters:
Praise the God and Father of our Lord Jesus Christ
for the spiritual blessings that Christ has brought us
from heaven!
Before the world was created,
God let Christ choose us to live with him
and to be his holy and innocent and loving people.
God was kind
and decided that Christ would choose us
to be God's own adopted children.
God was very kind to us because of the Son he dearly loves,
and so we should praise God.

The word of the Lord.

449

ONE

Responsorial Psalm

Psalm 113:1–2, 3–4, 5–6, 7–8 (see 2)

R. Blessed be the name of the Lord
for ever.
or:
R. Alleluia.

Shout praises to the LORD!
Everyone who serves him,
come and praise his name.
Let the name of the LORD
be praised now and forever.

R. Blessed be the name of the Lord
for ever.
or:
R. Alleluia.

From dawn until sunset
the name of the LORD
deserves to be praised.
The LORD is far above
all of the nations;
he is more glorious
than the heavens.

R. Blessed be the name of the Lord
for ever.
or:
R. Alleluia.

No one can compare
with the LORD our God.
His throne is high above,
and he looks down to see
the heavens and the earth.

R. Blessed be the name of the Lord
for ever.
or:
R. Alleluia.

God lifts the poor and needy
from dust and ashes,
and he lets them take part
in ruling his people.

R. Blessed be the name of the Lord
for ever.
or:
R. Alleluia.

TWO

Responsorial Psalm

Luke 1:47–48b, 48c–49, 50–51, 52–53, 54–55 (49)

R. The Almighty has done
great things for me,
and holy is his name.

With all my heart I praise the Lord,
and I am glad because of God my Savior.
He cares for me, his humble servant.

R. The Almighty has done
great things for me,
and holy is his name.

From now on,
all people will say God has blessed me.
God All-Powerful has done great things
for me,
and his name is holy.

R. The Almighty has done
great things for me,
and holy is his name.

continued

He always shows mercy
to everyone who worships him.
The Lord has used his powerful arm
to scatter those who are proud.

R. The Almighty has done
great things for me,
and holy is his name.

He drags strong rulers from their thrones
and puts humble people
in places of power.
He gives the hungry good things to eat,
and he sends the rich away
with nothing in their hands.

R. The Almighty has done
great things for me,
and holy is his name.

He helps his servant Israel
and is always merciful to his people.
He made this promise to our ancestors,
to Abraham and his family forever!

R. The Almighty has done
great things for me,
and holy is his name.

450

Alleluia Verse and Verse before the Gospel
See Luke 1:28

Hail, Mary, full of grace,
the Lord is with you;
blessed are you among women.

451

ONE

GOSPEL

Luke 1:26–38

You will conceive and bear a son.

✚ A reading from the holy gospel according to Luke

God sent the angel Gabriel to the town of Nazareth
in Galilee with a message for a virgin named Mary.
She was engaged to Joseph from the family of King David.
The angel greeted Mary and said,
"You are truly blessed! The Lord is with you."

Mary was confused by the angel's words
and wondered what they meant.
Then the angel told Mary, "Don't be afraid!
God is pleased with you, and you will have a son.
His name will be Jesus.
He will be great
and will be called the Son of God Most High.
The Lord God will make him king,
as his ancestor David was.
He will rule the people of Israel forever,
and his kingdom will never end."

Mary asked the angel, "How can this happen?
I am not married!"

The angel answered,
"The Holy Spirit will come down to you,
and God's power will come over you.
So your child will be called the holy Son of God.

"Your relative Elizabeth is also going to have a son,
even though she is old.
No one thought she could ever have a baby,
but in three months she will have a son.
Nothing is impossible for God!"

Mary said, "I am the Lord's servant!
Let it happen as you have said."

And the angel left her.

The gospel of the Lord.

TWO

GOSPEL **✚ A reading from the holy gospel according to Luke**

Luke 2:41–51

Your father and I have been looking for you.

Every year Jesus' parents went to Jerusalem for Passover.
And when Jesus was twelve years old,
they all went there as usual for the celebration.

After Passover his parents left,
but they did not know that Jesus had stayed on in the city.
They thought he was traveling with some other people,
and they went a whole day
before they started looking for him.

When they could not find him
with their relatives and friends,
they went back to Jerusalem
and started looking for him there.

Three days later they found Jesus sitting in the temple,
listening to the teachers and asking them questions.
Everyone who heard him was surprised
at how much he knew and at the answers he gave.

When his parents found him, they were amazed.
His mother said, "Son, why have you done this to us?
Your father and I have been very worried,
and we have been searching for you!"

Jesus answered, "Why did you have to look for me?
Didn't you know that I would be in my Father's house?"
But they did not understand what he meant.

Jesus went back to Nazareth with his parents
and obeyed them.

The gospel of the Lord.

THREE

GOSPEL

John 19:25–27

Woman, this is your son. This is your mother.

✚ A reading from the holy gospel according to John

Jesus' mother stood beside his cross
with her sister and Mary the wife of Clopas.
Mary Magdalene was standing there too.

When Jesus saw his mother
and his favorite disciple with her,
he said to his mother,
"This man is now your son."
Then he said to the disciple,
"She is now your mother."

From then on, that disciple took her into his own home.

The gospel of the Lord.

452

ONE

New Testament Reading

Acts 3:1–10

What I have, I give you; in the name of Jesus stand up and walk.

A reading from the Acts of the Apostles

At the time of prayer,
which was about three o'clock in the afternoon,
Peter and John were going into the temple.
A man who had been born lame was being carried
to the temple door.
Each day he was placed beside this door,
known as the Beautiful Gate.
He sat there and begged from the people
who were going in.

The man saw Peter and John entering the temple,
and he asked them for money.
But they looked straight at him and said,
"Look up at us!"

The man stared at them
and thought he was going to get something.
But Peter said, "I don't have any silver or gold!
But I will give you what I do have.
In the name of Jesus Christ from Nazareth,
get up and start walking."
Peter then took him by the right hand and helped him up.

At once the man's feet and ankles became strong,
and he jumped up and started walking.
He went with Peter and John into the temple,
walking and jumping and praising God.

Everyone saw him walking around and praising God.
They knew that he was the beggar
who had been lying beside the Beautiful Gate,
and they were completely surprised.
They could not imagine what had happened to the man.

The word of the Lord.

TWO

A reading from the letter of Paul to the Ephesians

NEW TESTAMENT READING

Ephesians 2:20–22

You are like a building with the apostles and prophets as the foundation.

Brothers and sisters:
You are like a building with the apostles and prophets
as the foundation
and with Christ as the most important stone.
Christ is the one who holds the building together
and makes it grow into a holy temple for the Lord.
And you are part of that building Christ has built
as a place for God's own Spirit to live.

The word of the Lord.

453

Responsorial Psalm

Psalm 19:1–2, 3–4abcd (5a)

R. Their message goes
through all the earth.

The heavens keep telling
the wonders of God,
and the skies declare
what he has done.
Each day informs
the following day;
each night announces
to the next.

R. Their message goes
through all the earth.

continued

They don't speak a word,
and there is never
the sound of a voice.
Yet their message reaches
all the earth,
and it travels
around the world.

R. Their message goes
through all the earth.

454

Alleluia Verse and Verse before the Gospel
See Luke 11:28

Blessed are they
who hear the word of God
and keep it.

455

ONE

GOSPEL

✚ A reading from the holy gospel according to Matthew

Matthew 20:26b–28

Anyone among you who wishes to be first must be your servant.

Jesus said to his disciples:
"If you want to be great,
you must be the servant of all the others.
And if you want to be first,
you must be the slave of the rest.

"The Son of Man did not come to be a slave master,
but a slave who will give his life to rescue many people."

The gospel of the Lord.

TWO

✚ A reading from the holy gospel according to Luke

GOSPEL

Luke 6:12–16

Jesus spent the night in prayer. He chose twelve from them whom he named apostles.

Jesus went off to a mountain to pray,
and he spent the whole night there.

The next morning he called his disciples together
and chose twelve of them to be his apostles.

One was Simon, and Jesus named him Peter.
Another was Andrew, Peter's brother.
There were also James, John, Philip, Bartholomew,
Matthew, Thomas, and James the son of Alphaeus.

The rest of the apostles were Simon,
known as the Eager One,
Jude, who was the son of James,
and Judas Iscariot, who later betrayed Jesus.

The gospel of the Lord.

456

OLD TESTAMENT READING

2 Maccabees 7:1, 20–23

A reading from the second book of Maccabees

King Antiochus arrested seven Jewish brothers
  and their mother.
He had them beaten with heavy whips
  and tried to make them eat the meat of pigs,
which was against their religion.

The mother of these young men was a wonderful woman,
and she deserves to be remembered with praise.
She saw all seven of her sons die on the same day,
but she was brave and never gave up her hope in the LORD.
She cheered each of her sons
  by speaking to them in their native language.

Because of her hope in the Lord, this admirable mother bore their deaths with honor.

This mother was very special.
With the feelings of a woman and with the courage of a man,
she told her sons:
"I don't understand how you grew inside me.
I didn't give you life and breath or give shape to your bodies.
The Creator of the world made all people
  and started everything.
Now you are giving up your lives,
so that you can obey his laws.
But he will be merciful and give life and breath back to you."

The word of the Lord.

457

ONE

A reading from the Acts of the Apostles

New Testament Reading

Acts 7:55–60

Stephen was filled with the Holy Spirit.
He looked toward heaven,
where he saw our glorious God
 and Jesus standing at his right side.
Then Stephen said, "I see heaven open
 and the Son of Man standing at the right side of God!"

The council members shouted and covered their ears.
At once they all attacked Stephen
 and dragged him out of the city.
Then they started throwing stones at him.
The men who had brought charges against him
 put their coats at the feet of a young man named Saul.

Lord Jesus, receive my spirit.

As Stephen was being stoned to death, he called out,
"Lord Jesus, please welcome me!"
He kneeled down and shouted,
"Lord, don't blame them for what they have done."
Then he died.

The word of the Lord.

TWO

NEW TESTAMENT READING

2 Corinthians 6:4–10

We are said to be dying and yet here we are alive.

A reading from the second letter of Paul to the Corinthians

Brothers and sisters:
In everything and in every way we show that we truly are God's servants.

We have always been patient,
though we have had a lot of trouble, suffering,
and hard times.
We have been beaten, put in jail, and hurt in riots.
We have worked hard and have gone without sleep or food.
But we have kept ourselves pure
and have been understanding, patient, and kind.

The Holy Spirit has been with us,
and our love has been real.
We have spoken the truth,
and God's power has worked in us.
In all our struggles we have said and done only what is right.

Whether we were honored or dishonored
or praised or cursed,
we always told the truth about ourselves.
But some people said we did not.

We were unknown to others, but well known to you.
We seem to be dying,
and yet we are still alive.
We have been punished, but never killed,
and we are always happy, even in times of suffering.

Although we are poor,
we have made many people rich.
And though we own nothing,
everything is ours.

The word of the Lord.

458

ONE

Responsorial Psalm

Psalm 31:1–2a, 2bcde–3, 19 (6a)

R. Into your hands, O Lord,
I entrust my spirit.

I come to you, LORD,
for protection.
Don't let me be ashamed.
Do as you have promised
and rescue me.
Listen to my prayer.

R. Into your hands, O Lord,
I entrust my spirit.

Hurry to save me.
Be my mighty rock
and the fortress
where I am safe.
You, LORD God,
are my mighty rock
and my fortress.
Lead me and guide me,
so that your name
will be honored.

R. Into your hands, O Lord,
I entrust my spirit.

You are wonderful,
and while everyone watches,
you store up blessings for all
who honor and trust you.

R. Into your hands, O Lord,
I entrust my spirit.

TWO

Responsorial Psalm

Psalm 34:1–2, 3–4, 7–8 (5b)

R. The Lord set me free from all my fears.

I will always praise the LORD.
With all my heart,
I will praise the LORD.
Let all who are helpless
listen and be glad.

R. The Lord set me free from all my fears.

Honor the LORD *with me!*
Celebrate his great name.
I asked the LORD *for help,*
and he saved me
from all my fears.

R. The Lord set me free from all my fears.

If you honor the LORD,
his angel will protect you.
Discover for yourself
that the LORD *is kind.*
Come to him for protection,
and you will be glad.

R. The Lord set me free from all my fears.

459

Alleluia Verse and Verse before the Gospel
2 Corinthians 1:3b–4a

Blessed be the Father of mercies
and the God of all comfort,
who consoles us
in all our afflictions.

460

GOSPEL

John 12.24–26

If a grain of wheat falls on the ground and dies, it yields a rich harvest.

✚ A reading from the holy gospel according to John

Jesus said to his disciples:
"I tell you for certain that a grain of wheat
that falls on the ground
will never be more than one grain unless it dies.
But if it dies, it will produce lots of wheat.

"If you love your life, you will lose it.
If you give it up in this world,
you will be given eternal life.

"If you serve me, you must go with me.
My servants will be with me wherever I am.
If you serve me, my Father will honor you."

The gospel of the Lord.

461

OLD TESTAMENT READING

Ezekiel 34:11–16abce

As a shepherd keeps all his flock in view, so shall I keep my sheep in view.

A reading from the book of the prophet Ezekiel

The LORD says this:
"I, the LORD God, will look for my people
and take care of them myself.
As a shepherd looks for sheep that have wandered away,
I will search for my scattered people.
I will rescue them from all the places where they went
on that dark and gloomy day.
I will bring them back from the foreign countries
and protect them on the mountains,
in the valleys, and wherever they settle.

"My people will be like sheep grazing and resting
in good pastures and on Israel's mountains.
I, the LORD All-Powerful, will lead them there
and watch over them.
"I will look for the lost sheep
and bring back the ones that have wandered off.
If any are hurt,
I will bandage their wounds.
If any are weak,
I will help them.
I will take good care of my people!"

The word of the Lord.

462

ONE

Responsorial Psalm

Psalm 23:1–3a, 3b–4, 6 (1)

R. The Lord is my shepherd;
there is nothing I shall want.

You, LORD, are my shepherd.
I will never be in need.
You let me rest in fields
of green grass.
You lead me to streams
of peaceful water,
and you refresh my life.

R. The Lord is my shepherd;
there is nothing I shall want.

You are true to your name,
and you lead me
along the right paths.
I may walk through valleys
as dark as death,
but I won't be afraid.
You are with me,
and your shepherd's rod
makes me feel safe.

R. The Lord is my shepherd;
there is nothing I shall want.

Your kindness and love
will always be with me
each day of my life,
and I will live forever
in your house, LORD.

R. The Lord is my shepherd;
there is nothing I shall want.

TWO

Responsorial Psalm

Psalm 96:1–2a, 2b–3, 7–8a, 10 (3)

R. Proclaim God's marvelous deeds
to all the nations.

Sing a new song to the LORD!
Everyone on this earth,
sing praises to the LORD,
sing and praise his name.

R. Proclaim God's marvelous deeds
to all the nations.

Day after day announce,
"The LORD has saved us!"
Tell every nation on earth,
"The LORD is wonderful
and does marvelous things!"

R. Proclaim God's marvelous deeds
to all the nations.

Tell everyone of every nation,
"Praise the glorious power
of the LORD.
He is wonderful! Praise him!"

R. Proclaim God's marvelous deeds
to all the nations.

Announce to the nations,
"The LORD is King!
The world stands firm,
never to be shaken,
and he will judge its people
with fairness."

R. Proclaim God's marvelous deeds
to all the nations.

463

Alleluia Verse and Verse before the Gospel
Matthew 28:19a, 20b

Go and teach all people my gospel;
I am with you always,
until the end of the world.

464

GOSPEL

[For Missionaries]

Matthew 28:16–20

Go and teach all people my gospel.

ONE

✚ A reading from the holy gospel according to Matthew

Jesus' eleven disciples went to a mountain in Galilee,
where Jesus had told them to meet him.
They saw him and worshiped him,
but some of them doubted.

Jesus came to them and said:
"I have been given all authority in heaven and on earth!
Go to the people of all nations and make them my disciples.
Baptize them in the name of the Father,
the Son, and the Holy Spirit,
and teach them to do everything I have told you.

"I will be with you always,
even until the end of the world."

The gospel of the Lord.

TWO

GOSPEL **✚ A reading from the holy gospel according to Mark**

Mark 1:14–20

After John was arrested,
Jesus went to Galilee and told the good news
that comes from God.
He said, "The time has come!
God's kingdom will soon be here.
Turn back to God and believe the good news!"

I will make you fishers of people.

As Jesus was walking along the shore of Lake Galilee,
he saw Simon and his brother Andrew.
They were fishermen and were casting their nets
into the lake.
Jesus said to them, "Come with me!
I will teach you how to bring in people instead of fish."
Right then the two brothers dropped their nets
and went with him.

Jesus walked on and soon saw James and John,
the sons of Zebedee.
They were in a boat, mending their nets.
At once Jesus asked them to come with him.
They left their father in the boat with the hired workers
and went with him.

The gospel of the Lord.

THREE

✚ A reading from the holy gospel according to John

GOSPEL

[For a Pope]

John 21:15–17

Feed my lambs; feed my sheep.

When Jesus and his disciples had finished eating, he asked,
"Simon son of John,
do you love me more than the others do?"

Simon Peter answered, "Yes, Lord, you know I do!"
"Then feed my lambs," Jesus said.

Jesus asked a second time, "Simon son of John,
do you love me?"
Peter answered, "Yes, Lord, you know I love you!"
"Then take care of my sheep," Jesus told him.

Jesus asked a third time, "Simon son of John,
do you love me?"

Peter was hurt because Jesus had asked him three times
if he loved him.
So he told Jesus, "Lord, you know everything.
You know I love you."

Jesus replied, "Feed my sheep."

The gospel of the Lord.

465

OLD TESTAMENT READING

A reading from the first book of Kings

1 Kings 3:11–14

The LORD said to Solomon:
"I will answer your prayer.
You will be wise and know more than anyone
who has ever lived or ever will live.
You didn't ask to live a long time or to be rich,
and you didn't ask for your enemies to be destroyed.
All you wanted was to be honest and fair.

I give you a heart wise and shrewd.

"But I will give you more than you have asked for.
I will make you rich and respected.
You will be the most famous king of your time.
And if you obey me and keep all my laws and commands,
as your father David did,
I will give you a long life."

The word of the Lord.

466

ONE

A reading from the letter of Paul to the Ephesians

New Testament Reading

Ephesians 4:1–7

Unity in the work of service, building up the body of Christ.

Brothers and sisters:
As a prisoner of the Lord,
I beg you to live in a way that is worthy of the people
God has chosen to be his own.
Always be humble and gentle.
Patiently put up with each other and love each other.
Try your best to let God's Spirit keep your hearts united.
Do this by living at peace.

All of you are part of the same body.
There is only one Spirit of God,
just as you were given one hope
when you were chosen to be God's people.

We have only one Lord, one faith, and one baptism.
There is one God who is the Father of all people.
Not only is God above all others,
but he works by using all of us,
and he lives in all of us.
Christ has generously divided out his gifts to us.

The word of the Lord.

TWO

NEW TESTAMENT READING

Ephesians 4:11–13

God chose some of us so that his people would learn to serve and his body grow strong.

A reading from the letter of Paul to the Ephesians

Brothers and sisters:
Christ chose some of us to be apostles, prophets,
missionaries, pastors, and teachers,
so that his people would learn to serve
and his body would grow strong.

This will continue until we are united by our faith
and by our understanding of the Son of God.
Then we will be mature, just as Christ is,
and we will be completely like him.

The word of the Lord.

467

Responsorial Psalm

Psalm 19:7, 8 (John 6:63c)

R. Your words, Lord, are spirit and life.

The Law of the LORD is perfect;
it gives us new life.
His teachings last forever,
and they give wisdom
to ordinary people.

R. Your words, Lord, are spirit and life.

The LORD's instruction is right;
it makes our hearts glad.
His commands shine brightly,
and they give us light.

R. Your words, Lord, are spirit and life.

468

Alleluia Verse and Verse before the Gospel

The seed is the word of God,
Christ is the sower;
all who come to him
will live for ever.

469

GOSPEL

✚ A reading from the holy gospel according to Mark

Mark 4:1–9

The next time Jesus taught beside Lake Galilee,
a big crowd gathered.
It was so large that he had to sit in a boat out on the lake,
while the people stood on the shore.
He used stories to teach them many things,
and this is part of what he taught:

The sower went out to sow seed.

"Now listen!
A farmer went out to scatter seed in a field.
While the farmer was scattering the seed,
some of it fell along the road and was eaten by birds.

"Other seeds fell on thin, rocky ground
and quickly started growing
because the soil was not very deep.
But when the sun came up,
the plants were scorched and dried up,
because they did not have enough roots.

"Some other seeds fell where thorn bushes grew up
and choked out the plants.
So they did not produce any grain.

"But a few seeds did fall on good ground
where the plants grew and produced thirty or sixty
or even a hundred times as much as was scattered."

Then Jesus said, "If you have ears, pay attention."

The gospel of the Lord.

470

ONE

NEW TESTAMENT READING

[For Religious]

Acts 4:32–35

The whole group of believers was united, heart and soul.

A reading from the Acts of the Apostles

The followers of Jesus all felt the same way
about everything.
None of them claimed that their belongings were their own,
and they shared everything they had with each other.

In a powerful way the apostles told everyone
that the Lord Jesus was now alive.

God greatly blessed his followers,
and no one went in need of anything.
Everyone who owned land or houses would sell them
and bring the money to the apostles.
Then they would give the money to anyone who needed it.

The word of the Lord.

TWO

A reading from the first letter of Paul to the Corinthians

NEW TESTAMENT READING

1 Corinthians 1:26–31

God has chosen what is weak by human reckoning.

My dear friends,
remember what you were when God chose you.
The people of this world didn't think
 that many of you were wise.
Only a few of you were in places of power,
and not many of you came from important families.

But God chose the foolish things of this world
 to put the wise to shame.
He chose the weak things of this world
 to put the powerful to shame.

What the world thinks is worthless, useless,
 and nothing at all is what God has used
 to destroy what the world considers important.
God did all this to keep anyone from bragging to him.
You are God's children.
He sent Christ Jesus to save us
 and to make us wise, acceptable, and holy.
So if you want to brag,
do what the Scriptures say and brag about the Lord.

The word of the Lord.

THREE

NEW TESTAMENT READING

1 Corinthians 13:4–13

A reading from the first letter of Paul to the Corinthians

Brothers and sisters:
Love is kind and patient,
never jealous, boastful, proud, or rude.
Love isn't selfish or quick tempered.
It doesn't keep a record of wrongs that others do.
Love rejoices in the truth, but not in evil.
Love is always supportive, loyal, hopeful, and trusting.
Love never fails!

Love never ends.

Everyone who prophesies will stop,
and unknown languages will no longer be spoken.
All that we know will be forgotten.
We don't know everything,
and our prophecies are not complete.
But what is perfect will someday appear,
and what is not perfect will then disappear.

When we were children,
we thought and reasoned as children do.
But when we grew up,
we quit our childish ways.

Now all we can see of God is like a cloudy picture
in a mirror.
Later we will see him face to face.
We don't know everything,
but then we will,
just as God completely understands us.

For now there are faith, hope, and love.
But of these three, the greatest is love.

The word of the Lord.

FOUR

New Testament Reading

Philippians 4:4–9

Fill your minds with everything that is holy.

A reading from the letter of Paul to the Philippians

Brothers and sisters:
Always be glad because of the Lord!
I will say it again: Be glad.

Always be gentle with others.
The Lord will soon be here.
Don't worry about anything,
but pray about everything.

With thankful hearts offer up your prayers and requests
to God.
Then, because you belong to Christ Jesus,
God will bless you with peace
that no one can completely understand.
And this peace will control the way you think and feel.

Finally, my friends,
keep your minds on whatever is true, pure, right,
holy, friendly, and proper.
Don't ever stop thinking about what is truly worthwhile
and worthy of praise.
You know the teachings I gave you,
and you know what you heard me say and saw me do.

So follow my example.
And God, who gives peace, will be with you.

The word of the Lord.

FIVE

NEW TESTAMENT READING

1 Peter 4:7b–11

A reading from the first letter of Peter

Each one of you has received a special gift; put yourselves at the service of others.

Brothers and sisters:
Be serious and be sensible enough to pray.

Most important of all, you must sincerely love each other,
because love wipes away many sins.

Welcome people into your home and don't grumble about it.

Each of you has been blessed
with one of God's many wonderful gifts
to be used in the service of others.
So use your gift well.

If you have the gift of speaking,
preach God's message.
If you have the gift of helping others,
do it with the strength that God supplies.

Everything should be done in a way that will bring honor
to God because of Jesus Christ,
who is glorious and powerful forever. Amen.

The word of the Lord.

SIX

New Testament Reading

1 John 3:16–18

We should lay down our lives for our brothers and sisters.

A reading from the first letter of John

Beloved:
We know what love is because Jesus gave his life for us.
That's why we must give our lives for each other.

If we have all we need and see one of our own people
in need,
we must have pity on that person,
or else we cannot say we love God.

Children, you show love for others by truly helping them,
and not merely by talking about it.

The word of the Lord.

SEVEN

New Testament Reading

1 John 5:2–5

This is the victory over the world—our faith.

A reading from the first letter of John

Beloved:
If we love and obey God,
we know that we will love his children.
We show our love for God by obeying his commandments,
and they are not hard to follow.

Every child of God can defeat the world,
and our faith is what gives us this victory.
No one can defeat the world
without having faith in Jesus as the Son of God.

The word of the Lord.

471

ONE

Responsorial Psalm

Psalm 34:1–2, 3–4, 8–9 (2a) (9a)

R. I will bless the Lord at all times.
or:
R. Taste and see the goodness of the Lord.

I will always praise the LORD.
With all my heart,
I will praise the LORD.
Let all who are helpless
listen and be glad.

R. I will bless the Lord at all times.
or:
R. Taste and see the goodness of the Lord.

Honor the LORD with me!
Celebrate his great name.
I asked the LORD for help,
and he saved me
from all my fears.

R. I will bless the Lord at all times.
or:
R. Taste and see the goodness of the Lord.

Discover for yourself
that the LORD is kind.
Come to him for protection,
and you will be glad.
Honor the LORD!
You are his special people.
No one who honors the LORD
will ever be in need.

R. I will bless the Lord at all times.
or:
R. Taste and see the goodness of the Lord.

TWO

Responsorial Psalm

Psalm 103:1–2, 3–4, 17–18a (1a)

R. O bless the Lord, my soul!

With all my heart
I praise the LORD,
and with all that I am
I praise his holy name!
With all my heart
I praise the LORD!
I will never forget
how kind he has been.

R. O bless the Lord, my soul!

The LORD forgives our sins,
heals us when we are sick,
and protects us from death.
His kindness and love
are a crown on our heads.

R. O bless the Lord, my soul!

The LORD is always kind
to those who worship him,
and he keeps his promises
to their descendants
who faithfully obey him.

R. O bless the Lord, my soul!

472

Alleluia Verse and Verse before the Gospel
Matthew 23:11, 12

Whoever is greatest among you
will serve the rest.
All who humble themselves
shall be exalted.

473

ONE

GOSPEL

✚ A reading from the holy gospel according to Matthew

Matthew 18:1–4

The disciples came to Jesus and asked him
who would be the greatest in the kingdom of heaven.
Jesus called a child over and had the child stand near him.

Unless you become like children, you will not enter the kingdom of heaven.

Then he said: "I promise you this.
If you don't change and become like this child,
you will never get into the kingdom of heaven.
But if you are as humble as this child,
you are the greatest in the kingdom of heaven."

The gospel of the Lord.

TWO

GOSPEL

[For Those Who Work for the Underprivileged]

Matthew 25:31–40

Whatever you have done to the very least of my brothers and sisters, you have done to me.

✚ A reading from the holy gospel according to Matthew

Jesus said to his disciples:
"When the Son of Man comes in his glory
with all of his angels,
he will sit on his royal throne.

"The people of all nations will be brought before him,
and he will separate them,
as shepherds separate their sheep from their goats.

"He will place the sheep on his right
and the goats on his left.
Then the king will say to those on his right,
'My father has blessed you!
Come and receive the kingdom that was prepared for you
before the world was created.
When I was hungry, you gave me something to eat,
and when I was thirsty, you gave me something to drink.
When I was a stranger, you welcomed me,
and when I was naked, you gave me clothes to wear.
When I was sick, you took care of me,
and when I was in jail, you visited me.'

"Then the ones who pleased the Lord will ask,
'When did we give you something to eat or drink?
When did we welcome you as a stranger
or give you clothes to wear
or visit you while you were sick or in jail?'

"The king will answer,
'Whenever you did it for any of my people,
no matter how unimportant they seemed,
you did it for me.'"

The gospel of the Lord.

THREE

GOSPEL **✠ A reading from the holy gospel according to Mark**

[For Educators]

Mark 9:33–37

Whenever you have accepted graciously a small child, you have accepted me.

Jesus and his disciples went to his home in Capernaum.
After they were inside the house, Jesus asked them,
"What were you arguing about along the way?"
They had been arguing about which one of them
was the greatest,
and so they did not answer.

After Jesus sat down and told the twelve disciples
to gather around him,
he said, "If you want the place of honor,
you must become a slave and serve others!"

Then Jesus had a child stand near him.
He put his arm around the child and said,
"When you welcome even a child because of me,
you welcome me.
And when you welcome me,
you welcome the one who sent me."

The gospel of the Lord.

FOUR

GOSPEL

[For Religious]

Luke 12:32–34

It has pleased the Father to give you the kingdom.

✚ A reading from the holy gospel according to Luke

Jesus said to his disciples:
"My little group of disciples, don't be afraid!
Your Father wants to give you the kingdom.

"Sell what you have and give the money to the poor.
Make yourselves moneybags that never wear out.
Make your treasure safe in heaven,
where thieves cannot steal it and moths cannot destroy it.
Your heart will always be where your treasure is."

The gospel of the Lord.

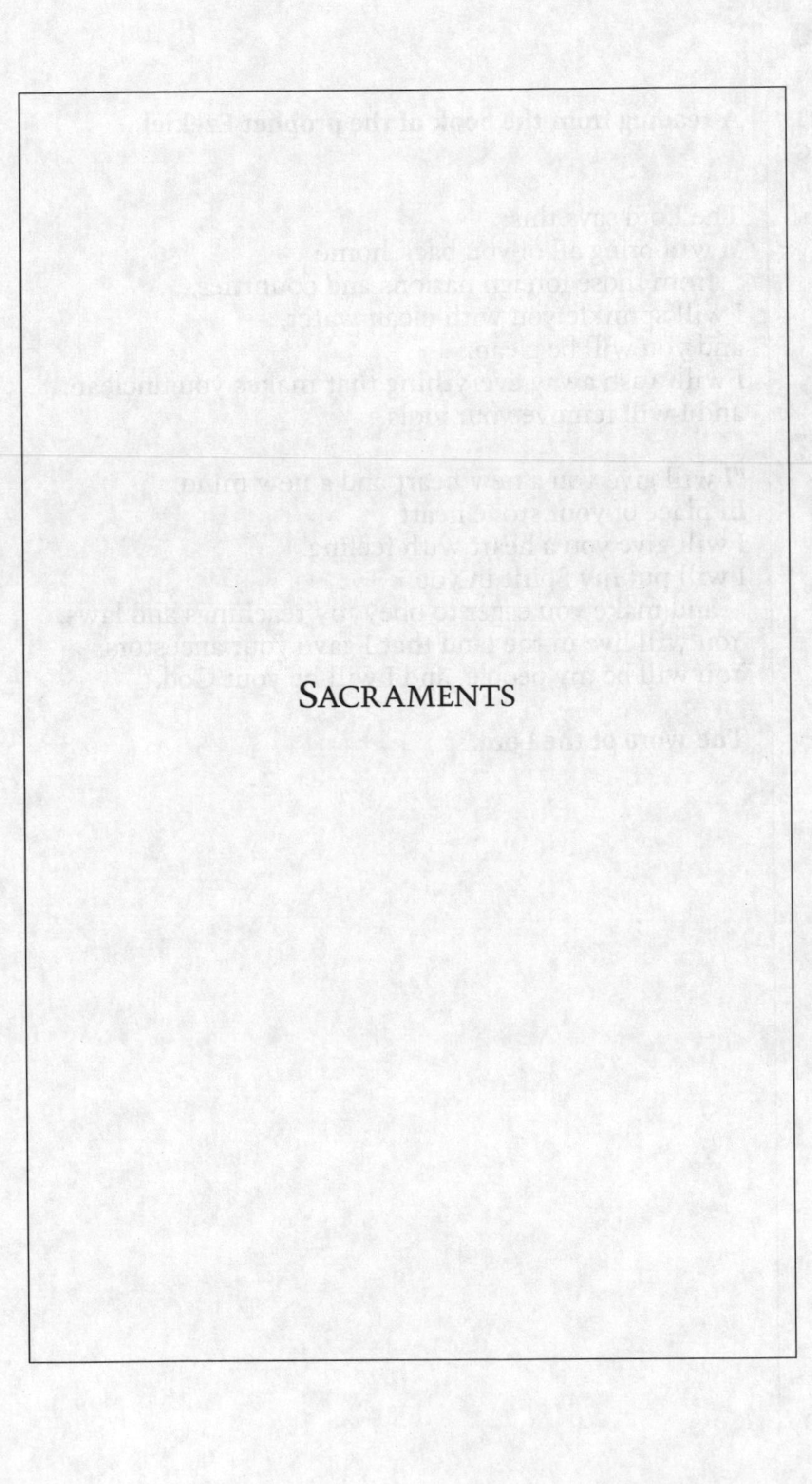
SACRAMENTS

474

Old Testament Reading

Ezekiel 36:24–28

I shall pour clean water over you and you will be cleansed from all your sins.

A reading from the book of the prophet Ezekiel

The Lord says this:
"I will bring all of you back home
  from those foreign nations and countries.
I will sprinkle you with clean water,
and you will be clean.
I will wash away everything that makes you unclean,
and I will remove your idols.

"I will give you a new heart and a new mind.
In place of your stone heart,
I will give you a heart with feeling.
I will put my Spirit in you
  and make you eager to obey my teachings and laws.
You will live in the land that I gave your ancestors.
You will be my people, and I will be your God."

The word of the Lord.

475

ONE

A reading from the first letter of Paul to the Corinthians

New Testament Reading

1 Corinthians 12:12–13

In the one Spirit we were all baptized into one body.

Brothers and sisters:
The body of Christ has many different parts,
just as any other body does.
Some of us are Jews, and others are Gentiles.
Some of us are slaves, and others are free.
But God's Spirit baptized each of us
  and made us part of the body of Christ.
Now we each drink from that same Spirit.

The word of the Lord.

TWO

A reading from the letter of Paul to the Galatians

New Testament Reading

Galatians 3:26–28

All baptized in Christ have put on Christ.

Brothers and sisters:
All of you are God's children
  because of your faith in Christ Jesus.
And when you were baptized,
it was as though you had put on Christ
  in the same way you put on new clothes.

Faith in Christ Jesus is what makes each of you equal
  with each other,
whether you are a Jew or a Greek,
a slave or a free person,
a man or a woman.

The word of the Lord.

476

ONE

Responsorial Psalm

Psalm 23:1–3a, 3b–4, 5–6 (1)

R. The Lord is my shepherd;
there is nothing I shall want.

You, LORD, are my shepherd.
I will never be in need.
You let me rest in fields
of green grass.
You lead me to streams
of peaceful water,
and you refresh my life.

R. The Lord is my shepherd;
there is nothing I shall want.

You are true to your name,
and you lead me
along the right paths.
I may walk through valleys
as dark as death,
but I won't be afraid.
You are with me,
and your shepherd's rod
makes me feel safe.

R. The Lord is my shepherd;
there is nothing I shall want.

You treat me to a feast,
while my enemies watch.
You honor me as your guest,
and you fill my cup
until it overflows.
Your kindness and love
will always be with me
each day of my life,
and I will live forever
in your house, LORD.

R. The Lord is my shepherd;
there is nothing I shall want.

TWO

Responsorial Psalm

Psalm 27:1, 4, 13–14 (1a)

R. The Lord is my light and my salvation.

You, LORD, are the light
that keeps me safe.
I am not afraid of anyone.
You protect me,
and I have no fears.

R. The Lord is my light and my salvation.

I ask only one thing, LORD:
Let me live in your house
every day of my life
to see how wonderful you are
and to pray in your temple.

R. The Lord is my light and my salvation.

I know that I will live
to see how kind you are.
Trust the LORD!
Be brave and strong
and trust the LORD!

R. The Lord is my light and my salvation.

Alleluia Verse and Verse before the Gospel

John 14:6

I am the way, the truth,
and the life, says the Lord;
no one comes to the Father,
except through me.

478

ONE

GOSPEL **✚ A reading from the holy gospel according to Matthew**

Matthew 22:35–40

This is the greatest and the first commandment.

One of the Pharisees was an expert in the Jewish Law.
He tried to test Jesus by asking,
"Teacher, what is the most important commandment
in the Law?"

Jesus answered:
"'Love the Lord your God with all your heart, soul,
and mind.'
This is the first and most important commandment.
The second most important commandment is like this one.
And it is, 'Love others as much as you love yourself.'
All the Law of Moses and the Books of the Prophets
are based on these two commandments."

The gospel of the Lord.

TWO

✚ A reading from the holy gospel according to Mark

GOSPEL

Mark 10:13–16

Do not keep the children from me.

Some people brought their children to Jesus
so that he could bless them by placing his hands on them.
But his disciples told the people to stop bothering him.

When Jesus saw this, he became angry and said,
"Let the children come to me!
Don't try to stop them.
People who are like these little children
belong to the kingdom of God.
I promise you that you cannot get into God's kingdom,
unless you accept it the way a child does."

Then Jesus took the children in his arms
and blessed them by placing his hands on them.

The gospel of the Lord.

THREE

GOSPEL ✚ **A reading from the holy gospel according to John**

John 15:1–4

Jesus said to his disciples:
"I am the true vine,
and my Father is the gardener.
He cuts away every branch of mine
that does not produce fruit.
But he trims clean every branch that does produce fruit,
so that it will produce even more fruit.

Those who live in me, and I in them, will bear much fruit.

"You are already clean because of what I have said to you.

"Stay joined to me,
and I will stay joined to you.
Just as a branch cannot produce fruit
unless it stays joined to the vine,
you cannot produce fruit unless you stay joined to me."

The gospel of the Lord.

FOUR

GOSPEL ✚ **A reading from the holy gospel according to John**

John 15:5–8

Those who live in me, and I in them, will bear much fruit.

Jesus said to his disciples:
"I am the vine, and you are the branches.
If you stay joined to me, and I stay joined to you,
then you will produce lots of fruit.
But you cannot do anything without me.

"If you don't stay joined to me,
you will be thrown away.
You will be like dry branches
that are gathered up and burned in a fire.

"Stay joined to me and let my teachings become part of you.
Then you can pray for whatever you want,
and your prayer will be answered.

"When you become fruitful disciples of mine,
my Father will be honored."

The gospel of the Lord.

FIVE

GOSPEL

✚ A reading from the holy gospel according to John

John 15:9–11

I have loved you as my Father has loved me.

Jesus said to his disciples:
"I have loved you,
just as my Father has loved me.
So make sure that I keep on loving you.
If you obey me,
I will keep loving you,
just as my Father keeps loving me,
because I have obeyed him.

"I have told you this to make you as completely happy
as I am."

The gospel of the Lord.

CONFIRMATION
(Holy Spirit)

479

ONE

OLD TESTAMENT READING

A reading from the book of the prophet Ezekiel

Ezekiel 36:24–28

I will place a new Spirit in your midst.

The Lord says this:
"I will bring all of you back home
  from those foreign nations and countries.
I will sprinkle you with clean water,
and you will be clean.
I will wash away everything that makes you unclean,
and I will remove your idols.

"I will give you a new heart and a new mind.
In place of your stone heart,
I will give you a heart with feeling.
I will put my Spirit in you
  and make you eager to obey my teachings and laws.
You will live in the land that I gave your ancestors.
You will be my people, and I will be your God."

The word of the Lord.

TWO

A reading from the book of the prophet Joel

OLD TESTAMENT READING

Joel 3:1–3a

I will pour out my Spirit on all people.

The LORD said:
"When that time comes,
I will give my Spirit to everyone.
Your sons and daughters will prophesy.

"Your young men will see visions,
and your old men will have dreams.
In those days I will give my Spirit to my servants,
both men and women.
I will work miracles in the sky above
and wonders on the earth below."

The word of the Lord.

480

ONE

NEW TESTAMENT READING

Acts 2:1–6, 14, 22b–23, 32–33

A reading from the Acts of the Apostles

On the day of Pentecost
all the Lord's followers were together in one place.
Suddenly there was a noise from heaven
like the sound of a mighty wind!
It filled the house where they were meeting.
Then they saw what looked like fiery tongues
moving in all directions,
and a tongue came and settled on each person there.
The Holy Spirit took control of everyone,
and they began speaking
whatever languages the Spirit let them speak.

They were all filled with the Holy Spirit, and began to speak different languages.

Many religious Jews from every country in the world
were living in Jerusalem.
And when they heard this noise, a crowd gathered.
But they were surprised,
because they were hearing everything
in their own languages.

Peter stood with the eleven apostles
and spoke in a loud and clear voice to the crowd:
"Friends and everyone else living in Jerusalem,
listen carefully to what I have to say!

"God proved that he sent Jesus to you
by having him work miracles, wonders, and signs.
All of you know this.

"God had already planned and decided
that Jesus would be handed over to you.
So you took him and had evil men put him to death
on a cross.

"All of us can tell you that God has raised Jesus to life!

"Jesus was taken up to sit at the right side of God,
and he was given the Holy Spirit,
just as the Father had promised.
Jesus is also the one who has given the Spirit to us,
and that is what you are now seeing and hearing."

The word of the Lord.

TWO

A reading from the letter of Paul to the Romans

NEW TESTAMENT READING

Romans 8:14–17

Brothers and sisters:
Only those people who are led by God's Spirit
are his children.
God's Spirit doesn't make us slaves who are afraid of him.
Instead, we become his children and call him our Father.
God's Spirit makes us sure that we are his children.

The Spirit and our spirit bear united witness that we are children of God.

His Spirit lets us know that together with Christ
we will be given what God has promised.
We will also share in the glory of Christ,
because we have suffered with him.

The word of the Lord.

THREE

NEW TESTAMENT READING

A reading from the first letter of Paul to the Corinthians

1 Corinthians 12:4–13

Brothers and sisters:
There are different kinds of spiritual gifts,
but they all come from the same Spirit.
There are different ways to serve the same Lord,
and we can each do different things.
Yet the same God works in all of us
and helps us in everything we do.

There is one and the same Spirit giving to each as the Spirit wills.

The Spirit has given each of us a special way
of serving others.
Some of us can speak with wisdom,
while others can speak with knowledge,
but these gifts come from the same Spirit.

To others the Spirit has given great faith
or the power to heal the sick
or the power to work mighty miracles.

Some of us are prophets,
and some of us recognize when God's Spirit is present.
Others can speak different kinds of languages,
and still others can tell what these languages mean.

But it is the Spirit who does all this
and decides which gifts to give to each of us.

The body of Christ has many different parts,
just as any other body does.
Some of us are Jews,
and others are Gentiles.
Some of us are slaves,
and others are free.
But God's Spirit baptized each of us
and made us part of the body of Christ.
Now we each drink from that same Spirit.

The word of the Lord.

481

Responsorial Psalm

Psalm 104:1abc and 24bcd, 30–31 (30)

R. Lord, send out your Spirit,
and renew the face of the earth.

I praise you, L*ORD* *God,*
with all my heart.
You are glorious and majestic.
Our L*ORD, you made so many things;*
the whole earth is covered
with your living creatures.

R. Lord, send out your Spirit,
and renew the face of the earth.

You created all of them
by your Spirit,
and you give new life
to the earth.
Our L*ORD, we pray*
that your glory
will last forever
and that you will be pleased
with what you have done.

R. Lord, send out your Spirit,
and renew the face of the earth.

TWO

Responsorial Psalm

Psalm 23:1–3a, 3b–4, 5, 6 (1)

R. The Lord is my shepherd;
there is nothing I shall want.

You, LORD, are my shepherd.
I will never be in need.
You let me rest in fields
of green grass.
You lead me to streams
of peaceful water,
and you refresh my life.

R. The Lord is my shepherd;
there is nothing I shall want.

You are true to your name,
and you lead me
along the right paths.
I may walk through valleys
as dark as death,
but I won't be afraid.
You are with me,
and your shepherd's rod
makes me feel safe.

R. The Lord is my shepherd;
there is nothing I shall want.

You treat me to a feast,
while my enemies watch.
You honor me as your guest,
and you fill my cup
until it overflows.

R. The Lord is my shepherd;
there is nothing I shall want.

Your kindness and love
will always be with me
each day of my life,
and I will live forever
in your house, LORD.

R. The Lord is my shepherd;
there is nothing I shall want.

482

Alleluia Verse and Verse before the Gospel
John 14:16

I will ask the Father
and he will send you
the Holy Spirit,
to be with you for ever.

483

ONE

GOSPEL **✚ A reading from the holy gospel according to John**

John 14:15–17

Jesus said to his disciples:
"If you love me, you will do as I command.
Then I will ask the Father to send you the Holy Spirit
who will help you and always be with you.
The Spirit will show you what is true.

The Spirit of truth will be with you for ever.

"The people of this world cannot accept the Spirit,
because they don't see or know him.
But you know the Spirit, who is with you
and will keep on living in you."

The gospel of the Lord.

TWO

GOSPEL

✚ A reading from the holy gospel according to John

John 14:23–26

The Holy Spirit will teach you everything.

Jesus said:
"If anyone loves me, they will obey me.
Then my Father will love them,
and we will come to them and live in them.
But anyone who doesn't love me,
won't obey me.
What they have heard me say doesn't really come from me,
but from the Father who sent me.

"I have told you these things while I am still with you.
But the Holy Spirit will come and help you,
because the Father will send the Spirit to take my place.
The Spirit will teach you everything
and will remind you of what I said while I was with you."

The gospel of the Lord.

484

NEW TESTAMENT READING

Acts 2:42–47

They continued in fellowship with the apostles and in the breaking of bread.

A reading from the Acts of the Apostles

The followers of Jesus spent their time
learning from the apostles,
and they were like family to each other.
They also broke bread and prayed together.

Everyone was amazed at the many miracles and wonders
that the apostles worked.

All the Lord's followers often met together,
and they shared everything they had.
They would sell their property and possessions
and give the money to whoever needed it.
Day after day they met together in the temple.
They broke bread together in different homes
and shared their food happily and freely,
while praising God.
Everyone liked them,
and each day the Lord added to their group
others who were being saved.

The word of the Lord.

485

ONE

Responsorial Psalm

Psalm 23:1–3a, 3b–4, 5, 6
(1)

R. The Lord is my shepherd;
there is nothing I shall want.

You, LORD, are my shepherd.
I will never be in need.
You let me rest in fields
of green grass.
You lead me to streams
of peaceful water,
and you refresh my life.

R. The Lord is my shepherd;
there is nothing I shall want.

You are true to your name,
and you lead me
along the right paths.
I may walk through valleys
as dark as death,
but I won't be afraid.
You are with me,
and your shepherd's rod
makes me feel safe.

R. The Lord is my shepherd;
there is nothing I shall want.

You treat me to a feast,
while my enemies watch.
You honor me as your guest,
and you fill my cup
until it overflows.

R. The Lord is my shepherd;
there is nothing I shall want.

continued

Your kindness and love
will always be with me
each day of my life,
and I will live forever
in your house, LORD.

R. The Lord is my shepherd;
there is nothing I shall want.

TWO

Responsorial Psalm

Psalm 34:1–2, 3–4, 5–6, 9–10 (9a)

R. Taste and see the goodness of the Lord.

I will always praise the LORD.
With all my heart,
I will praise the LORD.
Let all who are helpless
listen and be glad.

R. Taste and see the goodness of the Lord.

Honor the LORD with me!
Celebrate his great name.
I asked the LORD for help,
and he saved me
from all my fears.

R. Taste and see the goodness of the Lord.

Keep your eyes on the LORD!
You will shine like the sun
and never blush with shame.
I was a nobody, but I prayed,
and the LORD saved me
from all my troubles.

R. Taste and see the goodness of the Lord.

Honor the LORD!
You are his special people.
No one who honors the LORD
will ever be in need.
Young lions may go hungry
or even starve,
but if you trust the LORD,
you will never miss out
on anything good.

R. Taste and see the goodness of the Lord.

THREE

Responsorial Psalm

Psalm 145:10–11, 15–16, 17–18 (16)

R. You open your hand to feed us, Lord;
you answer all our needs.

All creation will thank you,
and your loyal people
will praise you.
They will tell about
your marvelous kingdom
and your power.

R. You open your hand to feed us, Lord;
you answer all our needs.

Everyone depends on you,
and when the time is right,
you provide them with food.
By your own hand you satisfy
the desires of all who live.

continued

R. You open your hand to feed us, Lord;
you answer all our needs.

Our LORD, *everything you do*
is kind and thoughtful,
and you are near to everyone
whose prayers are sincere.

R. You open your hand to feed us, Lord;
you answer all our needs.

486

Alleluia Verse and Verse before the Gospel
John 6:51

I am the living bread from heaven,
says the Lord;
whoever eats this bread
will live for ever.

487

ONE

GOSPEL

✚ A reading from the holy gospel according to Mark

Mark 14:12–16, 22–26

This is my body.
This is my blood.

It was the first day of the Feast of Thin Bread,
and the Passover lambs were being killed.
Jesus' disciples asked him,
"Where do you want us to prepare the Passover meal?"

Jesus said to two of the disciples,
"Go into the city,
where you will meet a man carrying a jar of water.
Follow him, and when he goes into a house,
say to the owner,
'Our teacher wants to know if you have a room
where he can eat the Passover meal with his disciples.'
The owner will take you upstairs and show you a large room
furnished and ready for you to use.
Prepare the meal there."

The two disciples went into the city
and found everything just as Jesus had told them.
So they prepared the Passover meal.

During the meal Jesus took some bread in his hands.
He blessed the bread and broke it.
Then he gave it to his disciples and said,
"Take this. It is my body."

Jesus picked up a cup of wine and gave thanks to God.
He then gave it to his disciples and said,
"Drink it!"
So they all drank some.

Then he said,
"This is my blood,
which is poured out for many people,
and with it God makes his agreement.
From now on I will not drink any wine,
until I drink new wine in God's kingdom."

Then they sang a hymn
and went out to the Mount of Olives.

The gospel of the Lord.

TWO

GOSPEL **✚ A reading from the holy gospel according to John**

John 6:51–58

Jesus said to the crowd:
"I am the bread from heaven!
Everyone who eats it will live forever.
My flesh is the life-giving bread
that I give to the people of this world."

They started arguing with each other and asked,
"How can he give us his flesh to eat?"

My flesh is real food and my blood is real drink.

Jesus answered:
"I tell you for certain that you won't live
unless you eat the flesh and drink the blood
of the Son of Man.
But if you do eat my flesh and drink my blood,
you will have eternal life,
and I will raise you to life on the last day.

"My flesh is the true food,
and my blood is the true drink.
If you eat my flesh and drink my blood,
you are one with me, and I am one with you.

"The living Father sent me,
and I have life because of him.
Now everyone who eats my flesh will live because of me.

"The bread that comes down from heaven
is not like what your ancestors ate.
They died,
but whoever eats this bread will live forever."

The gospel of the Lord.

RECONCILIATION

488

ONE

New Testament Reading

Ephesians 5:1–2, 8–10

You were once in darkness; now you are light in the Lord; so walk as children of the light.

A reading from the letter of Paul to the Ephesians

Brothers and sisters:
Do as God does.
After all, you are his dear children.
Let love be your guide.
Christ loved us and offered his life for us
as a sacrifice that pleases God.

You used to be like people living in the dark,
but now you are people of the light
because you belong to the Lord.
So act like people of the light
and make your light shine.
Be good and honest and truthful,
as you try to please the Lord.

The word of the Lord.

TWO

A reading from the letter of James

New Testament Reading

James 2:14–17

What use is it if someone says that he or she believes and does not manifest it in works!

My friends,
what good is it to say you have faith,
when you don't do anything
to show that you really do have faith?
Can that kind of faith save you?

If you know someone who doesn't have any clothes or food,
you shouldn't just say, "I hope all goes well for you.
I hope you will be warm and have plenty to eat."

What good is it to say this,
unless you do something to help?
Faith that doesn't lead us to do good deeds
is all alone and dead!

The word of the Lord.

THREE

New Testament Reading

Revelation 21:1–8

Those who conquer will inherit all this, and I will be their God, and they will be my children.

A reading from the book of Revelation

I, John, saw a new heaven and a new earth.
The first heaven and the first earth had disappeared,
and so had the sea.
Then I saw New Jerusalem, that holy city,
coming down from God in heaven.
It was like a bride dressed in her wedding gown
and ready to meet her husband.

I heard a loud voice shout from the throne:
"God's home is now with his people.
He will live with them,
and they will be his own.
Yes, God will make his home among his people.
He will wipe all tears from their eyes,
and there will be no more death, suffering, crying, or pain.
These things of the past are gone forever."

Then the one sitting on the throne said:
"I am making everything new.
Write down what I have said.
My words are true and can be trusted.
Everything is finished!

"I am Alpha and Omega,
the beginning and the end.
I will freely give water from the life-giving fountain
to everyone who is thirsty.
All who win the victory will be given these blessings.
I will be their God, and they will be my people.

"But I will tell you what will happen to cowards
and to everyone who is unfaithful or dirty-minded
or who murders or is sexually immoral
or uses witchcraft or worships idols or tells lies.
They will be thrown into that lake of fire
and burning sulphur.
This is the second death."

The word of the Lord.

489

ONE

Responsorial Psalm

Psalm 25:4–5abc, 8–9, 10 and 14 (1)

R. To you, O Lord, I lift my soul.

Show me your paths
and teach me to follow;
guide me by your truth
and instruct me.
You keep me safe.

R. To you, O Lord, I lift my soul.

You are honest and merciful,
and you teach sinners
how to follow your path.
You lead humble people
to do what is right
and to stay on your path.

R. To you, O Lord, I lift my soul.

continued

In everything you do,
you are kind and faithful
to everyone who keeps
our agreement with you.
Our LORD, you are the friend
of your worshipers,
and you make an agreement
with all of us.

R. To you, O Lord, I lift my soul.

TWO

Responsorial Psalm

Psalm 119:1–2, 4–5, 17–18, 33–34 (1)

R. Happy are they who follow
the law of the Lord!

Our LORD, you bless everyone
who lives right
and obeys your Law.
You bless all of those
who follow your commands
from deep in their hearts.

R. Happy are they who follow
the law of the Lord!

You have ordered us always
to obey your teachings;
I don't ever want to stray
from your laws.

R. Happy are they who follow
the law of the Lord!

Treat me with kindness, Lord,
so that I may live
and do what you say.
Open my mind
and let me discover
the wonders of your Law.

R. Happy are they who follow
the law of the Lord!

Point out your rules to me,
and I won't disobey
even one of them.
Help me to understand your Law;
I promise to obey it
with all my heart.

R. Happy are they who follow
the law of the Lord!

490

Alleluia Verse and Verse before the Gospel
Psalm 33:22

Lord, let your mercy be on us,
as we place our trust in you.

491

ONE

GOSPEL

✚ A reading from the holy gospel according to Matthew

Matthew 5:13–16

Jesus said to his disciples:
"You are like salt for everyone on earth.
But if salt no longer tastes like salt,
how can it make food salty?
All it is good for is to be thrown out and walked on.

Let your light shine before all.

"You are like light for the whole world.
A city built on top of a hill cannot be hidden,
and no one would light a lamp and put it under a clay pot.
A lamp is placed on a lamp stand,
where it can give light to everyone in the house.
Make your light shine,
so that others will see the good that you do
and will praise your Father in heaven."

The gospel of the Lord.

TWO

Gospel

Luke 15:1–3, 11–32

Father, I have sinned.

✚ **A reading from the holy gospel according to Luke**

Tax collectors and sinners were all crowding around
to listen to Jesus.
So the Pharisees and the teachers of the Law of Moses
started grumbling,
"This man is friendly with sinners.
He even eats with them."
Then Jesus told them this story:

"Once a man had two sons.
The younger son said to his father,
'Give me my share of the property.'
So the father divided his property between his two sons.

"Not long after that,
the younger son packed up everything he owned
and left for a foreign country,
where he wasted all his money in wild living.
He had spent everything,
when a bad famine spread through that whole land.
Soon he had nothing to eat.

"He went to work for a man in that country,
and the man sent him out to take care of his pigs.
He would have been glad to eat what the pigs were eating,
but no one gave him a thing.

"Finally, he came to his senses and said,
'My father's workers have plenty to eat,
and here I am, starving to death!
I will leave and go to my father and say to him,
"Father, I have sinned against God in heaven
and against you.
I am no longer good enough to be called your son.
Treat me like one of your workers."'

continued

"The younger son got up and started back to his father.
But when he was still a long way off,
his father saw him and felt sorry for him.
He ran to his son and hugged and kissed him.

"The son said,
'Father, I have sinned against God in heaven and against you.
I am no longer good enough to be called your son.'

"But his father said to the servants,
'Hurry and bring the best clothes and put them on him.
Give him a ring for his finger and sandals for his feet.
Get the best calf and prepare it,
so we can eat and celebrate.
This son of mine was dead,
but has now come back to life.
He was lost and has now been found.'
And they began to celebrate.

"The older son had been out in the field.
But when he came near the house,
he heard the music and dancing.
So he called one of the servants over and asked,
'What's going on here?'

"The servant answered,
'Your brother has come home safe and sound,
and your father ordered us to kill the best calf.'
The older brother got so mad
that he would not even go into the house.

"His father came out and begged him to go in.
But he said to his father,
'For years I have worked for you like a slave
and have always obeyed you.
But you have never even given me a little goat,
so that I could give a dinner for my friends.
This other son of yours wasted your money on bad women.
And now that he has come home,
you ordered the best calf to be killed for a feast.'

"His father replied,
'My son, you are always with me,
and everything I have is yours.
But we should be glad and celebrate!
Your brother was dead,
but he is now alive.
He was lost and has now been found.'"

The gospel of the Lord.

MASSES FOR VARIOUS NEEDS AND OCCASIONS

492

NEW TESTAMENT READING

2 Thessalonians 3:6–12, 16

Do not give any food to those who refuse to work.

A reading from the second letter of Paul to the Thessalonians

My dear friends,
in the name of the Lord Jesus,
I beg you not to have anything to do
with any of your people who loaf around
and refuse to obey the instructions we gave you.

You surely know that you should follow our example.
We didn't waste our time loafing,
and we didn't accept food from anyone without paying for it.
We didn't want to be a burden to any of you,
so night and day we worked as hard as we could.

We had the right not to work,
but we wanted to set an example for you.
We also gave you the rule that if you don't work,
you don't eat.

Now we learn that some of you just loaf around
and won't do any work,
except the work of a busybody.
So, for the sake of our Lord Jesus Christ,
we ask and beg these people to settle down
and start working for a living.

I pray that the Lord, who gives peace,
will keep blessing you with peace
no matter where you are.
May the Lord be with all of you.

The word of the Lord.

493

Responsorial Psalm

Psalm 95:1–2, 3–5, 6–7abcd (see 2)

R. Let us come before the Lord
and praise him.

Sing joyful songs to the LORD!
Praise the mighty rock
where we are safe.
Come to worship him
with thankful hearts
and songs of praise.

R. Let us come before the Lord
and praise him.

The LORD is the greatest God,
king over all other gods.
He holds the deepest part
of the earth in his hands,
and the mountain peaks
belong to him.
The ocean is the Lord's
because he made it,
and with his own hands
he formed the dry land.

R. Let us come before the Lord
and praise him.

Bow down and worship
the LORD our Creator!
The LORD is our God,
and we are his people,
the sheep he takes care of
in his own pasture.

R. Let us come before the Lord
and praise him.

494

Alleluia Verse and Verse before the Gospel
Philippians 3:8–9

I count all things worthless but this:
to gain Jesus Christ
and to be found in him.

495

ONE

GOSPEL

✚ A reading from the holy gospel according to Matthew

Matthew 13:44–46

He sold all that he had and bought the field.

Jesus said to his disciples:
"The kingdom of heaven is like what happens
when someone finds treasure hidden in a field
and buries it again.
A person like that is happy and goes and sells everything
in order to buy that field.

"The kingdom of heaven is like what happens
when a shop owner is looking for fine pearls.
After finding a very valuable one,
the owner goes and sells everything
in order to buy that pearl."

The gospel of the Lord.

TWO

GOSPEL

✚ A reading from the holy gospel according to Matthew

Matthew 25:14–30

Jesus told his disciples this story about the kingdom of God:

"The kingdom is also like what happened
when a man went away and put his three servants
in charge of all he owned.
The man knew what each servant could do.
So he handed five thousand coins to the first servant,
two thousand to the second,
and one thousand to the third.
Then he left the country.

Because you have been faithful in small matters, come into the joy of your master.

"As soon as the man had gone,
the servant with the five thousand coins
used them to earn five thousand more.
The servant who had two thousand coins
did the same with his money
and earned two thousand more.
But the servant with one thousand coins dug a hole
and hid his master's money in the ground.

"Some time later the master of those servants returned.
He called them in and asked what they had done
with his money.
The servant who had been given five thousand coins
brought them in with the five thousand
that he had earned.
He said, 'Sir, you gave me five thousand coins,
and I have earned five thousand more.'

" 'Wonderful!' his master replied.
'You are a good and faithful servant.
I left you in charge of only a little,
but now I will put you in charge of much more.
Come and share in my happiness!'

continued

"Next, the servant who had been given two thousand coins
  came in and said,
'Sir, you gave me two thousand coins,
and I have earned two thousand more.'
" 'Wonderful!' his master replied.
'You are a good and faithful servant.
I left you in charge of only a little,
but now I will put you in charge of much more.
Come and share in my happiness!'

"The servant who had been given one thousand coins
  then came in and said,
'Sir, I know that you are hard to get along with.
You harvest what you don't plant
  and gather crops where you have not scattered seed.
I was frightened and went out and hid your money
  in the ground.
Here is every single coin!'

"The master of the servant told him,
'You are lazy and good-for-nothing!
You know that I harvest what I don't plant
  and gather crops where I have not scattered seed.
You could have at least put my money in the bank,
so that I could have earned interest on it.'

"Then the master said,
'Now your money will be taken away
  and given to the servant with ten thousand coins!
Everyone who has something will be given more,
and they will have more than enough.
But everything will be taken from those
  who don't have anything.
You are a worthless servant,
and you will be thrown out into the dark
  where people will cry and grit their teeth in pain.' "

The gospel of the Lord.

THREE

✚ A reading from the holy gospel according to John

GOSPEL

John 14:23–26

The Holy Spirit will teach you everything.

Jesus said:
"If anyone loves me, they will obey me.
Then my Father will love them,
and we will come to them and live in them.
But anyone who doesn't love me,
won't obey me.
What they have heard me say doesn't really come from me,
but from the Father who sent me.

"I have told you these things while I am still with you.
But the Holy Spirit will come and help you,
because the Father will send the Spirit to take my place.
The Spirit will teach you everything
and will remind you of what I said while I was with you."

The gospel of the Lord.

END OF THE SCHOOL YEAR

496

OLD TESTAMENT READING

Isaiah 63:7

Let me sing the praises of the Lord's goodness.

A reading from the book of the prophet Isaiah

I will tell all the kind deeds that the LORD has done,
because they deserve praise.
The LORD has shown mercy to the people of Israel.
He has been loving and kind.

The word of the Lord.

497

NEW TESTAMENT READING

Colossians 3:12, 15b–17

A reading from the letter of Paul to the Colossians

Brothers and sisters:
God loves you and has chosen you as his own special people.
So be gentle, kind, humble, meek, and patient.

Let the peace that comes from Christ control your thoughts.
And be grateful.

Above all have love, which is the bond of perfection.

Let the message about Christ completely fill your lives,
while you use all your wisdom
 to teach and instruct each other.
With thankful hearts,
 sing psalms, hymns, and spiritual songs to God.
Whatever you say or do should be done in the name
 of the Lord Jesus,
as you give thanks to God the Father because of him.

The word of the Lord.

498

ONE

Responsorial Psalm

Psalm 113:1–2, 3–4, 5–6 (see 2)

R. Blessed be the name of the Lord
for ever.

Shout praises to the LORD!
Everyone who serves him,
come and praise his name.
Let the name of the LORD
be praised now and forever.

R. Blessed be the name of the Lord
for ever.

From dawn until sunset
the name of the LORD
deserves to be praised.
The LORD is far above
all of the nations;
he is more glorious
than the heavens.

R. Blessed be the name of the Lord
for ever.

No one can compare
with the LORD our God.
His throne is high above,
and he looks down to see
the heavens and the earth.

R. Blessed be the name of the Lord
for ever.

TWO

Responsorial Psalm

Psalm 150:1–2, 3–4, 5–6 (6)

R. Let everything that breathes
praise the Lord!
or:
R. Alleluia.

Shout praises to the LORD!
Praise God in his temple.
Praise him in heaven,
his mighty fortress.
Praise our God!
His deeds are wonderful,
too marvelous to describe.

R. Let everything that breathes
praise the Lord!
or:
R. Alleluia.

Praise God with trumpets
and all kinds of harps.
Praise him with tambourines
and dancing,
with stringed instruments
and woodwinds.

R. Let everything that breathes
praise the Lord!
or:
R. Alleluia.

Praise God with cymbals,
with clashing cymbals.
Let every living creature
praise the LORD.
Shout praises to the LORD!

R. Let everything that breathes
praise the Lord!
or:
R. Alleluia.

499

Alleluia Verse and Verse before the Gospel
Psalm 66:16

Come and listen,
and I will tell what great things
God has done for me.

500

ONE

✚ A reading from the holy gospel according to Matthew

GOSPEL

Matthew 13:31–32

When the mustard seed grows it is the biggest shrub of all and the birds of the air come and nest in its branches.

Jesus told the people this story:
"The kingdom of heaven is like what happens
when a farmer plants a mustard seed in a field.
Although it is the smallest of all seeds,
it grows larger than any garden plant and becomes a tree.
Birds even come and nest on its branches."

The gospel of the Lord.

TWO

GOSPEL

✚ A reading from the holy gospel according to Mark

Mark 5:18–20

When Jesus was getting into the boat,
the man who had been healed of the evil spirit
begged to go with him.
But Jesus would not let him.

Tell what the Lord has done for you.

Instead, he said, "Go home to your family
and tell them how much the Lord has done for you
and how good he has been to you."

The man went away into the region near the ten cities
known as Decapolis
and began telling everyone how much Jesus had done
for him.
Everyone who heard what happened was amazed.

The gospel of the Lord.

501

OLD TESTAMENT READING

A reading from the book of Sirach

Sirach 50:22–24

God does great deeds everywhere.

Now let's praise the God of all
who always does such wonderful things
and treats us with mercy from the day of our birth.
Pray for God to make us happy
and let Israel live in peace from this day onward.
Ask God to show mercy and save our nation now.

The word of the Lord.

502

ONE

Responsorial Psalm

Psalm 67:1–2, 4 (4a)

R. O God, let all the nations praise you!

Our God, be kind and bless us!
Be pleased and smile.
Then everyone on earth
will learn to follow you,
and all nations will see
your power to save us.

R. O God, let all the nations praise you!

Let the nations celebrate
with joyful songs,
because you judge fairly
and guide all nations.

R. O God, let all the nations praise you!

TWO

Responsorial Psalm

Psalm 113:1–2, 3–4, 5–6 (see 2)

R. Blessed be the name of the Lord
for ever.
or:
R. Alleluia.

Shout praises to the LORD*!*
Everyone who serves him,
come and praise his name.
Let the name of the LORD
be praised now and forever.

R. Blessed be the name of the Lord
for ever.
or:
R. Alleluia.

From dawn until sunset
the name of the LORD
deserves to be praised.
The LORD *is far above*
all of the nations;
he is more glorious
than the heavens.

R. Blessed be the name of the Lord
for ever.
or:
R. Alleluia.

No one can compare
with the LORD *our God.*
His throne is high above,
and he looks down to see
the heavens and the earth.

R. Blessed be the name of the Lord
for ever.
or:
R. Alleluia.

503

Alleluia Verse and Verse before the Gospel

Psalm 138:1bc

I will give thanks to you
with all my heart, O Lord,
for you have answered me.

504

GOSPEL

Luke 17:11–19

The man with leprosy threw himself at the feet of Jesus and thanked him.

✚ A reading from the holy gospel according to Luke

On his way to Jerusalem,
Jesus went along the border between Samaria and Galilee.
As he was going into a village,
ten men with leprosy came toward him.
They stood at a distance and shouted,
"Jesus, Master, have pity on us!"

Jesus looked at them and said,
"Go show yourselves to the priests."

On their way they were healed.
When one of them discovered that he was healed,
he came back, shouting praises to God.
He bowed down at the feet of Jesus and thanked him.
The man was from the country of Samaria.

Jesus asked, "Weren't ten men healed?
Where are the other nine?
Why was this foreigner the only one who came back
to thank God?"

Then Jesus told the man, "You may get up and go.
Your faith has made you well."

The gospel of the Lord.

505

ONE

Old Testament Reading

A reading from the book of Exodus

Exodus 3:1–6, 9–12

I shall be with you.

One day Moses was taking care of the sheep of Jethro
his father-in-law,
who was the priest of Midian.
Moses led the sheep along the edge of the desert to Sinai,
the mountain of God.
Suddenly the LORD's angel appeared to him
from a burning bush.
Moses saw that the bush was on fire,
but it was not burning up.
He said to himself, "This is strange!
I'll go over and see why the bush is not burning up."

When the LORD saw Moses coming near the bush,
he called out to him.

Moses answered, "LORD, here I am."

God replied, "Don't come any closer.
Take off your sandals,
because the ground where you are standing is holy.
I am the God who was worshiped by your ancestors,
Abraham, Isaac, and Jacob."

Moses was too afraid to look at God, and he hid his face.

The LORD said, "My people have cried out to me,
and I have seen how cruelly the Egyptians treat them.
Now go to the king.
I am sending you to bring my people out of his country."

But Moses said to God,
"Who am I to go to the king
and bring your people out of Egypt?"

God replied,
"I will be with you,
and you will lead my people out of Egypt.
Then you will know that I am the one who sent you,
and you will worship me on this mountain."

The word of the Lord.

TWO

OLD TESTAMENT READING

1 Samuel 3:1–10

Speak, O Lord,
your servant is listening.

A reading from the first book of Samuel

Samuel served the LORD by helping Eli the priest.
But in those days the LORD did not often speak to people
or appear to them in dreams.

One night Eli, who was almost blind, was in bed as usual.
Samuel was sleeping on a mat
in the place of worship near the sacred chest.
The lamp was still burning
when the LORD called out to Samuel.

"Here I am," Samuel answered.
He ran to Eli and said,
"Here I am, sir. What can I do for you?"

Eli replied, "I didn't call you. Go back to bed."
So Samuel went back.

continued

Once more the LORD called Samuel's name.
Samuel got up.
He went to Eli and said,
"Here I am. What can I do for you?"

But Eli told him, "Son, I didn't call you.
Now go back to sleep."

Samuel did not realize that the LORD was speaking,
because this was the first time the LORD had spoken to him.
When the LORD spoke a third time that night,
Samuel again went to Eli and said,
"Here I am. What can I do for you?"

Eli now knew that it was the LORD who was speaking
to Samuel.
So Eli told him, "Go back to bed.
If someone speaks to you again,
answer, 'LORD, I am your servant.
Speak, and I will listen.'"
Once again Samuel went back and lay down.

The LORD came and stood beside Samuel.
Then he called out as he had done before, "Samuel! Samuel!"

The boy replied, "LORD, I am your servant.
Speak, and I will listen."

The word of the Lord.

THREE

A reading from the book of the prophet Jeremiah

OLD TESTAMENT READING

Jeremiah 1:4–9

The LORD said to Jeremiah,
"Before I gave you life,
and before you were born,
I chose you to be a prophet to the nations."

I replied, "LORD God, how can I speak for you?
I'm too young."

Go to those to whom I send you.

The LORD answered, "Don't say you're too young.
Go to everyone I send you to
and tell them everything I command you.
Don't be afraid of them!
I, the LORD, will be with you to keep you safe."

Then the LORD reached out his hand.
He touched my lips and said,
"I have now given you the words to say."

The word of the Lord.

506

Responsorial Psalm

Psalm 27:1, 4 (8b)

R. I long to see your face, O Lord.

You, LORD, are the light
that keeps me safe.
I am not afraid of anyone.
You protect me,
and I have no fears.

R. I long to see your face, O Lord.

I ask only one thing, LORD:
Let me live in your house
every day of my life
to see how wonderful you are
and to pray in your temple.

R. I long to see your face, O Lord.

507

Alleluia Verse and Verse before the Gospel

See John 15:16

I have chosen you from the world,
says the Lord,
to go and bear fruit that will last.

508

ONE

GOSPEL

Matthew 9:35–38

The harvest is rich but the laborers are few.

✚ A reading from the holy gospel according to Matthew

Jesus went to every town and village.
He taught in their meeting places
and preached the good news about God's kingdom.
Jesus also healed every kind of disease and sickness.

When he saw the crowds,
he felt sorry for them.
They were confused and helpless,
like sheep without a shepherd.

He said to his disciples,
"A large crop is in the fields,
but there are only a few workers.
Ask the Lord in charge of the harvest
to send out workers to bring it in."

The gospel of the Lord.

TWO

GOSPEL **✚ A reading from the holy gospel according to Mark**

Mark 10:28–30

You will not be without persecutions but you will be repaid a hundred times over in this life and in the world to come, you will have eternal life.

Peter said to Jesus,
"Remember, we left everything to be your followers!"

Jesus told him:
"You can be sure that anyone who gives up home
or brothers or sisters
or mother or father or children or land
for me and for the good news will be rewarded.
In this world they will be given a hundred times as many
houses and brothers and sisters
and mothers and children
and pieces of land,
though they will also be mistreated.

"And in the world to come,
they will have eternal life."

The gospel of the Lord.

THREE

GOSPEL **✚ A reading from the holy gospel according to Luke**

[For Vocations to Holy Orders]

Luke 5:1–11

From this moment on, you will be fishers of people.

Jesus was standing on the shore of Lake Gennesaret,
teaching the people as they crowded around him
to hear God's message.
Near the shore he saw two boats
left there by some fishermen
who had gone to wash their nets.

Jesus got into the boat that belonged to Simon
and asked him to row it out a little way from the shore.
Then Jesus sat down in the boat to teach the crowd.

When Jesus had finished speaking, he told Simon,
"Row the boat out into the deep water
and let your nets down to catch some fish."

"Master," Simon answered,
"we have worked hard all night long
and have not caught a thing.
But if you tell me to, I will let the nets down."

They did it and caught so many fish
that their nets began ripping apart.
Then they signaled for their partners in the other boat
to come and help them.
The men came,
and together they filled the two boats so full
that they both began to sink.

When Simon Peter saw this happen,
he kneeled down in front of Jesus and said,
"Lord, don't come near me!
I am a sinner."

Peter and everyone with him
were completely surprised at all the fish they had caught.
His partners James and John, the sons of Zebedee,
were surprised too.

Jesus told Simon, "Don't be afraid!
From now on you will bring in people instead of fish."
The men pulled their boats up on the shore.
Then they left everything and went with Jesus.

The gospel of the Lord.

FOR UNITY OF CHRISTIANS

509

OLD TESTAMENT READING

Ezekiel 36:24–28

I shall take you from among the nations, and I shall give you a new heart.

A reading from the book of the prophet Ezekiel

The Lord says this:
"I will bring all of you back home
  from those foreign nations and countries.
I will sprinkle you with clean water,
and you will be clean.
I will wash away everything that makes you unclean,
and I will remove your idols.

"I will give you a new heart and a new mind.
In place of your stone heart,
I will give you a heart with feeling.
I will put my Spirit in you
  and make you eager to obey my teachings and laws.
You will live in the land that I gave your ancestors.
You will be my people, and I will be your God."

The word of the Lord.

510

ONE

Responsorial Psalm

Psalm 23:1–3a, 3b–4, 5, 6 (1)

R. The Lord is my shepherd;
there is nothing I shall want.

You, LORD, are my shepherd.
I will never be in need.
You let me rest in fields
of green grass.
You lead me to streams
of peaceful water,
and you refresh my life.

R. The Lord is my shepherd;
there is nothing I shall want.

You are true to your name,
and you lead me
along the right paths.
I may walk through valleys
as dark as death,
but I won't be afraid.
You are with me,
and your shepherd's rod
makes me feel safe.

R. The Lord is my shepherd;
there is nothing I shall want.

You treat me to a feast,
while my enemies watch.
You honor me as your guest,
and you fill my cup
until it overflows.

R. The Lord is my shepherd;
there is nothing I shall want.

Your kindness and love
will always be with me
each day of my life,
and I will live forever
in your house, LORD.

R. The Lord is my shepherd;
there is nothing I shall want.

TWO

Responsorial Psalm

Psalm 100:1–2, 3, 4, 5 (3c) (2c)

R. We are God's people:
the sheep of his flock.
or:
R. Come with joy into the presence of the Lord.

Shout praises to the LORD,
everyone on this earth.
Be joyful and sing
as you come in
to worship the LORD!

R. We are God's people:
the sheep of his flock.
or:
R. Come with joy into the presence of the Lord.

You know the LORD is God!
He created us,
and we belong to him;
we are his people,
the sheep in his pasture.

R. We are God's people:
the sheep of his flock.
or:
R. Come with joy into the presence of the Lord.

Be thankful and praise the LORD
as you enter his temple.

R. We are God's people:
the sheep of his flock.
or:
R. Come with joy into the presence
of the Lord.

The LORD *is good!*
His love and faithfulness
will last forever.

R. We are God's people:
the sheep of his flock.
or:
R. Come with joy into the presence
of the Lord.

511

Alleluia Verse and Verse before the Gospel
Colossians 3:15

May the peace of Christ
rule in your hearts,
that peace to which all of you
are called as one body.

512

ONE

GOSPEL **✚ A reading from the holy gospel according to Matthew**

Matthew 5:1–12ab

When Jesus saw the crowds,
he went up on the side of a mountain and sat down.

Jesus' disciples gathered around him, and he taught them:

"God blesses those people who depend only on him.
They belong to the kingdom of heaven!

Theirs is the kingdom of heaven.

"God blesses those people who grieve.
They will find comfort!

"God blesses those people who are humble.
The earth will belong to them!

"God blesses those people who want to obey him
more than to eat or drink.
They will be given what they want!

"God blesses those people who are merciful.
They will be treated with mercy!

"God blesses those people whose hearts are pure.
They will see him!

"God blesses those people who make peace.
They will be called his children!

"God blesses those people who are treated badly
for doing right.
They belong to the kingdom of heaven.

"God will bless you when people insult you, mistreat you,
and tell all kinds of evil lies about you because of me.
Be happy and excited!
You will have a great reward in heaven."

The gospel of the Lord.

TWO

GOSPEL

Matthew 18:19–22

Where two or three meet in my name, I shall be there with them.

✚ A reading from the holy gospel according to Matthew

Jesus said to his disciples:
"I promise that when any two of you on earth
agree about something you are praying for,
my Father in heaven will do it for you.
Whenever two or three of you come together in my name,
I am there with you."

Peter came up to the Lord and asked,
"How many times should I forgive someone
who does something wrong to me?
Is seven times enough?"

Jesus answered:
"Not just seven times, but seventy-seven times!"

The gospel of the Lord.

513

OLD TESTAMENT READING

Isaiah 32:15–20

A reading from the book of the prophet Isaiah

When the Spirit is given to us from heaven,
deserts will become orchards,
and orchards will turn into fertile forests.
Honesty and justice will prosper in the deserts and orchards.

The effect of justice will be peace.

Then justice will produce unending peace and quiet.
My people will live in peace, secure and undisturbed,
even if hailstones flatten forests and cities.
They will have my blessing,
as they plant their crops beside streams
and let their donkeys roam freely about.

The word of the Lord.

514

ONE

A reading from the letter of Paul to the Philippians

NEW TESTAMENT READING

Philippians 4:6–9

May the peace of God guard your hearts and your thoughts.

Brothers and sisters:
Don't worry about anything,
but pray about everything.

With thankful hearts offer up your prayers and requests
to God.
Then, because you belong to Christ Jesus,
God will bless you with peace
that no one can completely understand.
And this peace will control the way you think and feel.

Finally, my friends,
keep your minds on whatever is true, pure, right,
holy, friendly, and proper.
Don't ever stop thinking about what is truly worthwhile
and worthy of praise.
You know the teachings I gave you,
and you know what you heard me say and saw me do.

So follow my example.
And God, who gives peace, will be with you!

The word of the Lord.

TWO

NEW TESTAMENT READING

Colossians 3:12–15

May the peace of Christ rule in your hearts.

A reading from the letter of Paul to the Colossians

Brothers and sisters:
God loves you and has chosen you as his own special people.
So be gentle, kind, humble, meek, and patient.
Put up with each other,
and forgive anyone who does you wrong,
just as Christ has forgiven you.
Love is more important than anything else.
It is what ties everything completely together.

Each one of you is part of the body of Christ,
and you were chosen to live together in peace.
So let the peace that comes from Christ
  control your thoughts.
And be grateful.

The word of the Lord.

515

ONE

Responsorial Psalm

Psalm 72:1–2, 7–8, 12–13 (see 7)

R. Justice shall flourish in his time,
and fullness of peace for ever.

Please help the king
to be honest and fair
just like you, our God.
Let him be honest and fair
with all your people,
especially the poor.

R. Justice shall flourish in his time,
and fullness of peace for ever.

Let the king be fair
with everyone,
and let there be peace
until the moon
falls from the sky.
Let his kingdom reach
from sea to sea,
from the Euphrates River
across all the earth.

R. Justice shall flourish in his time,
and fullness of peace for ever.

Do this because the king
rescues the homeless
when they cry out,
and he helps everyone
who is poor and in need.
The king has pity
on the weak and helpless
and protects those in need.

R. Justice shall flourish in his time,
and fullness of peace for ever.

TWO

Responsorial Psalm

Psalm 122:1–2, 8–9
(see Sirach 36:18)

R. Give peace, O Lord,
to those who wait for you.

It made me glad to hear them say,
"Let's go to the house
of the LORD!"
Jerusalem, we are standing
inside your gates.

R. Give peace, O Lord,
to those who wait for you.

Because of my friends
and my relatives,
I will pray for peace.
And because of the house
of the LORD our God,
I will work for your good.

R. Give peace, O Lord,
to those who wait for you.

516

Alleluia Verse and Verse before the Gospel

Matthew 5:9

Blessed are the peacemakers;
they shall be called children of God.

517

GOSPEL

Matthew 5:1–12ab

Blessed are the peacemakers: they shall be called children of God.

✚ A reading from the holy gospel according to Matthew

When Jesus saw the crowds,
he went up on the side of a mountain and sat down.
Jesus' disciples gathered around him, and he taught them:

"God blesses those people who depend only on him.
They belong to the kingdom of heaven!

"God blesses those people who grieve.
They will find comfort!

"God blesses those people who are humble.
The earth will belong to them!

"God blesses those people who want to obey him
more than to eat or drink.
They will be given what they want!

"God blesses those people who are merciful.
They will be treated with mercy!

"God blesses those people whose hearts are pure.
They will see him!

"God blesses those people who make peace.
They will be called his children!

"God blesses those people who are treated badly
for doing right.
They belong to the kingdom of heaven.

"God will bless you when people insult you, mistreat you,
and tell all kinds of evil lies about you because of me.
Be happy and excited!
You will have a great reward in heaven."

The gospel of the Lord.

518

ONE

Old Testament Reading

A reading from the book of Genesis

Genesis 1:11–12

Let the earth produce vegetation and seed-bearing plants.

God said to the earth,
"Make all kinds of green things grow!
Produce grain and fruit trees."

So the earth made all kinds of green things grow.
It produced grain and fruit trees.

The word of the Lord.

TWO

Old Testament Reading

A reading from the book of Deuteronomy

Deuteronomy 8:7–10

Moses told the people:
"The LORD your God is bringing you into a good land.
It has a lot of streams and springs
that flow from underground rivers in the valleys and hills.
Wheat and barley grow there,
and you will also find grapes, figs,
pomegranates, olives, and honey.

You will have all you want to eat.

"You will have all you want to eat,
and you will never run out of food.
You can make iron from the stones in that land,
and from its hills you can dig copper.

"You will have all you want to eat,
and you will praise the LORD your God
for giving you this good land."

The word of the Lord.

519

NEW TESTAMENT READING

2 Corinthians 9:8–11

God will provide bread for people to eat.

A reading from the second letter of Paul to the Corinthians

Brothers and sisters:
God can bless you with everything you need,
and you will always have more than enough
to do all kinds of good things for others.

The Scriptures say,

"God freely gives his gifts to the poor,
and always does right."

God gives seed to farmers and provides everyone with food.
He will increase what you have,
so that you can give even more to those in need.

You will be blessed in every way,
and you will be able to keep on being generous.
Then many people will thank God
when we deliver your gift.

The word of the Lord.

520

Responsorial Psalm

Psalm 147:5 and 7, 8 (1)

R. Shout praises to the Lord!
Our God is kind.

Our LORD is great and powerful!
He understands everything.
Celebrate and sing!
Play your harps
for the LORD our God.

R. Shout praises to the Lord!
Our God is kind.

He fills the sky with clouds
and sends rain to the earth,
so that the hills
will be green with grass.

R. Shout praises to the Lord!
Our God is kind.

521

Alleluia Verse and Verse before the Gospel

Psalm 126:5

Those who sow in tears
shall reap with shouts of joy.

522

GOSPEL

Luke 12:15–21

Life is not made secure by worldly possessions even when a person owns them in abundance.

✚ A reading from the holy gospel according to Luke

Jesus said to the crowd, "Don't be greedy!
Owning a lot of things won't make your life safe."

So Jesus told them this story:

"A rich man's farm produced a big crop,
and he said to himself, 'What can I do?
I don't have a place large enough to store everything.'

"Later, he said, 'Now I know what I'll do.
I'll tear down my barns and build bigger ones,
where I can store all my grain and other goods.
Then I'll say to myself,
"You have stored up enough good things
to last for years to come.
Live it up! Eat, drink, and enjoy yourself."'

"But God said to him, 'You fool!
Tonight you will die.
Then who will get what you have stored up?'

"This is what happens to people who store up everything
for themselves,
but are poor in the sight of God."

The gospel of the Lord.

FOR REFUGEES AND EXILES

523

OLD TESTAMENT READING

Hebrews 13:1–3, 14–16

Be sure to welcome strangers into your home.

A reading from the letter to the Hebrews

Brothers and sisters:
Keep being concerned about each other
as the Lord's followers should.

Be sure to welcome strangers into your home.
By doing this, some people have welcomed angels as guests,
without even knowing it.

Remember the Lord's people who are in jail
and be concerned for them.
Don't forget those who are suffering,
but imagine that you are there with them.

On this earth we don't have a city that lasts forever,
but we are waiting for such a city.

Our sacrifice is to keep offering praise to God
in the name of Jesus.
But don't forget to help others
and to share your possessions with them.
This too is like offering a sacrifice that pleases God.

The word of the Lord.

524

Responsorial Psalm

Psalm 121:1–2, 5–6, 7–8
(2)

R. Our help is from the Lord,
who made heaven and earth.

I look to the hills!
Where will I find help?
It will come from the LORD,
who created the heavens
and the earth.

R. Our help is from the Lord,
who made heaven and earth.

The LORD is your protector,
there at your right side
to shade you from the sun.
You won't be harmed
by the sun during the day
or by the moon at night.

R. Our help is from the Lord,
who made heaven and earth.

The LORD will protect you
and keep you safe
from all dangers.
The LORD will protect you
now and always
wherever you are.

R. Our help is from the Lord,
who made heaven and earth.

525

Alleluia Verse and Verse before the Gospel
2 Corinthians 1:3b–4a

Blessed be the Father of mercies and
the God of all comfort,
who consoles us in all our
afflictions.

526

GOSPEL **✚ A reading from the holy gospel according to Luke**

Luke 10:25–37

Who is my neighbor?

An expert in the Law of Moses stood up
and asked Jesus a question to see what he would say.
"Teacher," he asked,
"What must I do to have eternal life?"

Jesus answered, "What is written in the Scriptures?
How do you understand them?"

The man replied, "The Scriptures say,
'Love the Lord your God with all your heart, soul,
strength, and mind.'
They also say, 'Love your neighbors
as much as you love yourself.'"

Jesus said, "You have given the right answer.
If you do this, you will have eternal life."

But the man wanted to show
that he knew what he was talking about.
So he asked Jesus, "Who are my neighbors?"

Jesus replied:
"As a man was going down from Jerusalem to Jericho,
robbers attacked him and grabbed everything he had.
They beat him up and ran off, leaving him half dead.

"A priest happened to be going down the same road.
But when he saw the man,
he walked by on the other side.
Later a temple helper came to the same place.
But when he saw the man who had been beaten up,
he also went by on the other side.

"A man from Samaria then came traveling along that road.
When he saw the man,
he felt sorry for him and went over to him.
He treated his wounds with olive oil and wine
and bandaged them.
Then he put him on his own donkey and took him to an inn,
where he took care of him.

"The next morning he gave the innkeeper two silver coins
and said,
'Please take care of the man.
If you spend more than this on him,
I will pay you when I return.' "

Then Jesus asked,
"Which of these three people was a real neighbor
to the man who was beaten up by robbers?"

The teacher answered, "The one who showed pity."
Jesus said, "Go and do the same!"

The gospel of the Lord.

527

NEW TESTAMENT READING

James 5:13–16

The prayer of faith will save the one who is ill.

A reading from the letter of James

Brothers and sisters:
If you are having trouble, you should pray.
And if you are feeling good, you should sing praises.

If you are sick, ask the church leaders to come
and pray for you.
Ask them to pour olive oil on you in the name of the Lord.
If you have faith when you pray for sick people,
they will get well.
The Lord will heal them,
and if they have sinned, he will forgive them.

If you have sinned,
you should tell each other what you have done.
Then you can pray for one another and be healed.

The prayer of an innocent person is powerful,
and it can help a lot.

The word of the Lord.

528

ONE

Responsorial Psalm

Psalm 25:4–5abc, 8–9, 10 and 14, 15–16 (1)

R. To you, O Lord, I lift my soul.

Show me your paths
and teach me to follow;
guide me by your truth
and instruct me.
You keep me safe.

R. To you, O Lord, I lift my soul.

You are honest and merciful,
and you teach sinners
how to follow your path.
You lead humble people
to do what is right
and to stay on your path.

R. To you, O Lord, I lift my soul.

In everything you do,
you are kind and faithful
to everyone who keeps
our agreement with you.
Our LORD, you are the friend
of your worshipers,
and you make an agreement
with all of us.

R. To you, O Lord, I lift my soul.

I always look to you,
because you rescue me
from every trap.
I am lonely and troubled.
Show that you care
and have pity on me.

R. To you, O Lord, I lift my soul.

TWO

Responsorial Psalm

Psalm 34:1–2, 3–4, 16 and 18 (9a)

R. Taste and see the goodness of the Lord.

I will always praise the LORD.
With all my heart,
I will praise the LORD.
Let all who are helpless
listen and be glad.

R. Taste and see the goodness of the Lord.

Honor the LORD with me!
Celebrate his great name.
I asked the LORD for help,
and he saved me
from all my fears.

R. Taste and see the goodness of the Lord.

God despises evil people,
and he will wipe them all
from the earth,
till they are forgotten.
The LORD is there to rescue
all who are discouraged
and have given up hope.

R. Taste and see the goodness of the Lord.

529

Alleluia Verse and Verse before the Gospel

Christ bore our sickness,
and endured our suffering.

Matthew 8:17

530

GOSPEL

Matthew 8:14–17

Christ bore our sickness.

✚ A reading from the holy gospel according to Matthew

Jesus went to the home of Peter,
where he found that Peter's mother-in-law
was sick in bed with fever.
He took her by the hand,
and the fever left her.
Then she got up and served Jesus a meal.

That evening many people with demons in them
were brought to Jesus.
And with only a word he forced out the evil spirits
and healed everyone who was sick.

So God's promise came true,
just as the prophet Isaiah had said,

"He healed our diseases and made us well."

The gospel of the Lord.

531

OLD TESTAMENT READING

Isaiah 25:6a, 7–9

The Lord God will destroy death for ever.

A reading from the book of the prophet Isaiah

On this mountain the LORD All-Powerful
will prepare for all nations a feast of the finest foods.

Here the LORD will strip away
the funeral clothes that cover the nations.
The LORD All-Powerful will destroy the power of death
and wipe away each tear.
No longer will his people be embarrassed everywhere.
The LORD has spoken!

On that day, people will say,
"The LORD God has saved us!
Let's celebrate.
We waited and waited, and now he is here."

The word of the Lord.

532

ONE

A reading from the letter of Paul to the Ephesians

New Testament Reading

Ephesians 1:3–5

The Father chose us in Christ, before the creation of the world, to be holy.

Brothers and sisters:
Praise the God and Father of our Lord Jesus Christ
for the spiritual blessings
that Christ has brought us from heaven!
Before the world was created,
God let Christ choose us to live with him
and to be his holy and innocent and loving people.
God was kind
and decided that Christ would choose us
to be God's own adopted children.

The word of the Lord.

TWO

A reading from the first letter of Paul to the Thessalonians

New Testament Reading

1 Thessalonians 4:13–14, 18

We shall stay with the Lord for ever.

My friends, we want you to understand how it will be
for those followers who have already died.
Then you won't grieve over them
and be like people who don't have any hope.

We believe that Jesus died and was raised to life.
We also believe that when God brings Jesus back again,
he will bring with him all who had faith in Jesus
before they died.

Encourage each other with these words.

The word of the Lord.

THREE

NEW TESTAMENT READING

1 John 3:1–2

A reading from the first letter of John

Beloved:
Think how much the Father loves us.
He loves us so much that he lets us be called his children,
as we truly are.

We shall see God as he really is.

But since the people of this world did not know
who Christ is,
they don't know who we are.

My dear friends, we are already God's children,
though what we will be has not yet been seen.
But we do know that when Christ returns,
we will be like him,
because we will see him as he truly is.

The word of the Lord.

FOUR

NEW TESTAMENT READING

Revelation 14:13

A reading from the book of Revelation

I, John, heard a voice from heaven say,
"Put this in writing.
From now on, the Lord will bless everyone
who has faith in him when they die."

Blessed are those who die in the Lord.

The Spirit answered, "Yes, they will rest
from their hard work,
and they will be rewarded for what they have done."

The word of the Lord.

533

ONE

Responsorial Psalm

Psalm 23:1–3a, 3b–4, 5, 6 (1)

R. The Lord is my shepherd;
there is nothing I shall want.

You, LORD, are my shepherd.
I will never be in need.
You let me rest in fields
of green grass.
You lead me to streams
of peaceful water,
and you refresh my life.

R. The Lord is my shepherd;
there is nothing I shall want.

You are true to your name,
and you lead me
along the right paths.
I may walk through valleys
as dark as death,
but I won't be afraid.
You are with me,
and your shepherd's rod
makes me feel safe.

R. The Lord is my shepherd;
there is nothing I shall want.

You treat me to a feast,
while my enemies watch.
You honor me as your guest,
and you fill my cup
until it overflows.

R. The Lord is my shepherd;
there is nothing I shall want.

continued

Your kindness and love
will always be with me
each day of my life,
and I will live forever
in your house, LORD.

R. The Lord is my shepherd;
there is nothing I shall want.

TWO

Responsorial Psalm

Psalm 27:1, 4, 13–14 (1a)

R. The Lord is my light and my salvation.

You, LORD, are the light
that keeps me safe.
I am not afraid of anyone.
You protect me, and I have no fears.

R. The Lord is my light and my salvation.

I ask only one thing, LORD:
Let me live in your house
every day of my life
to see how wonderful you are
and to pray in your temple.

R. The Lord is my light and my salvation.

I know that I will live to see
how kind you are.
Trust the LORD*!*
Be brave and strong and trust the LORD*!*

R. The Lord is my light and my salvation.

534

Alleluia Verse and Verse before the Gospel
John 11:25a, 26

I am the resurrection and the life,
says the Lord,
whoever believes in me
will not die for ever.

535

ONE

GOSPEL

✚ A reading from the holy gospel according to Matthew

Matthew 11:25–26, 28–30

On one occasion Jesus said:
"My Father, Lord of heaven and earth,
I am grateful that you hid all this
  from wise and educated people
  and showed it to ordinary people.
Yes, Father, that is what pleased you."

You have hidden these things from the learned and the clever and have revealed them to children.

Then Jesus said:
"If you are tired from carrying heavy burdens,
come to me and I will give you rest.
Take the yoke I give you.
Put it on your shoulders and learn from me.
I am gentle and humble,
and you will find rest.
This yoke is easy to bear,
and this burden is light."

The gospel of the Lord.

TWO

✚ A reading from the holy gospel according to Luke

GOSPEL

Luke 7:11–17

Young man,
I say to you, arise.

Jesus and his disciples were on their way
to the town of Nain,
and a big crowd was going along with them.
As they came near the gate of the town,
they saw people carrying out the body of a widow's only son.
Many people from the town were walking along with her.

When the Lord saw the woman,
he felt sorry for her and said, "Don't cry!"

Jesus went over and touched the stretcher
on which the people were carrying the dead boy.
They stopped, and Jesus said,
"Young man, get up!"
The man sat up and began to speak.
Jesus then gave him back to his mother.

Everyone was frightened and praised God.
They said, "A great prophet is here with us!
God has come to his people."

News about Jesus spread all over Judea
and everywhere else in that part of the country.

The gospel of the Lord.

THREE

GOSPEL

✚ A reading from the holy gospel according to John

John 11:21–27

Martha said to Jesus,
"Lord, if you had been here,
my brother would not have died.
Yet even now I know that God will do anything you ask."

Jesus told her, "Your brother will live again!"

I am the resurrection and the life.

Martha answered,
"I know that he will be raised to life on the last day,
when all the dead are raised."

Jesus then said,
"I am the one who raises the dead to life!
Everyone who has faith in me will live,
even if they die.
And everyone who lives because of faith in me
will never die.
Do you believe this?"

"Yes, Lord!" she replied.
"I believe that you are Christ, the Son of God.
You are the one we hoped would come into the world."

The gospel of the Lord.

CALENDAR

SUNDAY/FEAST DAY	1993	1994	1995	1996
	Year A	*Year B*	*Year C*	*Year A*
1st Sunday of Advent	Nov. 29, 1992	Nov. 28, 1993	Nov. 27, 1994	Dec. 3, 1995
2nd Sunday of Advent	Dec. 6, 1992	Dec. 5, 1993	Dec. 4, 1994	Dec. 10, 1995
Immaculate Conception, December 8	Tuesday	Wednesday	Thursday	Friday
3rd Sunday of Advent	Dec. 13, 1992	Dec. 12, 1993	Dec. 11, 1994	Dec. 17, 1995
4th Sunday of Advent	Dec. 29, 1992	Dec. 19, 1993	Dec. 18, 1994	Dec. 24, 1995
Christmas, December 25	Friday	Saturday	Sunday	Monday
Holy Family	Dec. 27, 1992	Dec. 26, 1993	Dec. 30, 1994*	Dec. 31, 1995
Mary, Mother of God, January 1	Friday	Saturday	Sunday	Monday
Epiphany	Jan. 3, 1993	Jan. 2, 1994	Jan. 8, 1995	Jan. 7, 1996
Baptism of the Lord	Jan. 10, 1993	Jan. 9, 1994	Jan. 9, 1995*	Jan. 8, 1996*
2nd Sunday in Ordinary Time	Jan. 17	Jan. 16	Jan. 15	Jan. 14
3rd Sunday in Ordinary Time	Jan. 24	Jan. 23	Jan. 22	Jan. 21
4th Sunday in Ordinary Time	Jan. 31	Jan. 30	Jan. 29	Jan. 28
Presentation of the Lord, February 2	Tuesday	Wednesday	Thursday	Friday
5th Sunday in Ordinary Time	Feb. 7	Feb. 6	Feb. 5	Feb. 4
6th Sunday in Ordinary Time	Feb. 14	Feb. 13	Feb. 12	Feb. 11
7th Sunday in Ordinary Time	Feb. 21	■	Feb. 19	Feb. 18
8th Sunday in Ordinary Time	■	■	Feb. 26	■
9th Sunday in Ordinary Time	■	■	■	■
Ash Wednesday	Feb. 24	Feb. 16	Mar. 1	Feb. 21
1st Sunday of Lent	Feb. 28	Feb. 20	Mar. 5	Feb. 25
2nd Sunday of Lent	Mar. 7	Feb. 27	Mar. 12	Mar. 3
3rd Sunday of Lent	Mar. 14	Mar. 6	Mar. 19	Mar. 10
4th Sunday of Lent	Mar. 21	Mar. 13	Mar. 26	Mar. 17
5th Sunday of Lent	Mar. 28	Mar. 20	Apr. 2	Mar. 24
Passion (Palm) Sunday	Apr. 4	Mar. 27	Apr. 9	Mar. 31
• Joseph, Husband of Mary, March 19	Friday	Saturday	Mar. 20†	Tuesday
• Annunciation, Mar. 25	Thursday	Friday	Saturday	Monday
Holy Thursday	Apr. 8	Mar. 31	Apr. 13	Apr. 4
Good Friday	Apr. 9	Apr. 1	Apr. 14	Apr. 5
Easter Sunday	Apr. 11	Apr. 3	Apr. 16	Apr. 7
2nd Sunday of Easter	Apr. 18	Apr. 10	Apr. 23	Apr. 14
3rd Sunday of Easter	Apr. 25	Apr. 17	Apr. 30	Apr. 21
4th Sunday of Easter	May 2	Apr. 24	May 7	Apr. 28
5th Sunday of Easter	May 9	May 1	May 14	May 5

** This feast is celebrated this year on a weekday.* *† This solemnity has been transferred to this date.*

SUNDAY/FEAST DAY	1993 *Year A*	1994 *Year B*	1995 *Year C*	1996 *Year A*
6th Sunday of Easter	May 16	May 8	May 21	May 12
Ascension	May 20	May 12	May 25	May 16
7th Sunday of Easter	May 23	May 15	May 28	May 19
Pentecost	May 30	May 22	June 4	May 26
Trinity Sunday	June 6	May 29	June 11	June 2
Body and Blood of Christ	June 13	June 5	June 18	June 9
Sacred Heart	June 18	June 10	June 23	June 14
9th Sunday in Ordinary Time	■	■	■	■
10th Sunday in Ordinary Time	■	■	■	■
11th Sunday in Ordinary Time	■	June 12	■	June 16
12th Sunday in Ordinary Time	June 20	June 19	June 25	June 23
Birth of John the Baptist, June 24	Thursday	Friday	Saturday	Monday
13th Sunday in Ordinary Time	June 27	June 26	July 2	June 30
Peter and Paul, Apostles, June 29	Tuesday	Wednesday	Thursday	Saturday
14th Sunday in Ordinary Time	July 4	July 3	July 9	July 7
15th Sunday in Ordinary Time	July 11	July 10	July 16	July 14
16th Sunday in Ordinary Time	July 18	July 17	July 23	July 21
17th Sunday in Ordinary Time	July 25	July 24	July 30	July 28
18th Sunday in Ordinary Time	Aug. 1	July 31	■	Aug. 4
Transfiguration, August 6	Friday	Saturday	Sunday	Tuesday
19th Sunday in Ordinary Time	Aug. 8	Aug. 7	Aug. 13	Aug. 11
Assumption, August 15	Sunday	Monday	Tuesday	Thursday
20th Sunday in Ordinary Time	■	Aug. 14	Aug. 20	Aug. 18
21st Sunday in Ordinary Time	Aug. 22	Aug. 21	Aug. 27	Aug. 25
22nd Sunday in Ordinary Time	Aug. 29	Aug. 28	Sept. 3	Sept. 1
23rd Sunday in Ordinary Time	Sept. 5	Sept. 4	Sept. 10	Sept. 8
Triumph of the Cross, September 14	Tuesday	Wednesday	Thursday	Saturday
24th Sunday in Ordinary Time	Sept. 12	Sept. 11	Sept. 17	Sept. 15
25th Sunday in Ordinary Time	Sept. 19	Sept. 18	Sept. 24	Sept. 22
26th Sunday in Ordinary Time	Sept. 26	Sept. 25	Oct. 1	Sept. 29
27th Sunday in Ordinary Time	Oct. 3	Oct. 2	Oct. 8	Oct. 6
28th Sunday in Ordinary Time	Oct. 10	Oct. 9	Oct. 15	Oct. 13
29th Sunday in Ordinary Time	Oct. 17	Oct. 16	Oct. 22	Oct. 20
30th Sunday in Ordinary Time	Oct. 24	Oct. 23	Oct. 29	Oct. 27
31st Sunday in Ordinary Time	Oct. 31	Oct. 30	Nov. 5	Nov. 3
All Saints, November 1	Monday	Tuesday	Wednesday	Friday
All Souls, November 2	Tuesday	Wednesday	Thursday	Saturday
32nd Sunday in Ordinary Time	Nov. 7	Nov. 6	Nov. 12	Nov. 10
Dedication of St. John Lateran, November 9	Tuesday	Wednesday	Thursday	Saturday
33rd Sunday in Ordinary Time	Nov. 14	Nov. 13	Nov. 19	Nov. 17
Christ the King	Nov. 21	Nov. 20	Nov. 26	Nov. 24

SUNDAY/FEAST DAY	1997 *Year B*	1998 *Year C*	1999 *Year A*	2000 *Year B*
1st Sunday of Advent	Dec. 1, 1996	Nov. 30, 1997	Nov. 29, 1998	Nov 28, 1999
2nd Sunday of Advent	Dec. 8, 1996	Dec. 7, 1997	Dec. 6, 1998	Dec. 5, 1999
Immaculate Conception, December 8	Dec. 9, 1996†	Monday	Tuesday	Wednesday
3rd Sunday of Advent	Dec. 15, 1996	Dec. 14, 1997	Dec. 13, 1998	Dec. 12, 1999
4th Sunday of Advent	Dec. 22, 1996	Dec. 21, 1997	Dec. 20, 1998	Dec. 19, 1999
Christmas, December 25	Wednesday	Thursday	Friday	Saturday
Holy Family	Dec. 29, 1996	Dec. 28, 1997	Dec. 27, 1998	Dec. 26, 1999
Mary, Mother of God, January 1	Wednesday	Thursday	Friday	Saturday
Epiphany	Jan. 5, 1997	Jan. 4, 1998	Jan. 3, 1999	Jan. 2, 2000
Baptism of the Lord	Jan. 12, 1997	Jan. 11, 1998	Jan. 10, 1999	Jan. 9, 2000
2nd Sunday in Ordinary Time	Jan. 19	Jan. 18	Jan. 17	Jan. 16
3rd Sunday in Ordinary Time	Jan. 26	Jan. 25	Jan. 24	Jan. 23
4th Sunday in Ordinary Time	■	Feb. 1	Jan. 31	Jan. 30
Presentation of the Lord, Feb. 2	Sunday	Monday	Tuesday	Wednesday
5th Sunday in Ordinary Time	Feb. 9	Feb. 8	Feb. 7	Feb. 6
6th Sunday in Ordinary Time	■	Feb. 15	Feb. 14	Feb. 13
7th Sunday in Ordinary Time	■	Feb. 22	■	Feb. 20
8th Sunday in Ordinary Time	■	■	■	Feb. 27
9th Sunday in Ordinary Time	■	■	■	Mar. 5
Ash Wednesday	Feb. 12	Feb. 25	Feb. 17	Mar. 8
1st Sunday of Lent	Feb. 16	Mar. 1	Feb. 21	Mar. 12
2nd Sunday of Lent	Feb. 23	Mar. 8	Feb. 28	Mar. 19
3rd Sunday of Lent	Mar. 2	Mar. 15	Mar. 7	Mar. 26
4th Sunday of Lent	Mar. 9	Mar. 22	Mar. 14	Apr. 2
5th Sunday of Lent	Mar. 16	Mar. 29	Mar. 21	Apr. 9
Passion (Palm) Sunday	Mar. 23	Apr. 5	Mar 28	Apr. 16
• Joseph, Husband of Mary, March 19	Tuesday	Thursday	Friday	Mar. 20†
• Annunciation, March 25	Apr. 7†	Wednesday	Thursday	Saturday
Holy Thursday	Mar. 27	Apr. 9	Apr. 1	Apr. 20
Good Friday	Mar. 28	Apr. 10	Apr. 2	Apr. 21
Easter Sunday	Mar. 30	Apr. 12	Apr. 4	Apr. 23
2nd Sunday of Easter	Apr. 6	Apr. 19	Apr. 11	Apr. 30
3rd Sunday of Easter	Apr. 13	Apr. 26	Apr. 18	May 7
4th Sunday of Easter	Apr. 20	May 3	Apr. 25	May 14
5th Sunday of Easter	Apr. 27	May 10	May 2	May 21

† This solemnity has been transferred to this date.

SUNDAY/FEAST DAY	1997 *Year B*	1998 *Year C*	1999 *Year A*	2000 *Year B*
6th Sunday of Easter	May 4	May 17	May 9	May 28
Ascension	May 8	May 21	May 13	June 1
7th Sunday of Easter	May 11	May 24	May 16	June 4
Pentecost	May 18	May 31	May 23	June 11
Trinity Sunday	May 25	June 7	May 30	June 18
Body and Blood of Christ	June 1	June 14	June 6	June 25
Sacred Heart	June 6	June 19	June 11	June 30
9th Sunday in Ordinary Time	■	■	■	■
10th Sunday in Ordinary Time	June 8	■	■	■
11th Sunday in Ordinary Time	June 15	■	June 13	■
12th Sunday in Ordinary Time	June 22	June 21	June 20	■
Birth of John the Baptist, June 24	Tuesday	Wednesday	Thursday	Saturday
13th Sunday in Ordinary Time	■	June 28	June 27	July 2
Peter and Paul, Apostles, June 29	Sunday	Monday	Tuesday	Thursday
14th Sunday in Ordinary Time	July 6	July 5	July 4	July 9
15th Sunday in Ordinary Time	July 13	July 12	July 11	July 16
16th Sunday in Ordinary Time	July 20	July 19	July 18	July 23
17th Sunday in Ordinary Time	July 27	July 26	July 25	July 30
18th Sunday in Ordinary Time	Aug. 3	Aug. 2	Aug. 1	■
Transfiguration, August 6	Wednesday	Thursday	Friday	Sunday
19th Sunday in Ordinary Time	Aug. 10	Aug. 9	Aug. 8	Aug. 13
Assumption, August 15	Friday	Saturday	Sunday	Tuesday
20th Sunday in Ordinary Time	Aug. 17	Aug. 16	■	Aug. 20
21st Sunday in Ordinary Time	Aug. 24	Aug. 23	Aug. 22	Aug. 27
22nd Sunday in Ordinary Time	Aug. 31	Aug. 30	Aug. 29	Sept. 3
23rd Sunday in Ordinary Time	Sept. 7	Sept. 6	Sept. 5	Sept. 10
Triumph of the Cross, September 14	Sunday	Monday	Tuesday	Thursday
24th Sunday in Ordinary Time	■	Sept. 13	Sept. 12	Sept. 17
25th Sunday in Ordinary Time	Sept. 21	Sept. 20	Sept. 19	Sept. 24
26th Sunday in Ordinary Time	Sept. 28	Sept. 27	Sept. 26	Oct. 1
27th Sunday in Ordinary Time	Oct. 5	Oct. 4	Oct. 3	Oct. 8
28th Sunday in Ordinary Time	Oct. 12	Oct. 11	Oct. 10	Oct. 15
29th Sunday in Ordinary Time	Oct. 19	Oct. 18	Oct. 17	Oct. 22
30th Sunday in Ordinary Time	Oct. 26	Oct. 25	Oct. 24	Oct. 29
31st Sunday in Ordinary Time	■	■	Oct. 31	Nov. 5
All Saints, November 1	Saturday	Sunday	Monday	Wednesday
All Souls, November 2	Sunday	Monday	Tuesday	Thursday
32nd Sunday in Ordinary Time	■	Nov. 8	Nov. 7	Nov. 12
Dedication of St. John Lateran, November 9	Sunday	Monday	Tuesday	Thursday
33rd Sunday in Ordinary Time	Nov. 16	Nov. 15	Nov. 14	Nov. 19
Christ the King	Nov. 23	Nov. 22	Nov. 21	Nov. 26

SUNDAY/FEAST DAY	2001 *Year C*	2002 *Year A*	2003 *Year B*	2004 *Year C*
1st Sunday of Advent	Dec. 3, 2000	Dec. 2, 2001	Dec. 1, 2002	Nov. 30, 2003
2nd Sunday of Advent	Dec. 10, 2000	Dec. 9, 2001	Dec. 8, 2002	Dec. 7, 2003
Immaculate Conception, December 8	Friday	Saturday	Dec. 9, 2002†	Monday
3rd Sunday of Advent	Dec. 17, 2000	Dec. 16, 2001	Dec. 15, 2002	Dec. 14, 2003
4th Sunday of Advent	Dec. 24, 2000	Dec. 23, 2001	Dec. 22, 2002	Dec. 21, 2003
Christmas, December 25	Monday	Tuesday	Wednesday	Thursday
Holy Family	Dec. 31, 2000	Dec. 30, 2001	Dec. 29, 2002	Dec. 28, 2003
Mary, Mother of God, January 1	Monday	Tuesday	Wednesday	Thursday
Epiphany	Jan. 7, 2001	Jan. 6, 2002	Jan. 5, 2003	Jan. 4, 2004
Baptism of the Lord	Jan. 8, 2001*	Jan. 13, 2002	Jan. 12, 2003	Jan. 11, 2004
2nd Sunday in Ordinary Time	Jan. 14	Jan. 20	Jan. 19	Jan. 18
3rd Sunday in Ordinary Time	Jan. 21	Jan. 27	Jan. 26	Jan. 25
4th Sunday in Ordinary Time	Jan. 28	Feb. 3	■	Feb. 1
Presentation of the Lord, February 2	Friday	Saturday	Sunday	Monday
5th Sunday in Ordinary Time	Feb. 4	Feb. 10	Feb. 9	Feb. 8
6th Sunday in Ordinary Time	Feb. 11	■	Feb. 16	Feb. 15
7th Sunday in Ordinary Time	Feb. 18	■	Feb. 23	Feb. 22
8th Sunday in Ordinary Time	Feb. 25	■	Mar. 2	■
9th Sunday in Ordinary Time	■	■	■	■
Ash Wednesday	Feb. 28	Feb. 13	Mar. 5	Feb. 25
1st Sunday of Lent	Mar. 4	Feb. 17	Mar. 9	Feb. 29
2nd Sunday of Lent	Mar. 11	Feb. 24	Mar. 16	Mar. 7
3rd Sunday of Lent	Mar. 18	Mar. 3	Mar. 23	Mar. 14
4th Sunday of Lent	Mar. 25	Mar. 10	Mar. 30	Mar. 21
5th Sunday of Lent	Apr. 1	Mar. 17	Apr. 6	Mar. 28
Passion (Palm) Sunday	Apr. 8	Mar. 24	Apr. 13	Apr. 4
• Joseph, Husband of Mary, March 19	Monday	Tuesday	Wednesday	Friday
• Annunciation, March 25	Mar. 26†	Apr. 8†	Tuesday	Thursday
Holy Thursday	Apr. 12	Mar. 28	Apr. 17	Apr. 8
Good Friday	Apr. 13	Mar. 29	Apr. 18	Apr. 9
Easter Sunday	Apr. 15	Mar. 31	Apr. 20	Apr. 11
2nd Sunday of Easter	Apr. 22	Apr. 7	Apr. 27	Apr. 18
3rd Sunday of Easter	Apr. 29	Apr. 14	May 4	Apr. 25
4th Sunday of Easter	May 6	Apr. 21	May 11	May 2
5th Sunday of Easter	May 13	Apr. 28	May 18	May 9

** This feast is celebrated this year on a weekday.* *† This solemnity has been transferred to this date.*

SUNDAY/FEAST DAY	2001 *Year C*	2002 *Year A*	2003 *Year B*	2004 *Year C*
6th Sunday of Easter	May 20	May 5	May 25	May 16
Ascension	May 24	May 9	May 29	May 20
7th Sunday of Easter	May 27	May 12	June 1	May 23
Pentecost	June 3	May 19	June 8	May 30
Trinity Sunday	June 10	May 26	June 15	June 6
Body and Blood of Christ	June 17	June 2	June 22	June 13
Sacred Heart	June 22	June 7	June 27	June 18
9th Sunday in Ordinary Time	■	■	■	■
10th Sunday in Ordinary Time	■	June 9	■	■
11th Sunday in Ordinary Time	■	June 16	■	■
12th Sunday in Ordinary Time	■	June 23	■	June 20
Birth of John the Baptist, June 24	Sunday	Monday	Tuesday	Thursday
13th Sunday in Ordinary Time	July 1	June 30	■	June 27
Peter and Paul, Apostles, June 29	Friday	Saturday	Sunday	Tuesday
14th Sunday in Ordinary Time	July 8	July 7	July 6	July 4
15th Sunday in Ordinary Time	July 15	July 14	July 13	July 11
16th Sunday in Ordinary Time	July 22	July 21	July 20	July 18
17th Sunday in Ordinary Time	July 29	July 28	July 27	July 25
18th Sunday in Ordinary Time	Aug. 5	Aug. 4	Aug. 3	Aug. 1
Transfiguration, August 6	Monday	Tuesday	Wednesday	Friday
19th Sunday in Ordinary Time	Aug. 12	Aug. 11	Aug. 10	Aug. 8
Assumption, August 15	Wednesday	Thursday	Friday	Sunday
20th Sunday in Ordinary Time	Aug. 19	Aug. 18	Aug. 17	■
21st Sunday in Ordinary Time	Aug. 26	Aug. 25	Aug. 24	Aug. 22
22nd Sunday in Ordinary Time	Sept. 2	Sept. 1	Aug. 31	Aug. 29
23rd Sunday in Ordinary Time	Sept. 9	Sept. 8	Sept. 7	Sept. 5
Triumph of the Cross, September 14	Friday	Saturday	Sunday	Tuesday
24th Sunday in Ordinary Time	Sept. 16	Sept. 15	■	Sept. 12
25th Sunday in Ordinary Time	Sept. 23	Sept. 22	Sept. 21	Sept. 19
26th Sunday in Ordinary Time	Sept. 30	Sept. 29	Sept. 28	Sept. 26
27th Sunday in Ordinary Time	Oct. 7	Oct. 6	Oct. 5	Oct. 3
28th Sunday in Ordinary Time	Oct. 14	Oct. 13	Oct. 12	Oct. 10
29th Sunday in Ordinary Time	Oct. 21	Oct. 20	Oct. 19	Oct. 17
30th Sunday in Ordinary Time	Oct. 28	Oct. 27	Oct. 26	Oct. 24
31st Sunday in Ordinary Time	Nov. 4	Nov. 3	■	Oct. 31
All Saints, November 1	Thursday	Friday	Saturday	Monday
All Souls, November 2	Friday	Saturday	Sunday	Tuesday
32nd Sunday in Ordinary Time	Nov. 11	Nov. 10	■	Nov. 7
Dedication of St. John Lateran, November 9	Friday	Saturday	Sunday	Tuesday
33rd Sunday in Ordinary Time	Nov. 18	Nov. 17	Nov. 16	Nov. 14
Christ the King	Nov. 25	Nov. 24	Nov. 23	Nov. 21

SUNDAY/FEAST DAY	2005 *Year A*	2006 *Year B*	2007 *Year C*	2008 *Year A*
1st Sunday of Advent	Nov. 28, 2004	Nov. 27, 2005	Dec. 3, 2006	Dec. 2, 2007
2nd Sunday of Advent	Dec. 5, 2004	Dec. 4, 2005	Dec. 10, 2006	Dec. 9, 2007
Immaculate Conception, December 8	Wednesday	Thursday	Friday	Saturday
3rd Sunday of Advent	Dec. 12, 2004	Dec. 11, 2005	Dec. 17, 2006	Dec. 16, 2007
4th Sunday of Advent	Dec. 19, 2004	Dec. 18, 2005	Dec. 24, 2006	Dec. 23, 2007
Christmas, December 25	Saturday	Sunday	Monday	Tuesday
Holy Family	Dec. 26, 2004	Dec. 30, 2005*	Dec. 31, 2006	Dec. 30, 2007
Mary, Mother of God, January 1	Saturday	Sunday	Monday	Tuesday
Epiphany	Jan. 2, 2005	Jan. 8, 2006	Jan. 7, 2007	Jan. 6, 2008
Baptism of the Lord	Jan. 9, 2005	Jan. 9, 2006*	Jan. 8, 2007*	Jan. 13, 2008
2nd Sunday in Ordinary Time	Jan. 16	Jan. 15	Jan. 14	Jan. 20
3rd Sunday in Ordinary Time	Jan. 23	Jan. 22	Jan. 21	Jan. 27
4th Sunday in Ordinary Time	Jan. 30	Jan. 29	Jan. 28	Feb. 3
Presentation of the Lord, February 2	Wednesday	Thursday	Friday	Saturday
5th Sunday in Ordinary Time	Feb. 6	Feb. 5	Feb. 4	■
6th Sunday in Ordinary Time	■	Feb. 12	Feb. 11	■
7th Sunday in Ordinary Time	■	Feb. 19	Feb. 18	■
8th Sunday in Ordinary Time	■	Feb. 26	■	■
9th Sunday in Ordinary Time	■	■	■	■
Ash Wednesday	Feb. 9	Mar. 1	Feb. 21	Feb. 6
1st Sunday of Lent	Feb. 13	Mar. 5	Feb. 25	Feb. 10
2nd Sunday of Lent	Feb. 20	Mar. 12	Mar. 4	Feb. 17
3rd Sunday of Lent	Feb. 27	Mar. 19	Mar. 11	Feb. 24
4th Sunday of Lent	Mar. 6	Mar. 26	Mar. 18	Mar. 2
5th Sunday of Lent	Mar. 13	Apr. 2	Mar. 25	Mar. 9
Passion (Palm) Sunday	Mar. 20	Apr. 9	Apr. 1	Mar. 16
• Joseph, Husband of Mary, March 19	Saturday	Mar. 20†	Monday	Mar. 31†
• Annunciation, March 25	Apr. 4†	Saturday	Mar. 26†	Apr. 1†
Holy Thursday	Mar. 24	Apr. 13	Apr. 5	Mar. 20
Good Friday	Mar. 25	Apr. 14	Apr. 6	Mar. 21
Easter Sunday	Mar. 27	Apr. 16	Apr. 8	Mar. 23
2nd Sunday of Easter	Apr. 3	Apr. 23	Apr. 15	Mar. 30
3rd Sunday of Easter	Apr. 10	Apr. 30	Apr. 22	Apr. 6
4th Sunday of Easter	Apr. 17	May 7	Apr. 29	Apr. 13
5th Sunday of Easter	Apr. 24	May 14	May 6	Apr. 20

* *This feast is celebrated this year on a weekday.* † *This solemnity has been transferred to this date.*

SUNDAY/FEAST DAY	2005 *Year A*	2006 *Year B*	2007 *Year C*	2008 *Year A*
6th Sunday of Easter	May 1	May 21	May 13	Apr. 27
Ascension	May 5	May 25	May 17	May 1
7th Sunday of Easter	May 8	May 28	May 20	May 4
Pentecost	May 15	June 4	May 27	May 11
Trinity Sunday	May 22	June 11	June 3	May 18
Body and Blood of Christ	May 29	June 18	June 10	May 25
Sacred Heart	June 3	June 23	June 15	May 30
9th Sunday in Ordinary Time	■	■	■	June 1
10th Sunday in Ordinary Time	June 5	■	■	June 8
11th Sunday in Ordinary Time	June 12	■	June 17	June 15
12th Sunday in Ordinary Time	June 19	June 25	■	June 22
Birth of John the Baptist, June 24	Friday	Saturday	Sunday	Tuesday
13th Sunday in Ordinary Time	June 26	July 2	July 1	■
Peter and Paul, Apostles, June 29	Wednesday	Thursday	Friday	Sunday
14th Sunday in Ordinary Time	July 3	July 9	July 8	July 6
15th Sunday in Ordinary Time	July 10	July 16	July 15	July 13
16th Sunday in Ordinary Time	July 17	July 23	July 22	July 20
17th Sunday in Ordinary Time	July 24	July 30	July 29	July 27
18th Sunday in Ordinary Time	July 31	■	Aug. 5	Aug. 3
Transfiguration, August 6	Saturday	Sunday	Monday	Wednesday
19th Sunday in Ordinary Time	Aug. 7	Aug. 13	Aug. 12	Aug. 10
Assumption, August 15	Monday	Tuesday	Wednesday	Friday
20th Sunday in Ordinary Time	Aug. 14	Aug. 20	Aug. 19	Aug. 17
21st Sunday in Ordinary Time	Aug. 21	Aug. 27	Aug. 26	Aug. 24
22nd Sunday in Ordinary Time	Aug. 28	Sept. 3	Sept. 2	Aug. 31
23rd Sunday in Ordinary Time	Sept. 4	Sept. 10	Sept. 9	Sept. 7
Triumph of the Cross, September 14	Wednesday	Thursday	Friday	Sunday
24th Sunday in Ordinary Time	Sept. 11	Sept. 17	Sept. 16	■
25th Sunday in Ordinary Time	Sept. 18	Sept. 24	Sept. 23	Sept. 21
26th Sunday in Ordinary Time	Sept. 25	Oct. 1	Sept. 30	Sept. 28
27th Sunday in Ordinary Time	Oct. 2	Oct. 8	Oct. 7	Oct. 5
28th Sunday in Ordinary Time	Oct. 9	Oct. 15	Oct. 14	Oct. 12
29th Sunday in Ordinary Time	Oct. 16	Oct. 22	Oct. 21	Oct. 19
30th Sunday in Ordinary Time	Oct. 23	Oct. 29	Oct. 28	Oct. 26
31st Sunday in Ordinary Time	Oct. 30	Nov. 5	Nov. 4	■
All Saints, November 1	Tuesday	Wednesday	Thursday	Saturday
All Souls, November 2	Wednesday	Thursday	Friday	Sunday
32nd Sunday in Ordinary Time	Nov. 6	Nov. 12	Nov. 11	■
Dedication of St. John Lateran, November 9	Wednesday	Thursday	Friday	Sunday
33rd Sunday in Ordinary Time	Nov. 13	Nov. 19	Nov. 18	Nov. 16
Christ the King	Nov. 20	Nov. 26	Nov. 25	Nov. 23

SUNDAY/FEAST DAY	2009 *Year B*	2010 *Year C*	2011 *Year A*	2012 *Year B*
1st Sunday of Advent	Nov. 30, 2008	Nov. 29, 2009	Nov. 28, 2010	Nov. 27, 2011
2nd Sunday of Advent	Dec. 7, 2008	Dec. 6, 2009	Dec. 5, 2010	Dec. 4, 2011
Immaculate Conception, December 8	Monday	Tuesday	Wednesday	Thursday
3rd Sunday of Advent	Dec. 14, 2008	Dec. 13, 2009	Dec. 12, 2010	Dec. 11, 2011
4th Sunday of Advent	Dec. 21, 2008	Dec. 20, 2009	Dec. 19, 2010	Dec. 18, 2011
Christmas, Dec. 25	Thursday	Friday	Saturday	Sunday
Holy Family	Dec. 28, 2008	Dec. 27, 2009	Dec. 26, 2010	Dec. 30, 2011*
Mary, Mother of God, January 1	Thursday	Friday	Saturday	Sunday
Epiphany	Jan. 4, 2009	Jan. 3, 2010	Jan. 2, 2011	Jan. 8, 2012
Baptism of the Lord	Jan. 11, 2009	Jan. 10, 2010	Jan. 9, 2011	Jan. 9, 2012*
2nd Sunday in Ordinary Time	Jan. 18	Jan. 17	Jan. 16	Jan. 15
3rd Sunday in Ordinary Time	Jan. 25	Jan. 24	Jan. 23	Jan. 22
4th Sunday in Ordinary Time	Feb. 1	Jan. 31	Jan. 30	Jan. 29
Presentation of the Lord, February 2	Monday	Tuesday	Wednesday	Thursday
5th Sunday in Ordinary Time	Feb. 8	Feb. 7	Feb. 6	Feb. 5
6th Sunday in Ordinary Time	Feb. 15	Feb. 14	Feb. 13	Feb. 12
7th Sunday in Ordinary Time	Feb. 22	■	Feb. 20	Feb. 19
8th Sunday in Ordinary Time	■	■	Feb. 27	■
9th Sunday in Ordinary Time	■	■	Mar. 6	■
Ash Wednesday	Feb. 25	Feb. 17	Mar. 9	Feb. 22
1st Sunday of Lent	Mar. 1	Feb. 21	Mar. 13	Feb. 26
2nd Sunday of Lent	Mar. 8	Feb. 28	Mar. 20	Mar. 4
3rd Sunday of Lent	Mar. 15	Mar. 7	Mar. 27	Mar. 11
4th Sunday of Lent	Mar. 22	Mar. 14	Apr. 3	Mar. 18
5th Sunday of Lent	Mar. 29	Mar. 21	Apr. 10	Mar. 25
Passion (Palm) Sunday	Apr. 5	Mar. 28	Apr. 17	Apr. 1
• Joseph, Husband of Mary, March 19	Thursday	Friday	Saturday	Monday
• Annunciation, March 25	Wednesday	Thursday	Friday	Mar. 26†
Holy Thursday	Apr. 9	Apr. 1	Apr. 21	Apr. 5
Good Friday	Apr. 10	Apr. 2	Apr. 22	Apr. 6
Easter Sunday	Apr. 12	Apr. 4	Apr. 24	Apr. 8
2nd Sunday of Easter	Apr. 19	Apr. 11	May 1	Apr. 15
3rd Sunday of Easter	Apr. 26	Apr. 18	May 8	Apr. 22
4th Sunday of Easter	May 3	Apr. 25	May 15	Apr. 29
5th Sunday of Easter	May 10	May 2	May 22	May 6

* *This feast is celebrated this year on a weekday.* † *This solemnity has been transferred to this date.*

SUNDAY/FEAST DAY	2009	2010	2011	2012
	Year B	*Year C*	*Year A*	*Year B*
6th Sunday of Easter	May 17	May 9	May 29	May 13
Ascension	May 21	May 13	June 2	May 17
7th Sunday of Easter	May 24	May 16	June 5	May 20
Pentecost	May 31	May 23	June 12	May 27
Trinity Sunday	June 7	May 30	June 19	June 3
Body and Blood of Christ	June 14	June 6	June 26	June 10
Sacred Heart	June 19	June 11	July 1	June 15
9th Sunday in Ordinary Time	■	■	■	■
10th Sunday in Ordinary Time	■	■	■	■
11th Sunday in Ordinary Time	■	June 13	■	June 17
12th Sunday in Ordinary Time	June 21	June 20	■	■
Birth of John the Baptist, June 24	Wednesday	Thursday	Friday	Sunday
13th Sunday in Ordinary Time	June 28	June 27	■	July 1
Peter and Paul, Apostles, June 29	Monday	Tuesday	Wednesday	Friday
14th Sunday in Ordinary Time	July 5	July 4	July 3	July 8
15th Sunday in Ordinary Time	July 12	July 11	July 10	July 15
16th Sunday in Ordinary Time	July 19	July 18	July 17	July 22
17th Sunday in Ordinary Time	July 26	July 25	July 24	July 29
18th Sunday in Ordinary Time	Aug. 2	Aug. 1	July 31	Aug. 5
Transfiguration, August 6	Thursday	Friday	Saturday	Monday
19th Sunday in Ordinary Time	Aug. 9	Aug. 8	Aug. 7	Aug. 12
Assumption, August 15	Saturday	Sunday	Monday	Wednesday
20th Sunday in Ordinary Time	Aug. 16	■	Aug. 14	Aug. 19
21st Sunday in Ordinary Time	Aug. 23	Aug. 22	Aug. 21	Aug. 26
22nd Sunday in Ordinary Time	Aug. 30	Aug. 29	Aug. 28	Sept. 2
23rd Sunday in Ordinary Time	Sept. 6	Sept. 5	Sept. 4	Sept. 9
Triumph of the Cross, September 14	Monday	Tuesday	Wednesday	Friday
24th Sunday in Ordinary Time	Sept. 13	Sept. 12	Sept. 11	Sept. 16
25th Sunday in Ordinary Time	Sept. 20	Sept. 19	Sept. 18	Sept. 23
26th Sunday in Ordinary Time	Sept. 27	Sept. 26	Sept. 25	Sept. 30
27th Sunday in Ordinary Time	Oct. 4	Oct. 3	Oct. 2	Oct. 7
28th Sunday in Ordinary Time	Oct. 11	Oct. 10	Oct. 9	Oct. 14
29th Sunday in Ordinary Time	Oct. 18	Oct. 17	Oct. 16	Oct. 21
30th Sunday in Ordinary Time	Oct. 25	Oct. 24	Oct. 23	Oct. 28
31st Sunday in Ordinary Time	■	Oct. 31	Oct. 30	Nov. 4
All Saints, November 1	Sunday	Monday	Tuesday	Thursday
All Souls, November 2	Monday	Tuesday	Wednesday	Friday
32nd Sunday in Ordinary Time	Nov. 8	Nov. 7	Nov. 6	Nov. 11
Dedication of St. John Lateran, November 9	Monday	Tuesday	Wednesday	Friday
33rd Sunday in Ordinary Time	Nov. 15	Nov. 14	Nov. 13	Nov. 18
Christ the King	Nov. 22	Nov. 21	Nov. 20	Nov. 25

INDEX OF READINGS

The numbers on this chart refer to sections, not to pages.

Reading	Volume A	Volume B	Volume C	Volume W
Genesis				
1:11 – 12				518
1:26 – 2:3				288
2:7 – 9; 3:1 – 7	18			
2:18 – 24		135		
3:9 – 15		84		
3:9 – 15, 20				429
9:8 – 15		19		
12:1 – 4a	21			
14:18 – 20			163	
18:1 – 10a			103	
18:20 – 32			106	
50:15 – 21				180
Exodus				
3:1 – 6, 9 – 12				505
3:1 – 8a, 13 – 15			26	
16:2 – 4, 12 – 15		108		
17:3 – 7	24			
19:1 – 6a	86			
20:1 – 3, 7 – 8, 12 – 17		25		
23:20 – 21a				384
24:3 – 8		162		
34:4b – 6, 8 – 9	158			
Leviticus				
19:1 – 2, 17 – 18	74			
Numbers				
6:22 – 27	15	15	15	
11:25 – 29		132		
21:4b – 9				370
Deuteronomy				
4:1 – 2, 6 – 8		120		
4:39 – 40		159		
5:12 – 15		81		
6:2 – 6		147		
7:6 – 11	164			
8:2 – 3, 14b – 16a	161			
8:7 – 10				518
10:12 – 14				182
11:18, 26 – 28	80			
18:18 – 19		66		
26:4 – 10			20	
30:10 – 14			100	
Joshua				
24:1 – 2a, 15 – 17, 18b		117		
1 Samuel				
3:1 – 10				505
3:4 – 10, 19		60		
1 Samuel (continued)				
16:1b, 6 – 7, 10 – 13a	27			
26:2, 7 – 9, 12 – 13, 22 – 23			76	
2 Samuel				
5:1 – 3			157	
7:4 – 5a, 12 – 14a, 16				272
12:7 – 10, 13 – 14			88	
1 Kings				
3:5, 7 – 12	104			
3:11 – 14				465
8:41 – 43			82	
17:10 – 16		150		
17:17 – 24			85	
19:4 – 8		111		
19:9a, 11 – 13a	110			
19:16b, 19 – 21			94	
2 Kings				
4:8 – 11, 14 – 16a	92			
4:42 – 44		105		
5:14 – 17			139	
Nehemiah				
8:1 – 4a, 5 – 6, 8 – 10			64	
2 Maccabees				
7:1, 20 – 23				456
7:1 – 2, 9 – 14			151	
Job				
7:1 – 4, 6 – 7		69		
38:1, 8 – 11		90		
Proverbs				
8:22 – 31			160	
9:1 – 6		114		
Wisdom				
1:13 – 15; 2:23 – 24a		93		
6:12 – 16	149			
7:7 – 11		138		
9:16c – 18			124	
11:22 — 12:1			148	
12:13, 16 – 19	101			
Sirach				
3:2 – 6	14	14	14	
3:17 – 18, 20			121	
15:15 – 20	71			
27:6 – 7			79	
28:2 – 5, 6b – 7	125			

The numbers on this chart refer to sections, not to pages.

READING	Volume A	B	C	W
Sirach (continued)				
35:12b – 14, 16 – 17			**145**	
50:22 – 24				**501**
Isaiah				
2:1 – 5	**1**			
5:1 – 7	**134**			
6:1 – 2a, 3 – 8			**70**	
9:2 – 3a, 6 – 7a				**447**
9:2 – 4	**62**			
9:2 – 4, 6 – 7	**13**	**13**	**13**	
11:1b, 5 – 9				**224**
11:1 – 4a, 5 – 6, 9b	**4**			
12:4b – 5				**179**
25:6 – 7, 9				**201**
25:6, 9				**229**
25:6a, 7 – 9				**531**
25:6 – 10a	**137**			
30:18				**210**
30:19 – 20, 23 – 24, 26				**205**
30:19, 23 – 24, 26				**173**
30:19b – 21				**172**
32:15 – 20				**513**
35:1 – 2, 5 – 6ab, 10	**7**			
35:4 – 7a		**123**		
40:3 – 5		**5**		
40:10 – 11				**218**
40:25 – 26, 29 – 31				**174**
41:10				**207**
41:14				**204**
42:1 – 2, 4, 6 – 7	**17**	**17**	**17**	
42:16				**208**
43:1 – 3a, 5				**211**
43:18 – 21			**32**	
43:22 – 25		**75**		
45:1, 4 – 6	**140**			
46:4				**197**
49:3, 5 – 6	**59**			
49:14 – 15	**77**			
50:4 – 8a		**126**		
50:6 – 7	**33**			
50:6 – 7			**35**	
50:6 – 7		**34**		
55:1 – 3	**107**			
55:6 – 9	**128**			
55:10 – 11	**98**			
55:10 – 11				**203**
56:1, 6 – 7	**113**			
56:1, 6 – 7				**442**
58:6 – 9				**176**
58:7 – 10	**68**			
60:1 – 6	**16**	**16**	**16**	
61:1 – 2		**8**		
Isaiah (continued)				
62:1 – 3			**61**	
63:7				**496**
66:10 – 14c			**97**	
Jeremiah				
1:4 – 5, 17ab, 18 – 19			**67**	
1:4 – 8				**213**
1:4 – 8				**316**
1:4 – 9				**505**
17:7 – 8			**73**	
20:7 – 9	**119**			
20:10 – 12a, 13	**89**			
23:3 – 6		**102**		
31:7 – 9		**144**		
31:31 – 34		**31**		
31:33				**222**
33:14 – 16			**3**	
38:4 – 6, 8 – 10			**115**	
Lamentations				
3:22 – 25				**183**
Baruch				
5:1 – 5, 7			**6**	
Ezekiel				
2:2 – 5		**96**		
17:22 – 24		**87**		
18:25 – 28	**131**			
33:7 – 9	**122**			
34:11 – 15				**218**
34:11 – 16abce			**166**	
34:11 – 16abce				**461**
34:11 – 12, 14 – 16abce	**155**			
36:24 – 28				**509**
36:24 – 28				**479**
36:24 – 28				**474**
37:12 – 14	**30**			
37:21 – 22, 24				**184**
Daniel				
7:13 – 14		**156**		
12:1 – 3		**153**		
Hosea				
2:16b, 17b, 21 – 22		**78**		
6:3 – 6	**83**			
11:1, 3 – 4, 8c – 9		**165**		
11:3 – 4				**221**
Joel				
3:1 – 3a				**479**

The numbers on this chart refer to sections, not to pages.

READING	Volume A	Volume B	Volume C	Volume W
Amos				
7:10 – 15		99		
Jonah				
3:1 – 5, 10		63		
Micah				
5:1 – 3			12	
Habakkuk				
1:2 – 3; 2:2 – 4			136	
Zephaniah				
2:3; 3:12 – 13	65			
3:14 – 15			9	
3:17 – 18a				302
Zechariah				
2:14 – 15				447
9:9 – 10	95			
Malachi				
2:8 – 10	146			
3:1 – 2b				252
3:19 – 20			154	
Matthew				
1:16, 18 – 21, 24a				272
1:18 – 24	10			
2:1 – 12	16	16	16	
2:13 – 15, 19 – 23	14	14	14	
2:13 – 18				439
3:1 – 9, 11	4			
4:1 – 11	18			
4:17 – 23	62			
4:18 – 22				423
5:1 – 12a	65			
5:1 – 12a				402
5:1 – 12a				517
5:1 – 12a				512
5:13 – 16	68			
5:13 – 16				491
5:14 – 16				193
5:20 – 24				180
5:23 – 24	71			
5:38 – 48	74			
5:43 – 48				181
5:43 – 48				194
6:1 – 4				176
6:1 – 6, 16 – 18				176
6:1, 5 – 6				176
6:1, 16 – 18				176
6:7 – 13				195

READING	Volume A	Volume B	Volume C	Volume W
Matthew (continued)				
6:7 – 15				178
6:19 – 21				196
6:24 – 34	77			
6:25b – 33				197
7:1 – 5				198
7:7 – 11				179
7:21, 24 – 27				228
7:21 – 27	80			
8:5 – 11				229
8:14 – 17				530
9:9 – 13	83			
9:9 – 13				376
9:35 – 38				508
9:35 — 10:1, 5a, 6 – 7				173
9:36 — 10:8	86			
10:26 – 31	89			
10:40 – 42	92			
11:2 – 11	7			
11:25 – 26, 28 – 30				535
11:25 – 30	95			
11:25 – 30	164			
11:29 – 30				199
13:1 – 9	98			
13:24 – 30	101			
13:31 – 32				500
13:44 – 46	104			
13:44 – 46				200
13:44 – 46				495
13:54 – 58				288
14:13 – 21	107			
14:22 – 33	110			
14:22 – 33				415
14:22 – 33				201
15:21 – 28	113			
16:13 – 19				319
16:13 – 19a				263
16:13 – 20	116			
16:21 – 25	119			
17:1 – 9	21			
17:1 – 9				344
18:1 – 4				473
18:1 – 5, 10				384
18:15 – 17	122			
18:19 – 22				512
18:21 – 35	125			
20:1 – 16a	128			
20:26b – 28				455
21:1 – 11	33			
21:28 – 32	131			
21:33 – 43	134			
22:1 – 10	137			
22:15 – 21	140			

The numbers on this chart refer to sections, not to pages.

READING	Volume A	B	C	W
Matthew (continued)				
22:34 – 40	143			
22:35 – 40				478
23:1 – 12	146			
24:37 – 44	1			
25:1 – 13	149			
25:14 – 15, 19 – 21	152			
25:14 – 29				202
25:14 – 30				495
25:31 – 40				473
25:31 – 40				177
25:31 – 46	155			
27:11 – 54	33			
28:16 – 20	52			
28:16 – 20		159		
28:16 – 20				464
Mark				
1:1 – 8		5		
1:12 – 15		19		
1:14 – 20		63		
1:14 – 20				464
1:21 – 28		66		
1:29 – 39		69		
1:40 – 45		72		
2:1 – 12		75		
2:18 – 22		78		
2:23 – 28		81		
3:20 – 21, 31 – 35		84		
3:20 – 26, 31 – 35		84		
4:1 – 9				203
4:1 – 9				469
4:30 – 34		87		
4:35 – 41		90		
4:35 – 41				204
5:18 – 20				500
5:21 – 24, 35b – 36, 38 – 42				205
5:21 – 24, 35 – 43		93		
6:1 – 6		96		
6:7 – 13		99		
6:17 – 29				365
6:30 – 34		102		
7:1 – 5, 14 – 15, 21 – 23		120		
7:31 – 37		123		
8:31 – 35		126		
9:2 – 10		22		
9:2 – 10				344
9:33 – 37		129		
9:33 – 37				206
9:33 – 37				473
9:38 – 41		132		
10:13 – 16		135		
10:13 – 16				207

READING	Volume A	B	C	W
Mark (continued)				
10:13 – 16				478
10:17 – 27		138		
10:28 – 30				508
10:35 – 45		141		
10:46 – 52		144		
10:46 – 52				208
11:1 – 10		34		
12:28 – 31		147		
12:28b – 31				182
12:41 – 44		150		
12:41 – 44				209
13:24 – 32		153		
13:33 – 37		2		
14:12 – 16, 22 – 26		162		
14:12 – 16, 22 – 26				487
15:1 – 39		34		
16:15 – 18				247
16:15 – 20				284
16:15 – 20		53		
Luke				
1:5 – 17				316
1:26 – 38		11		
1:26 – 38				274
1:26 – 38				429
1:26 – 38				451
1:39 – 45			12	
1:39 – 56				302
1:39 – 56				352
1:46 – 56				175
2:1 – 14	13	13	13	
2:16 – 21	15	15	15	
2:22 – 32				252
2:41 – 51				303
2:41 – 51				272
2:41 – 51				451
3:1a, 2 – 6			6	
3:10 – 16, 18			9	
3:15 – 16, 21 – 22	17	17	17	
4:1 – 13			20	
4:14 – 21			64	
4:20b – 24, 28 – 30			67	
5:1 – 11			70	
5:1 – 11				508
6:12 – 16				455
6:17, 20 – 23			73	
6:27 – 37			76	
6:39 – 45			79	
7:1 – 10			82	
7:1 – 10				210
7:11 – 17				211
7:11 – 17				535

The numbers on this chart refer to sections, not to pages.

Reading	Volume A	Volume B	Volume C	Volume W
Luke (continued)				
7:11 – 17			**85**	
7:17 – 26				**174**
7:36 – 50			**88**	
7:36 – 50				**212**
9:1 – 6				**192**
9:1 – 6				**213**
9:11b – 17			**163**	
9:18 – 24			**91**	
9:28b – 36			**23**	
9:28b – 36				**344**
9:57 – 62			**94**	
10:1 – 9			**97**	
10:1 – 9				**396**
10:25 – 37			**100**	
10:25 – 37				**214**
10:25 – 37				**526**
10:38 – 42			**103**	
11:1 – 10			**106**	
11:5 – 10				**215**
12:15 – 21				**522**
12:16 – 21			**109**	
12:32 – 34				**473**
12:35 – 38				**172**
12:35 – 40				**230**
12:35 – 40			**112**	
12:49 – 53			**115**	
13:6 – 9			**26**	
13:6 – 9				**216**
13:22 – 30			**118**	
14:1, 7 – 14			**121**	
14:12 – 14				**217**
14:25 – 27			**124**	
15:1 – 3, 11 – 32			**29**	
15:1 – 3, 11 – 32				**491**
15:1 – 7				**218**
15:3 – 7			**166**	
15:11 – 32			**127**	
16:10 – 13			**130**	
16:19 – 31			**133**	
17:5 – 10			**136**	
17:11 – 19			**139**	
17:11 – 19				**219**
17:11 – 19				**504**
17:20 – 21				**231**
18:1 – 8a				**220**
18:1 – 8			**142**	
18:9 – 14			**145**	
19:1 – 10			**148**	
19:1 – 10				**446**
19:28 – 40			**35**	
20:27 – 38			**151**	

Reading	Volume A	Volume B	Volume C	Volume W
Luke (continued)				
21:5 – 19			**154**	
21:25 – 28, 34 – 36			**3**	
23:1 – 49			**35**	
23:35 – 43			**157**	
24:13 – 35	**40**			
24:35 – 48		**41**		
24:50 – 53			**54**	
John				
1:19 – 28		**8**		
1:29 – 34	**59**			
1:35 – 42		**60**		
1:47 – 51				**381**
2:1 – 12			**61**	
2:13 – 22		**25**		
3:13 – 17				**370**
3:16 – 17				**221**
3:16 – 17		**28**		
3:16 – 17	**158**			
4:5 – 15, 19b – 26, 39a, 40 – 42	**24**			
4:46 – 53				**183**
6:1 – 15		**105**		
6:24 – 29		**108**		
6:48 – 51		**111**		
6:51 – 58		**114**		
6:51 – 58	**161**			
6:51 – 58				**487**
6:60 – 69		**117**		
8:1 – 11			**32**	
9:1, 6 – 12, 35 – 38	**27**			
10:1 – 10	**43**			
10:11 – 16		**44**		
10:14 – 16				**190**
10:27 – 30			**45**	
11:3 – 7, 17, 20 – 27, 31 – 45	**30**			
11:17 – 27				**337**
11:21 – 27				**535**
11:47 – 52				**184**
12:24 – 26				**460**
12:24 – 26		**31**		
13:31a, 33 – 35			**48**	
13:34 – 35				**222**
14:1 – 12	**46**			
14:12 – 14				**186**
14:15 – 17				**223**
14:15 – 17				**483**
14:15 – 21	**49**			
14:21 – 26				**189**
14:23 – 26			**51**	
14:23 – 26				**495**

The numbers on this chart refer to sections, not to pages.

READING	A	B	C	W
	Volume			
John (continued)				
14:23 – 26				**483**
14:27				**224**
15:1 – 4				**478**
15:1 – 5				**225**
15:1 – 5, 7 – 8		**47**		
15:5 – 8				**478**
15:9 – 11				**226**
15:9 – 11				**478**
15:9 – 14		**50**		
15:12 – 15				**227**
15:18 – 21				**188**
15:26 — 16:1				**191**
16:12 – 15			**160**	
17:6 – 9	**55**			
17:11		**56**		
17:20 – 21			**57**	
17:21 – 23				**187**
18:33b – 37		**156**		
19:25 – 27				**371**
19:25 – 27				**451**
19:31 – 37		**165**		
20:1 – 2, 11 – 18				**333**
20:1 – 9	**36**	**36**	**36**	
20:2 – 8				**438**
20:11 – 18				**185**
20:19 – 23	**58**	**58**	**58**	
20:19 – 29	**37**			
20:19 – 29			**39**	
20:19 – 29		**38**		
20:24 – 29				**322**
21:1 – 14			**42**	
21:15 – 17				**464**
Acts				
1:8 – 11		**53**		
1:8 – 11	**52**			
1:8 – 11			**54**	
1:12 – 13a, 14				**448**
1:12 – 14	**55**			
1:15 – 17, 20a, 20c – 26		**56**		
1:15 – 17, 20a, 20c – 26				**293**
2:1 – 6, 14, 22b – 23, 32 – 33				**480**
2:1 – 11	**58**	**58**	**58**	
2:14, 22 – 24	**40**			
2:14a, 36 – 41	**43**			
2:32 – 33				**185**
2:42 – 47				**484**
2:42 – 47	**37**			
3:1 – 10				**186**
3:1 – 10				**452**
3:13 – 15, 17 – 19		**41**		

READING	A	B	C	W
	Volume			
Acts (continued)				
4:8 – 12		**44**		
4:32 – 35		**38**		
4:32 – 35				**470**
4:32 – 35				**187**
5:12 – 16			**39**	
5:17 – 21				**188**
5:27 – 32				**189**
5:27b – 32, 40b – 41			**42**	
6:1 – 7a	**46**			
6:8 – 10; 7:54 – 60				**437**
7:55 – 60				**457**
7:55 – 60			**57**	
8:5 – 8, 14 – 17	**49**			
9:1 – 20				**190**
9:26 – 28		**47**		
10:25 – 26, 34 – 35, 44 – 48		**50**		
10:34 – 38	**17**	**17**	**17**	
10:34a, 37 – 43	**36**	**36**	**36**	
11:19 – 22, 26c				**191**
11:21 – 26; 13:1 – 3				**310**
11:27 – 30				**177**
12:1 – 11				**319**
13:43 – 44, 47 – 48			**45**	
14:21 – 27			**48**	
16:22 – 34				**192**
22:3 – 16				**247**
28:11 – 16				**415**
Romans				
1:1c – 4				**274**
1:2 – 4	**10**			
4:18 – 21	**83**			
5:5 – 11			**166**	
5:6 – 11	**86**			
5:10b – 11				**226**
6:3 – 4, 8 – 9	**92**			
8:9, 11	**95**			
8:14 – 17		**159**		
8:14 – 17				**480**
8:14 – 18	**98**			
8:26 – 27	**101**			
8:28 – 30	**104**			
8:31, 38 – 39		**22**		
8:35, 37 – 39	**107**			
11:33 – 36	**116**			
12:1 – 2	**119**			
12:9 – 12			**130**	
12:9 – 16b				**302**
12:17 – 18, 21				**181**
13:8 – 10	**122**			
13:11 – 13a	**1**			

The numbers on this chart refer to sections, not to pages.

Reading	Volume A	B	C	W
Romans (continued)				
14:7 – 9	125			
15:4 – 6	4			
16:25 – 27		11		
1 Corinthians				
1:3 – 9		2		
1:10 – 13, 17	62			
1:26 – 31	65			
1:26 – 31				470
2:1 – 5	68			
2:6 – 10	71			
3:18 – 20	74			
5:6b – 8	36	36	36	
9:16 – 18		69		
10:16 – 17	161			
10:31 — 11:1		72		
11:23 – 26			163	
12:4 – 7, 12 – 13	58	58	58	
12:4 – 11			61	
12:4 – 13				480
12:12 – 13				475
12:12 – 13				225
12:12 – 14, 27			64	
13:4 – 7				194
13:4 – 8a, 11 – 13			67	
13:4 – 13				470
15:3 – 8, 11			70	
15:12, 16 – 20			73	
15:20 – 24a	155			
2 Corinthians				
1:3 – 4				175
4:6 – 11		81		
4:16 — 5:1		84		
5:6 – 10		87		
5:14 – 17		90		
5:17 – 19			29	
6:4 – 10				457
8:1 – 3a, 12				209
8:7, 9, 13 – 14		93		
9:8 – 11				519
12:7 – 10		96		
13:11 – 13	158			
Galatians				
1:11 – 12, 15 – 19			85	
3:26 – 28				475
3:26 – 29			91	
5:1, 13 – 15			94	
5:22 – 23, 25 – 26				223

Reading	Volume A	B	C	W
Ephesians				
1:3 – 5				532
1:3 – 6				448
1:3 – 10		99		
1:15 – 16a, 18 – 19a				205
1:17 – 21			54	
1:17 – 21	52			
1:17 – 21		53		
2:4 – 10		28		
2:20 – 22				443
2:20 – 22				452
3:14 – 19		165		
3:16b – 17, 20 – 21				231
4:1 – 6		105		
4:1 – 7				466
4:11 – 13				466
4:31 — 5:2		111		
5:1 – 2, 8 – 10	27			
5:1 – 2, 8 – 10				488
5:8 – 10				193
5:15 – 20		114		
6:1 – 4		117		
6:18b – 19a, 20b				220
Philippians				
1:4 – 6			6	
2:1 – 5	131			
3:12 – 14			32	
3:20 — 4:1			23	
4:4 – 7			9	
4:4 – 7				230
4:4 – 9				470
4:6 – 9				514
4:6 – 9	134			
4:8 – 9				199
4:12 – 14, 19 – 20	137			
Colossians				
1:15 – 18			157	
1:18 – 20			100	
1:27 – 28			103	
2:6 – 7				216
3:1 – 2				196
3:1 – 4	36	36	36	
3:1 – 4			109	
3:12 – 13				198
3:12 – 14				178
3:12 – 15				514
3:12, 15b – 17				497
3:12 – 17	14	14	14	
3:15 – 16				224
3:17, 23 – 24				288

The numbers on this chart refer to sections, not to pages.

Reading	Volume A	Volume B	Volume C	Volume W
1 Thessalonians				
1:1 – 5b	140			
1:5 – 8a	143			
2:7 – 9, 13	146			
4:13 – 14, 18				532
4:13 – 18	149			
5:1 – 6	152			
5:16 – 18				219
5:16 – 24		8		
2 Thessalonians				
1:11 – 12			148	
2:16 — 3:5			151	
3:6 – 12, 16				492
3:7 – 12			154	
1 Timothy				
1:12 – 15b			127	
2:1 – 4				195
6:11b – 12a			133	
2 Timothy				
1:6 – 8			136	
1:1 – 8				248
2:11 – 13			139	
4:1 – 2			142	
4:6 – 8			145	
4:17 – 18				319
Titus				
1:1 – 5				248
3:4 – 6	13	13	13	
Hebrews				
4:12 – 13		138		
4:14 – 16		141		
5:1 – 6		144		
7:26		147		
11:1 – 2, 8 – 12			112	
12:1 – 4			115	
12:5a, 6 – 7, 11			118	
13:1 – 3, 14 – 16				523
James				
1:17 – 18, 21b – 22		120		
2:1 – 5		123		
2:14 – 17				228
2:14 – 17				488
2:14 – 18				217
2:14 – 18		126		
3:17 – 18		129		
5:1 – 6		132		
James (continued)				
5:7 – 10	7			
5:13 – 16				527
5:16b – 18				215
1 Peter				
1:3 – 4	37			
1:3 – 4				200
2:9 – 10				222
4:7b – 11				470
4:10 – 11				202
4:13 – 16	55			
5:1 – 4				263
5:12 – 14				284
2 Peter				
1:16 – 19				344
1 John				
2:29b — 3:1a				206
3:1, 23				227
3:1 – 2				532
3:1 – 2		44		
3:11, 18				214
3:16 – 18				470
3:18		47		
4:7 – 10		50		
4:7 – 10				212
4:7 – 11, 16b	164			
4:11 – 13		56		
5:1 – 3		38		
5:2 – 5				470
Revelation				
1:5 – 8		156		
7:9 – 10				402
12:7 – 12a				381
14:13				532
21:1 – 4				443
21:1 – 4			48	
21:1 – 8				488
21:10 – 14, 22 – 23			51